T0301628

TOO LITTLE, TOO LATE

INITIATIVE FOR POLICY DIALOGUE AT COLUMBIA
CHALLENGES IN DEVELOPMENT AND GLOBALIZATION

INITIATIVE FOR POLICY
DIALOGUE AT COLUMBIA

CHALLENGES IN DEVELOPMENT AND GLOBALIZATION

JOSÉ ANTONIO OCAMPO AND JOSEPH E. STIGLITZ, SERIES EDITORS

Escaping the Resource Curse, Macartan Humphreys,
Jeffrey D. Sachs, and Joseph E. Stiglitz, eds.

The Right to Know, Ann Florini, ed.

Privatization: Successes and Failures, Gérard Roland, ed.

Growth and Policy in Developing Countries: A Structuralist Approach,
José Antonio Ocampo, Codrina Rada, and Lance Taylor

Taxation in Developing Countries, Roger Gordon, ed.

Reforming the International Financial System for Development,
Jomo Kwame Sundaram, ed.

Development Cooperation in Times of Crisis, José Antonio Ocampo and
José Antonio Alonso

New Perspectives on International Migration and Development,
Jeronimo Cortina and Enrique Ochoa-Reza, eds.

Industrial Policy and Economic Transformation in Africa,
Akbar Noman and Joseph E. Stiglitz, eds.

*Macroeconomics and Development: Roberto Frenkel and
the Economics of Latin America*, Mario Damill, Martín Rapetti,
and Guillermo Rozenwurcell, eds.

TOO LITTLE, TOO LATE

The Quest to Resolve Sovereign Debt Crises

Martin Guzman,
José Antonio Ocampo,
and Joseph E. Stiglitz, eds.

COLUMBIA UNIVERSITY PRESS

NEW YORK

Columbia University Press
Publishers Since 1893
New York   Chichester, West Sussex
cup.columbia.edu

Library of Congress Cataloging-in-Publication Data

Names: Guzman, Martin, editor. | Ocampo, José Antonio, editor. |
Stiglitz, Joseph E., editor.
Title: Too little, too late : the quest to resolve sovereign debt crises /
Martin Guzman, Jose Antonio Ocampo, and Joseph E. Stiglitz, eds.
Description: New York City : Columbia University Press, 2016. | Series:
Initiative for policy dialogue at Columbia: challenges in development and
globalization | Includes bibliographical references and index.
Identifiers: LCCN 2015048091 | ISBN 9780231179263 (cloth : alk. paper)
Subjects: LCSH: Debts, Public. | Financial crises. | Monetary policy. |
International law.
Classification: LCC HJ8017 .T66 2016 | DDC 336.3—dc23
LC record available at http://lccn.loc.gov/2015048091

Columbia University Press books are printed
on permanent and durable acid-free paper.

Printed in the United States of Americac
c 10 9 8 7 6 5 4 3 2 1

Cover design: Jordan Wannemacher

INITIATIVE FOR POLICY DIALOGUE AT COLUMBIA

CHALLENGES IN DEVELOPMENT AND GLOBALIZATION

JOSÉ ANTONIO OCAMPO AND JOSEPH E. STIGLITZ, SERIES EDITORS

The Initiative for Policy Dialogue (IPD) at Columbia University brings together academics, policymakers, and practitioners from developed and developing countries to address the most pressing issues in economic policy today. IPD is an important part of Columbia's broad program on development and globalization. The Initiative for Policy Dialogue at Columbia: Challenges in Development and Globalization book series presents the latest academic thinking on a wide range of development topics and lays out alternative policy options and trade-offs. Written in a language accessible to policymakers and students alike, this series is unique in that it both shapes the academic research agenda and furthers the economic policy debate, facilitating a more democratic discussion of development policies.

The current non-system for resolving sovereign debt crises does not work. Sovereign debt restructurings come too late and too little. This imposes enormous costs on societies: restructurings are often not deep enough to provide the conditions for economic recovery, as the Greek debt restructuring of 2012 illustrates, impeding debtors in distress from escaping from recessions or depressions. Furthermore, if the debtor decides to play hardball and not to accept the terms demanded by the creditors, finalizing a restructuring can take a long time and, as the case of Argentina illustrates, be beset with legal challenges, especially from a small group of non-cooperative agents that have earned the epithet "vulture funds."

A fresh start for distressed debtors is a basic principle of a well functioning market economy. The absence of a fresh start may lead to large inefficiencies, where both the debtor and the creditors lose. This principle is well recognized in domestic bankruptcy laws. But there is no international bankruptcy framework that similarly governs sovereign debts. These problems are not new. They have been plaguing the functioning of sovereign debt markets for decades.

This book provides a thorough analysis of the main deficiencies of the current non-system for sovereign debt restructuring and of possible solutions. It includes fifteen chapters by world-leading academics and practitioners. Overall, the chapters in this book depict an overwhelming consensus on the need to reform the non-system that governs sovereign debt restructuring. And as this book emphasizes, if there is a better framework for debt restructuring, debt markets will function better, and societies will do better.

For more information about IPD and its upcoming books, visit www .policydialogue.org.

CONTENTS

ACKNOWLEDGMENTS

Most of the chapters in this volume were presented at a conference on Frameworks for Sovereign Debt Restructuring jointly organized by Columbia University Initiative for Policy Dialogue (IPD), the Centre for International Governance Innovation (CIGI), the Center of Global Economic Governance (CGEG) at Columbia University, and the United Nations Department of Economics and Social Affairs (UNDESA), held at Columbia University, New York, on November 17, 2014. We are thankful to all those institutions as well as Domenico Lombardi, Benu Schneider, and Jan Svejnar for their support, and to the participants for the excellent discussions. We are also thankful to the Institute for New Economic Thinking and its president, Rob Johnson, for hosting a panel on Sovereign Debt Restructuring in its annual conference at the OECD, Paris, April 2015. Some of the chapters of this book were presented in that panel, and the excellent discussions therein contributed to improve them. Several of the chapters of this book were also presented at the different meetings of the United Nations General Assembly Ad Hoc Committee on Sovereign Debt Restructuring Processes. The discussions during those meetings have also greatly contributed to the quality of this volume. Some of the chapters were presented at a follow-up conference on Sovereign Debt Restructuring jointly organized by Columbia University IPD and the CIGI, held at Columbia University on September 22, 2015. We are also grateful to CIGI for the financial support for that conference, and to the participants for the excellent discussions. Finally, we are thankful to all the authors of this volume for their efforts to turn this volume into an enriching and timely contribution.

TOO LITTLE, TOO LATE

———

Martin Guzman, José Antonio Ocampo, and Joseph E. Stiglitz

Sovereign debt crises are becoming, once again, frequent. In some cases, the costs to the citizens of those countries facing such crises have been enormous. Deficiencies in the mechanisms for resolving such crises cast a pallor over countries that are not yet in a crisis but worry that they might become so; and indeed, the high costs and uncertainties associated with debt restructuring dampen cross-border capital flows and force especially developing countries and emerging markets to pay higher interest rates than might be the case if there were better ways of resolving these debt problems.

A fresh start for distressed debtors is a basic principle of a well-functioning market economy. The absence of a fresh start may lead to large inefficiencies, wherein both the debtor and the creditors lose. This principle is well recognized in domestic bankruptcy laws. But there is no international bankruptcy framework that similarly governs sovereign debts. We refer to such a broad framework as a "framework for sovereign debt restructuring."

This lacuna is creating serious problems for nations facing sovereign debt crises. The issue has been brought to the fore especially by the difficulties recently faced by several countries attempting reasonable debt restructurings—most notably Argentina and Greece.

Sovereign debt restructuring has suffered from "too little, too late." The current system discourages incumbent governments from initiating debt restructurings. And when a restructuring is undertaken, it is often not deep enough to provide the conditions for an economic recovery, as the Greek debt restructuring of 2012 illustrates. And if the debtor decides to play hardball and not accept the terms demanded by the creditors, finalizing a restructuring can take a long time and, as the case of Argentina illustrates, be beset with legal challenges, especially from small groups of noncooperative agents (holdout creditors) that have earned the epithet "vulture funds." Under the current non-system, the gaps in the international legal architecture make possible the emergence of these vulture funds, who buy defaulted debt in secondary markets at very low prices and then litigate against the issuer for the payment of the full amount of the liabilities. This destabilizing speculative behavior, together with the favorable treatment these agents have been receiving from the U.S. courts, creates serious problems, as it encourages all creditors to hold out in debt restructuring negotiations—making debt restructurings de facto impossible.

Delays in debt restructurings have been costly for sovereigns and for good faith investors. These dysfunctions have ramifications for the entire sovereign debt market. They may lead to a reluctance on the part of countries to borrow, even when doing so might make sense; and they may lead to higher interest rates in sovereign debt markets.

These problems are not new. They have been plaguing the functioning of sovereign debt markets for decades. Over the past fifteen years discussions have explored many alternative ways of dealing with both situations in which sovereigns have difficulties in meeting their debt obligations and the subsequent economic, political, and social consequences. Each has to be evaluated in terms of ex ante incentives. Is there, in some sense, too much or too little lending? How is lending distributed across countries? Is lending done on the right terms? To the right countries? Do the lenders have the right incentives for due diligence? And do the borrowers have the incentives for prudent borrowing?

An assessment of alternative frameworks for resolving sovereign debt crises must also consider the ex post incentives: When a problem occurs, are there incentives for a timely resolution? Are there incentives for a fair and efficient resolution, one that enables the indebted country to return to growth quickly, that does not impose undue hardship on the debtor's citizens, and provides fair compensation to the creditors? Does it provide appropriate treatment for "implicit" creditors, such as old-age pensioners?

Some have suggested that simple modifications of the current contractual approach are all that are required. Others claim that some sovereign debt restructuring mechanism would be desirable; this is known as the "statutory approach." Others aver that at the very least, there is a need for an international agreement on the set of acceptable debt contracts—for instance, that countries cannot sign away their sovereign immunities.

At the time of publication of this book, the issue of fixing the frameworks for sovereign debt restructuring is in the center of the global debate. It has been explicitly addressed by the United Nations (in resolutions overwhelmingly passed by the General Assembly in September 2014 and in September 2015 over the opposition of some developed countries and the abstention of others), the International Capital Market Association (ICMA), the International Monetary Fund (IMF), and the G20, which made explicit reference to the need of resolving the current deficiencies in the final communiqué of the leaders' summit in November 2014.

There have been several important academic studies addressing various aspects of frameworks for sovereign debt restructuring and the advantages and disadvantages of these mechanisms relative to the private contractual approach. In light of the recent events and progress in our understanding of the issues, these studies need to be updated.

This book fills in this gap by providing a collection of essays from top academic economists, lawyers, and practitioners in the field, providing guidance on the most critical questions. (Many of these ideas were presented as part of an ongoing series of conferences held at Columbia University on frameworks for sovereign debt restructuring.)

Part I focuses on general issues of sovereign debt restructuring, with an emphasis on the goals of debt restructuring and the challenges imposed by the deficiencies in the current non-system, as well as the implications of recent events for the functioning of sovereign lending markets.

In chapter 1, Martin Guzman and Joseph E. Stiglitz review the existing problems in the world of sovereign debt restructuring, contrast how well existing structures and proposed alternatives fulfill the objectives of debt restructuring, and propose solutions. They argue that improvements in the language of contracts, although beneficial, cannot provide a comprehensive, efficient, and equitable solution to the problems faced in restructurings, but they note there are improvements within the contractual approach that should be implemented. They claim that ultimately the contractual approach must be complemented by a multinational legal framework that facilitates restructurings based on principles of efficiency and equity. Given the current geopolitical constraints, in the short run they advocate for the implementation of a "soft law" approach, one built on the recognition of the limitations of the private contractual approach and on a set of principles over which there may be consensus, as the restoration of sovereign immunity.

In chapter 2, Marilou Uy and Shichao Zhou provide an overview of the broadly favorable public debt trends in developing countries over the past decade. They also note that while the increased access to international debt markets provides more opportunities for investments that stimulate growth, it may also bring with it new sources of risk that could seriously affect some sovereign borrowers. They also highlight the unique challenges that some groups of countries face in managing sustainable levels of debt. Their paper further acknowledges countries' responsibility for managing their debt but also recognizes that the global community has a role in strengthening the system of sovereign debt resolution. Yet a global consensus on how to move forward on this has been elusive. In this context, their chapter documents the evolution of highly divergent views on how to reform the global system for sovereign debt in intergovernmental forums and the potential approaches that could pave the way for a wider consensus.

In chapter 3, Skylar Brooks and Domenico Lombardi examine two cases that help to explain why an international framework to facilitate sovereign debt restructuring has not been created yet: first, the IMF's attempt to establish a sovereign debt restructuring mechanism (SDRM) in 2001–2003; second, the creation of the European stability mechanism (ESM) in 2012. In the former case, they ask why the SDRM failed despite growing recognition of the need for such a mechanism. In the latter case, they analyze why eurozone countries responded to the European debt crisis by creating the ESM—a sovereign bailout rather than a debt restructuring mechanism. They argue that private creditor opposition best explains the failure to create a sovereign debt restructuring framework and advance the hypothesis that private creditor preferences shape outcomes through two distinct but intersecting forms of power: instrumental and structural. Instrumentally, private creditors engage in lobbying and "strategic reform" to preempt more far-reaching measures. Structurally, private creditor preferences are internalized by states with systemically important financial markets and states that rely on international markets for their borrowing.

Part II offers an analysis of two recent major cases—the resolution of Argentina's and Greece's debt crises. These cases illustrate the problems that the lack of mechanisms for sovereign debt restructuring may create.

In chapter 4, Sergio Chodos explores in depth Argentina's debt restructuring saga after its 2001 default. In his ruling in the country's dispute with vulture funds, Judge Thomas Griesa of the District of New York decided that Argentina breached a boilerplate pari passu clause included in sovereign bond issuances, and he created a novel "equitable remedy" that in effect prohibited Argentina from continuing to service its restructured debt until the vulture funds had been paid in advance in full. This decision, which was confirmed by the Court of Appeals of the Second Circuit in October 2012, became operational after the U.S. Supreme Court denied a petition for review in June 2014. The chapter describes the details of the case and argues that the decision constituted a game changer that affected the nature of restructurings to a point where the problems generated by the absence of a fair, effective, and efficient mechanism to deal with sovereign debt restructuring can no longer be neglected. Chodos also argues that one of the main consequences of such decision is to render untenable the marked-based approach for sovereign debt restructuring.

In chapter 5, Yanis Varoufakis presents the proposals from the Greek government during his appointment as Finance Minister of Tsipras's government. He argues that his ministry's priority was an ex-ante debt restructuring, because it would provide the "optimism shock" necessary to energize investment in Greece's private sector. He claims that in contrast, the troika program they inherited was always going to fail, because its logic was deeply flawed and, for this reason, guaranteed to deter investment. It was a logic based on incoherent backward induction, reflecting political expediency's triumph over sound macroeconomic thinking.

The case of Greek debt is fascinating because it is one of those curious situations in which creditors extend new loans under conditions that guarantee they will not get their money back. Why do Greece's creditors refuse to move on debt restructuring before any new loans are negotiated? And why did they ignore the Greek government's proposals? What is the reason for preferring a much larger new loan package than necessary? Varoufakis claims that the answers to these questions cannot be found by discussing sound finance, public or private, for they reside firmly in the realm of power politics. If Tsipras's government were to conclude a viable, mutually advantageous agreement with the troika of creditors, after having opposed its "program," its "success" would have seriously jeopardized the electoral prospects of troika-friendly governing parties in Portugal, Spain, and Ireland. But although these considerations were important factors in the perpetuation of the "Greek debt denial," he claims there is a more powerful explanation buried deep in the architectural faults of the eurozone and in the manner in which a significant European politician, the German finance minister Wolfgang Schäuble, (1) understands these faults and (2) is planning to resolve them.

He concludes that behind the Eurogroup rhetoric and decisions a war is waging between Berlin and Paris over the form of political union that must be introduced to bolster Europe's monetary union. Greek debt will not be restructured until this conflict is resolved.

Part III focuses on a set of possible improvements within the contractual approach, extending the set of measures proposed by Guzman and Stiglitz in chapter 1.

In chapter 6, Anna Gelpern, Ben Heller, and Brad Setser provide a comprehensive description of the recent reforms proposed by the International Capital Market Association (ICMA) for sovereign debt contracts (a process in which the three experts have been involved), i.e. the changes that would allow a supermajority of creditors to approve a debtor's restructuring proposal in one vote across multiple bond series. They start by reviewing the introduction of series-by-series voting to amend financial terms into New York–law bonds in 2003. Then, they look at the factors that helped create broad consensus on the need to move beyond series-by-series voting in 2012. Most of the essay is devoted to analyzing the key features of the new generation of aggregated CACs and the considerations that shaped decisions about these features. They conclude with observations on contract reform in sovereign debt restructuring and their views of the challenges ahead.

In chapter 7, Richard Gitlin and Brett House lay out a work program to reduce the ex ante costs of sovereign debt restructuring that is complemented by additional measures to mitigate the costs of restructuring. Among other measures, they propose the creation of a sovereign debt forum that would provide a standing, independent venue (outside of existing institutions like the IMF) in which creditors and debtors could meet on an ongoing basis to address incipient sovereign debt distress in a proactive fashion, and they suggest the implementation of state-contingent debt in the form of sovereign "cocos," which consists of bonds that automatically extend their maturity upon realization of a prespecified trigger linked to a liquidity crisis.

In chapter 8, James Haley makes three points regarding recent improvements for sovereign debt contracts suggested by the ICMA and later endorsed by the IMF. First, he argues that the new clauses are a useful and potentially important instrument to deal with the problem of holdout creditors. Second, he claims the new clauses are not a panacea.

This assessment reflects the fact that it will take some time for these clauses to be embedded in the stock of outstanding bonds and that whatever their merits the new clauses do not fully address the issues of unenforceability and discharge of sovereign debts. Third, he notes that the debate between voluntary/contractual and statutory approaches is a false dichotomy. Contractual approaches will necessarily be incomplete and the design of "institutions," whether bankruptcy provisions embodied in formal treaty or the responses of existing international financial institutions, will influence the outcome of sovereign debt restructurings.

In chapter 9, Timothy DeSieno points to the importance of creditor committees for achieving successful sovereign debt restructurings. He claims that a more widespread utilization of creditor committees would minimize the holdout problems and facilitate inter-creditor consensus, as most creditors will usually feel they can trust "a group of their own" more readily than they can trust the issuer.

Part IV turns to the specific proposals for the implementation of a multinational formal framework for sovereign debt restructuring. The chapters in this section lay out a set of principles, elements, and forms for institutionalizing such a framework.

In chapter 10, José Antonio Ocampo provides a history of debt crises resolution and the rise of the current non-system, which mixes the Paris Club for official debts, voluntary renegotiations with private creditors, and occasional ad hoc debt relief initiatives (the Brady Plan and the Highly Indebted Poor Countries and later Multilateral Debt Relief Initiatives). This system, he argues, not only provides inadequate solutions but also does not guarantee equitable treatment of different debtors or different creditors. He then proposes a multilateral mechanism for sovereign debt restructuring that offers a sequence of voluntary negotiations, mediation, and eventual arbitration with preestablished deadlines, similar in a sense to the World Trade Organization's dispute settlement mechanism.

In chapter 11, Barry Herman proposes that the UN General Assembly should formulate a set of principles to guide governments and international institution creditors when restructuring sovereign debt and as the representative of the international community should guide the IMF in assessing restructuring needs. The principles would also guide national courts, which would oversee restructuring of sovereign bonds and bank loans issued under national law. The UN Commission on International Trade Law (UNCITRAL) would prepare a model law for national governments that would provide common guidance across jurisdictions for court supervision of restructuring of private claims. While sovereigns would continue to negotiate restructurings separately with each class of creditors, the indebted government or creditor groups could appeal the workout to the Permanent Court of Arbitration in The Hague when either party believes there has been a violation of the principles.

In chapter 12, Jürgen Kaiser discusses the "institutionalization" of a multinational framework for sovereign debt restructuring. In Kaiser's view, the institutionalization should comply to three basic principles: first, it needs to restructure debt in a single comprehensive process, with no payment obligations being exempted from the process; second, it needs to allow for impartial decision making about the terms of any debt restructuring; and third, this decision must be based on an impartial assessment of the debtor's situation. Kaiser claims that there are not many historical precedents for a sovereign debt restructuring that complies with these conditions, but the case of Indonesia in 1969 may be inspiring. He argues that a "sovereign debt restructuring liaison office" mandated by the United Nations and run independently from any debtor or creditor interference could be a catalytic element with the potential to overcome the shortcomings of existing procedures. In this view, it could facilitate a comprehensive negotiation format with all stakeholders around the table; it could provide an impartial and thus realistic assessment of the need for debt relief; and it could suggest an unbiased solution. Such an "office" could be established immediately as an outcome of the present UN General Assembly consultation process and then develop its rules, regulations, and infrastructure over time.

In chapter 13, Richard Conn argues that the creation of an agreed-upon framework that interacts with private party contracts or restricts contractual options ex ante is a logical alternative to the status quo. This approach can provide greater stability and efficiency in the restructuring process while allowing for sufficient flexibility and certainty for market participants. He claims that there are procedural frameworks that could add value to the restructuring process with less risk of treading on the political terrain of sovereigns. This chapter discusses the catalyst for recent efforts to create a framework and context for evaluating sovereign debt restructuring; outlines a strategy to successfully adopt a framework that deals with problems that require resolution; highlights the deficiencies of relying solely upon private party contractual revisions; discusses practical impediments to a substantive-law approach to sovereign debt restructuring; and finally puts forward specific proposals for a consensual, procedural framework designed to earn broad political support.

In chapter 14, Robert Howse analyzes some of the possible elements of an international-law approach to a multilateral framework for sovereign debt restructuring. This chapter draws extensively from the deliberations and publications of the UN Conference on Trade and Development (UNCTAD) Working Group. He proposes the creation of a "counter-framework" using soft-law instruments of a kind generated by various UN processes and institutions, including the International Law Commission, UNCITRAL, and UNCTAD. The "counter-framework" would offer different norms, fora, legal mechanisms, expertise, and analyses to those that dominate the existing informal framework (IMF, Paris Club, U.S. Treasury, financial industry associations, private law firms, creditors' groups, etc.). It would offer alternatives for borrower-lender relationships and the restructuring of debt, alternatives that if the analysis in this chapter (and the other chapters of this book) is correct, would benefit both sovereign debtors and creditors. This proposal might be of particular interest to states that could be sources of new finance and do not want to keep within the existing informal framework (like perhaps China).

In chapter 15, Kunibert Raffer analyzes which elements are indispensable for any model to be rightly called insolvency: equality of parties instead of creditor diktat, debtor protection, fairness, and a solution in the best interest of all creditors. This chapter presents a model that fulfills all these requirements. It concludes by showing that since the 1980s there has been progress in moving toward such a model, although at snail speed.

Overall, the chapters in this book depict an overwhelming consensus among those who are well informed about sovereign debt markets but do not have a vested interest on either the creditor or debtor side on the need to reform the non-system that governs sovereign debt restructuring. Doing so requires the political willingness from both of debtor and creditor countries. Debtor countries have raised their voice at the United Nations, calling for an end to the suffering that debt crises bring under the current arrangements. But creditor countries, led by the United States, are reluctant to engage in reforms. The political reasons are clear: the reforms would lead to a redefinition of the balance of power between debtors and creditors—a redefinition that is necessary if we are to create a better-functioning sovereign debt market. But as this book explains, those concerns miss the point. A better system for debt restructuring may be a win-win, that is, a situation in which everyone—with the exception of the vulture funds—wins. The size of the pie distributed among debtors and creditors would be larger with a better system. The suffering of societies in debt crises would be lessened, and creditors would also benefit from the faster economic recoveries that better resolutions of debt crises would entail. And as this book emphasizes, if there is a better framework for debt restructuring, debt markets will function better.

PART I

General Issues of Sovereign Debt Restructuring

CHAPTER 1

Creating a Framework for Sovereign Debt Restructuring That Works

Martin Guzman and Joseph E. Stiglitz

Debt matters. In recessions, high uncertainty discourages private spending, weakening demand. Resolving the problem of insufficient demand requires expansionary macroeconomic policies. But "excessive" public debt may constrain the capacity for running expansionary policies.[1] Evidence shows that high public debt also exacerbates the effects of private sector deleveraging after crises, leading to deeper and more prolonged economic depressions (Jordà, Schularick, and Taylor, 2013).

Even if programs of temporary assistance (e.g., from the International Monetary Fund) make full repayment of what is owed possible in those situations, doing so could only make matters worse. If the assistance is accompanied by austerity measures, it would aggravate the economic situation of the debtor.[2,3]

Distressed debtors need a fresh start, not just temporary assistance. This is in the best interests of the debtor and the majority of its creditors: precluding a rapid fresh start for the debtor leads to large negative-sum games in which the debtor cannot recover and creditors cannot benefit from the larger capacity of repayment that the recovery would imply.

Lack of clarity for resolving situations in which a firm or a country cannot meet its obligations can lead to chaos. There can be extended periods of time during which the claims are not resolved and business (either of the firm or the country) cannot proceed—or at least cannot proceed in the most desirable way. In the meantime, assets may be tunneled out of the firm or country, or at the very least, productive investments that would enhance the value of the human and physical assets are not made.

Within a country, bankruptcy laws are designed to prevent this chaos, ensuring an orderly restructuring and discharge of debts. Such laws establish how restructuring will proceed, who will get paid first, what plans the debtor will implement, who will control the firm, and so on. Bankruptcies are typically resolved through bargaining among the claimants—but with the backdrop of a legal framework and with a judiciary that will decide what each party will get, based on well-defined principles.

Bankruptcy laws thus protect corporations and their creditors, facilitating the processes of debt restructuring. A more orderly process not only lowers transactions costs but precludes the deadweight losses associated with disorderly processes; in doing so, it may even lower the cost of borrowing.

Good bankruptcy laws facilitate efficient and equitable outcomes in other ways; for instance, in encouraging lenders to undertake adequate due diligence before making loans.

The benefits of a legal framework providing for orderly debt restructuring have also been extended to public bodies, for instance, through Chapter 9 of the U.S. Bankruptcy Code.

But there is no comprehensive international bankruptcy procedure to ensure proper resolution of sovereign debt crises. Instead, the current system for sovereign debt restructuring (SDR) features a decentralized market-based process in which the debtor engages in intricate and complicated negotiations with many creditors with different interests, often under the backdrop of conflicting national legal regimes. Outcomes are often determined on the basis not of principles but of economic power—often under the backdrop of political power. Restructurings come too little, too late.[4] And when they come, they may take too long.[5] The lack of a rule of law leads to ex ante and ex post inefficiencies and inequities both among creditors and between the debtor and its creditors.

Furthermore, unlike domestic bankruptcies, sovereign bankruptcy negotiations take place in an ambiguous legal context. Several different jurisdictions, all with different perspectives, influence the process. Different legal orders often reach different conclusions for the same problem. It may not be clear which will prevail (and possibly none will prevail) and how the implicit bargaining among different countries' judiciaries will be resolved.

At the time we write this chapter, events are making the reform of the frameworks for SDR a major issue. Countries in desperate need of addressing profound debt sustainability issues, like Greece at the moment, are confronting the risks of a chaotic restructuring, and this discourages them from undertaking the restructurings that are now recognized as desirable or even inevitable.

Besides, the gaps in the legal and financial international architecture favor behavior that severely distorts the workings of sovereign lending markets. The emergence of vulture funds—investors who buy defaulted debt on the cheap and litigate against the issuer, demanding full payment and disrupting the whole restructuring process—as recently seen in the case of Argentine restructuring, is a symptom of a flawed market-based approach for debt crisis resolution.

Recent decisions[6] have also highlighted the previously noted interplay among multiple jurisdictions, none of which seems willing to cede the right to adjudicate restructuring to the others (Guzman and Stiglitz, 2015b).

There is consensus on the necessity of moving to a different framework, but there are different views on the table about how to move forward.

The International Monetary Fund (IMF) and the financial community represented by the International Capital Markets Association (ICMA) recognize that the current system does not work well (ICMA, 2014; IMF, 2014). They are proposing modifications in the language of contracts, such as a better design of collective action clauses (CACs) and clarification of pari passu—a standard contractual clause that is supposed to ensure fair treatment of different creditors. These proposals are improvements over the old terms, but they are still insufficient to solve the variety of problems faced in SDRs. And it is almost surely the case that new problems will arise—some anticipated, some not—within the new contractual arrangements.

On the other hand, a large group of countries is supporting the creation of a multinational legal framework, as reflected in Resolution 69/304 of the General Assembly of the United Nations of September 2014, which was overwhelmingly passed (by 124 votes to 11, with 41 abstentions), and more recently in Resolution 69/L.84 of September 2015 that established a set of principles that should be the basis of a statutory framework for sovereign debt restructuring, passed with 136 votes in favor, 41 abstentions, and only 6 against (see Li, 2015).[7] The framework should complement contracts, putting in place mechanisms that would establish how to solve disputes fairly. Building it on a consensual basis will be essential for its success. This in turn requires fulfilling a set of principles on which the different parties involved would agree, an issue that we analyze in this chapter.

While the importance of the absence of an adequate mechanism for SDR has long been noted (see also Stiglitz, 2006), five changes have helped to bring the issue to the fore and motivate the global movement for reform of existing arrangements. (1) Once again, many countries seem likely to face a problem of debt burdens beyond their ability to pay. (2) Court rulings in the United States and United Kingdom have highlighted the incoherence of the current system and made debt restructurings, at least in some jurisdictions, more difficult if not impossible. (3) The movement of debt from banks to capital markets has greatly increased the difficulties of debt renegotiations, with so many creditors with often conflicting interests at the table. (4) The development of credit default swaps (CDSs)—financial instruments for shifting risk—has meant that the economic interests of those at the bargaining table may actually be advanced if there is no resolution. (5) The growth of the vulture funds, whose business model entails holding out on settlement and using litigation to get for themselves payments that are greater than the original purchase price and of those that will be received by the creditors who agreed to debt restructuring, has also made debt restructurings under existing institutional arrangements much more difficult.[8]

The sections in the remainder of this chapter are organized around the following topics: the objectives of restructuring; the current problems; the solution proposed by the ICMA and the IMF; analysis of the limitations of the ICMA-IMF solution; a set of further reforms that could be implemented within the contractual approach; and the principles that should guide the creation of a multinational formal framework for SDR.

THE OBJECTIVES OF RESTRUCTURING

In absence of information asymmetries and contracting costs, risk-sharing (equity) contracts would be optimal; there would be no bankruptcy. But under imperfect information and costly state verification, complete risk sharing is suboptimal, and the optimal contract is a debt contract (Townsend, 1979).[9]

Information asymmetries and costly monitoring characterize the world of sovereign lending, which explains the widespread utilization of sovereign debt contracts. The optimal debt contract may be associated with partial risk sharing, including default in bad states and a compensation for default risk in the form of a higher (than the risk-free) interest rate in good states.

If default were never possible, the borrower would absorb all the risk. Under the assumptions of risk-neutral lenders who can diversify their portfolios in a perfectly competitive environment, the expected utility of each lender (who is compensated for the opportunity cost)[10] would be the same, but the borrower's would be lower than it would be with good risk-sharing contracts. Moreover, if the possibility of default were ruled out in every state of nature (for instance, through sufficiently high penalization of default), the amount of lending would be severely limited.

The probability of entering into situations of debt distress depends on a range of economic conditions[11] but also on the actions of the debtor.[12] And once the distress arises, the debtor's capacity for production and repayment going forward will depend on how the debt situation is resolved. If the debtor defaults, he or she normally loses access to credit markets until a restructuring agreement is reached.[13]

The mechanisms in place for debt restructuring determine how all these tensions are resolved. A good system should incentivize lenders and debtors to behave in ways that are conducive to efficiency ex ante (i.e., the "right" decisions at the moment of lending) and ex post (i.e., at the moment of resolving a debt crisis). It should also ensure a fair treatment of all the parties involved.

EFFICIENCY ISSUES

A system that makes restructurings too costly induces political leaders to postpone the reckoning. When there are no mechanisms in place that would ensure orderly restructurings, the perceived costs of default to the party in power become too large. Therefore, "gambling for resurrection," delaying the recognition of debt unsustainability, may be the optimal strategy for the debtor.

Delays are inefficient. They make recessions more persistent and decrease what is available for creditors if a default occurs.[14] In the presence of cross-border contagion, furthermore, the delay is costly not only to the given country but to those with which it has economic relations (Orszag and Stiglitz, 2002).

The objective of the restructuring process itself must not be to maximize the flows of capital or to minimize short-term interest rates. Instead, the framework should ensure overall economic efficiency, a critical feature of which is ex post efficiency in a broader sense: it should provide the conditions for a rapid and sustained economic recovery. A system of

orderly discharge of debts would permit the debtor to make a more efficient use of its resources, which may be in the best interests of both the
debtor and the creditors. Normally, contractual and judicial arrangements
should support this kind of ex post efficiency that is necessary for achieving Pareto efficiency.[15]

A curious feature of the current restructuring process is that countries that are in the process of restructuring typically face massive underutilization of their resources. This is because such countries cannot get
access to external resources; financial markets often become very dysfunctional in the midst of a crisis, with adverse implications for both
aggregate demand and supply. Creditors, focusing narrowly and short-
sightedly on repayment, force a cutback in government expenditures
(austerity), and the combination of financial constraints and decreases
in private and public demand bring on a major recession or depression.
They wrongly reason that if the country is spending less on itself, it
has more to spend on others—to repay its debts. But they forget the
large multipliers that prevail at such times: the cutbacks in expenditure
decrease gross domestic product (GDP) and tax revenues. The underutilization of the country's resources makes it more difficult for it to fulfill
its debt obligations—the austerity policies are normally counterproductive even from the creditors' perspective.

Another critical feature is ex ante efficiency. A system that does not
put any burden on the lenders ex post does not provide the right incentives for due diligence ex ante. Selection of "good" borrowers requires,
in general, specific actions from the lenders, such as screening (before
lending) and monitoring (after lending). The existence of a mechanism
for SDR would act as a signal that money will be lost unless due diligence
is applied.

Note that good due diligence will result in better screening and
lending practices, so interest rates may actually be lowered as a result
of better bankruptcy laws (i.e., more punitive bankruptcy procedures
may so adversely affect lender moral hazard that financial markets
become more dysfunctional). This is especially the case when, as now,
large fractions of lending are mediated through capital markets, not
banks. Arguably, that was one of the consequences of the passage of the
creditor-friendly U.S. bankruptcy law reforms in 2005 (through the
Bankruptcy Abuse Prevention and Consumer Protection Act), which
made the discharge of debt more difficult and led to a substantial
increase in bad lending practices.

EQUITY ISSUES

The framework for restructuring determines the incentives for creditors' behavior. A system that favors holdout behavior creates a perverse moral hazard problem that makes restructurings more difficult, or, on occasion, impossible.

It also creates interdebtor inequities, as it increases the borrowing costs for those debtors more likely to need a restructuring (which is both an efficiency and an equity issue, as the lack of proper mechanisms affects all countries but those that are riskier more severely). Of course, debtors who are more likely to default should pay a higher interest rate. The problem is that if the restructuring mechanism is inefficient—as the current system is—it overpenalizes these borrowers, and the ex post inefficiency also gets translated into an ex ante inefficiency, as the unnecessarily high penalty discourages participation in the credit market.

A flawed system like the current one that relies more on mechanisms for "bailouts" (such as the European Stability Mechanism) instead of providing mechanisms for restructuring also creates large intercreditor inequities, as only the creditors that get paid with the resources of the "bailouts" benefit, while the expected value of the claims of the other claimants (such as the creditors whose debts mature in a longer term, or the workers and pensioners whose wages depend on a production capacity of an economy that decreases precisely as the consequence of the austerity often associated with those plans) decreases.

Finally, there is a problem of equity between formal and informal creditors—those who have a contract and those whose benefits are part of a social contract. This is one of the important ways in which sovereign debt is different from private debt. Typically, there are a large number of such claimants—pensioners or those depending on the government for health benefits or education. Though Chapter 9 of the U.S. Bankruptcy Code (pertaining to the bankruptcy of public bodies) recognizes the importance of these claimants, in the absence of an international rule of law that gives such claims formal recognition, their claims are at risk of being made subordinate to those of the formal creditors. And the recognition that this is so may itself have a distorting effect on the economy: it may encourage the formalization of such claims, even when such formalization may result in socially undesirable rigidities and undesirable institutional arrangements.

THE CURRENT PROBLEMS

The current non-system does not achieve the described objectives of restructuring. Instead, it creates a host of inequities as well as inefficiencies. It overpenalizes debtors in distress, causing delays in the recognition of the problems. It leads to the "too little, too late" syndrome. In some cases, there is too much lending—and too much suffering later on; in other cases, there may be too little lending. Moreover, the legal frameworks permit a situation in which a few specialized agents (the vulture funds) can block the finalization of a restructuring, imposing large costs on the debtor and on other creditors. This section describes various factors that lead to these problems.

THE VULTURE FUNDS

Restructurings involve a public good problem: each claimant wants to enjoy the benefit of the country's increased ability to repay from debt reduction, but each wants to be repaid in full.

The existing frameworks fail to solve the public-good problem. Instead, they provide the conditions for the emergence of vulture funds. The vulture funds are a class of holdouts that are not really in the business of providing credit to countries. Instead, they are engaged in "legal arbitrage." Their business consists in buying debt in default (or about to be in default) in secondary markets at a fraction of its face value. Then, they litigate in courts, demanding full payment on the principal plus interest (typically at an interest rate that already includes compensation for default risk). A victory in court brings exorbitant returns on the initial investment.

Their modus operandi relies on a legal framework that has weakened sovereign immunity and on a flawed design of contracts. They resort to activities (many of which are socially unproductive) to increase their bargaining power and to influence the decisions of the actors involved—including lobbying and threats about economic and political consequences of a failure to reach a settlement satisfactory to the creditors (some liken it to extortion) to affect the debtor's behavior. Economic "extortion" is especially effective in influencing countries needing to re-enter capital markets, and political extortion is especially effective in influencing governments whose officials have been engaged in illegal activities or who are motivated by a concern over their "standing" in the international community.

The presence of vulture funds creates huge inefficiencies and inequities in sovereign lending markets. It can even lead to the total impossibility of debt restructuring. Recent events—in particular, the Argentine debt restructuring, which pitted the country against NML Capital (a subsidiary of the hedge fund Elliott Management)—show that these inefficiencies are a major issue. In that case, the presiding U.S. federal judge, Thomas Griesa, ruled in favor of the vulture funds and ordered an injunction that obliged Argentina to make payments to vultures and the holders of bonds denominated in foreign currency issued by Argentina in the 2005 and 2010 debt exchanges on a ratable basis, an interpretation of pari passu that requires Argentina to pay to the vulture funds their full judgment whenever it makes any payment under the exchange bonds, even if it is just a coupon payment, or otherwise any holder of exchange bonds would be barred from receiving payments. The injunction was based on a peculiar interpretation of pari passu,[16] a contractual clause that is supposed to ensure equal treatment among equally ranked creditors.[17]

The design of contracts also facilitates the emergence of vulture funds. Many existing debt contracts do not have CACs—clauses that allow a majority of bondholders to agree to changes in bond terms (e.g., to reduce the value of the principal) that are legally binding to all the bondholders, including those who vote against the restructuring. Some contracts do include them, but most are defined at the level of each individual bond.[18]

Under a unanimity rule, vulture funds can easily emerge. With CACs at the level of each security, vultures' behavior is more constrained but is still possible. They can still buy the minimum fraction that would block the restructuring of a unique series of bonds, and by doing so they would be able to block the whole restructuring.

A formula for aggregation of CACs (over different classes of bonds), like the one proposed by ICMA discussed later in this chapter, would alleviate these problems. But it raises other questions: How are different bonds to be added together for purposes of voting (How do we adjust for differences in priorities and exchange rates)? It is clearly conceivable that a majority of junior bonds could vote to deprive more senior bonds of some of the returns they might have expected, given their seniority. There may even be ambiguity about which claimants should be included in the aggregation: Should foreign *and* domestic claimants be included?[19]

Clearly, the issues faced in SDRs go beyond the design of CACs. These clauses are no panacea. If they were, there would be no need for bankruptcy laws that spell out issues like precedence and fair treatment.

Evidence shows that no country has relied on markets to solve bankruptcies. Every country has a bankruptcy law. Theory also shows that under realistic conditions markets are not able to provide efficient restructurings on their own, as they are unable to reach efficient solutions on their own in general, except under very restrictive and unlikely conditions (Greenwald and Stiglitz, 1986).[20] There are important market failures that are present in restructurings—either for corporations or for sovereigns.

WEAKENING OF SOVEREIGN IMMUNITY AND THE CHAMPERTY DEFENSE

The evolution of the legal frameworks has been instrumental for the emergence of vultures and the debilitation of sovereign immunity. Sovereign immunity had first been challenged with the sanction of the Foreign Sovereign Immunity Act in 1976 (Schumacher, Trebesch, and Enderlein, 2014), and has more recently been challenged by litigation over the champerty defense—an English common-law doctrine, later adopted by U.S. state legislatures, that prohibited the purchase of debt with the intent of bringing a lawsuit against the debtor (Blackman and Mukhi, 2010).

The case *Elliott Associates, LP v. Republic of Peru* was a game changer for the interpretation of legal frameworks affecting sovereign immunity.[21] Elliott had bought Peruvian debt in default and sued the country for full payment in the New York courts. The U.S. District Court for the Southern District of New York ruled that champerty applied, dismissing Elliott's claims. But the Second Circuit of Appeals reversed the decision, stating that the plaintiff's intent in purchasing the Peruvian debt in default was to be paid in full or otherwise to sue. Then, according to the Second Circuit, Elliott's intent did not meet the champerty requirement because litigation was contingent. Such an interpretation is absurd, as it was not reasonable to expect to be paid in full over a promise that had already been broken. The exorbitant returns obtained based on an interpretation that was unreasonable to expect could have constituted a case of "unjust enrichment" (Guzman and Stiglitz, 2014c).

In 2004, the New York state legislature effectively eliminated the defense of champerty concerning any debt purchase above US$500,000 dollars. That decision constituted a change to the understanding over which hundreds of billions of dollars of debt had been issued, redefining property rights. This change in legislation ensured the good health of the vultures' business.

DISTORTIVE CREDIT DEFAULT SWAPS

The problems are aggravated by the nontransparent use of CDSs. A CDS separates ownership from economic consequences: the seeming owner of a bond could even be better off in the event of a default, as the payments over the CDS would be activated in such an event. The opacity of this market makes unclear the real economic interests of those who have a seat at the restructuring bargaining table. They provide another reason for delayed restructuring, with its associated inequities and inefficiencies.

THE UNBALANCED BACKGROUND FOR NEGOTIATIONS

The legal frameworks and the bailout policies of the IMF determine the background of the negotiations (cf. Brooks et al., 2015). The current arrangements favor short-term creditors against long-term creditors; included in the latter group are the "informal creditors" (citizens toward whom the sovereign has obligations, such as workers and pensioners).

IMF bailout policies only aim at ensuring repayment in the short run. In practice, they have not been designed with the purpose of favoring sustained economic recoveries. On occasion they even undermined them (both as a result of counterproductive conditionality and because of insufficiently deep restructuring), increasing the probability of a subsequent restructuring being needed down the road.

In the case of Europe, the European Stability Mechanism leads to the same perverse effects. By construction, it is not a mechanism for debt restructuring but a mechanism for bailouts that gives creditor countries enormous power in the negotiations with a debtor country (Brooks and Lombardi, 2015). In the case of Greece, it was the main instrument by which the eurozone countries enforced their demands for policy decisions that were not in the best interest of the country (at least as judged by the vast majority of people in the country, as reflected repeatedly in the polls, and by a large fraction of economists).

POLITICAL ECONOMY ISSUES

SDR mechanisms must take political economy issues into account. The costs of restructuring are usually borne by different political actors than those who created the problem. Political economy tensions increase in times of distress, when the incumbent government has larger incentives to achieve deals with short-term benefits but long-term costs that will be paid by the next government. One of the strategies for better short-term financing conditions is giving up on sovereign immunity.

Every bad loan is equally the result of bad lending and bad borrowing: these are voluntary agreements. But a system the puts the onus on the debtor (i.e., making it more likely that more of the debt will be repaid) encourages bad lending—it encourages banks to encourage the government today to borrow too much, exacerbating the already present distortion. (There is a further argument for putting more of the onus on the lenders: they are supposed to be the experts in risk analysis; that is supposed to be their comparative advantage. Government officials typically have no expertise and rely on the judgments of those in the financial market concerning reasonable debt levels.)

Political costs are also often borne disproportionately by those willing to take actions—that is, to actually do the restructuring. Thus, a system that makes restructurings too costly exacerbates these natural political economy tensions, because it incentivizes debtors to delay the recognition of problems.

Creditors' behavior may also worsen these distortions, for instance, by providing short-term lending at high interest rates to countries that are obviously in need of a restructuring, taking into account the distorted incentives of the distressed debtors to make use of those funds, the "gambling on resurrection" behavior that we described earlier. Such short-term lending is, of course, risky: when the situation is bad enough, eventually there will be a restructuring. But the short-term creditors can typically charge a sufficiently high interest rate to compensate them for this risk.

There are also political economy problems on the creditors' side. Sovereign bonds are an important form of collateral. A decrease in the value of bonds held by banks would decrease the value of collateral, affecting lending and (reported) profits. But when bonds (loans) are not marked to market,[22] what matters is the *recognition* of the loss. A debt write-off forces the recognition of the loss.[23] Thus, banks have incentives to resist debt write-offs. The incentives turn more perverse when the managers' relevant horizon is short—as is typically the case, especially when, with bad corporate governance, compensation is linked to short-term performance metrics.

THE MARKET-BASED APPROACH RESPONSE

The ICMA, with the support of the IMF, proposes to resolve the failures in SDR by modifying the debt contracts' language. The new terms include a formula for aggregation of CACs and a clarification of the pari passu clause.[24]

The formula for aggregation allows bondholders across different series of bonds to vote collectively in response to a restructuring proposal. The decisions of a supermajority (defined by acceptance of the aggregate principal amount[25] of outstanding debt securities of all of the affected series) would be binding to all the bondholders across all series.

The clarification of pari passu establishes that, unlike Judge Griesa's interpretation in Argentina's case, "the Issuer shall have no obligation to effect equal or ratable payment(s) at any time" with respect to any other external indebtedness of the issuer, and in particular the issuer "shall have no obligation to pay other External Indebtedness at the same time or as a condition of paying sums due on the Notes and vice versa" (ICMA, 2014, 1). In other words, ICMA states that pari passu does not mean what Judge Griesa interpreted it to mean.

These new terms are improvements over the previous ones but leave some important issues unaddressed. We analyze these issues in the next section.

LIMITATIONS OF THE PRIVATE CONTRACTUAL APPROACH: WHY A MARKET-BASED APPROACH WILL NOT SUFFICE

SDRs are more complex than private debt restructurings. They involve dealing with contracts issued under different terms, under different legislation from different jurisdictions, and different currencies, over which there may not be obvious ways for comparing values when the contracts need to be rewritten. At those times, distributive conflicts get magnified.[26] The private contractual approach does not solve these issues according to efficiency or equity considerations but on the basis of relative bargaining strength (related, for instance, to the ability to withstand large litigation costs and delays). Outcomes are generally inefficient and inequitable. That is why no government relies on the private contractual approach within its boundaries for private debts. The advocates of the private contractual approach have never explained why, if it were as good as they claim, it has been universally rejected. And as the complexities of SDR are greater, the need for a statutory approach is larger.

THE PROBLEM WITH EXISTING CONTRACTS

The IMF estimates that roughly 30 percent of the $900 billion in outstanding bonds issued under the old terms will mature in more than ten years. Approximately 20 percent of those stocks do not include any kind of CACs, and virtually all of the 80 percent that does include them have CACs that operate only at the level of each security (IMF, 2014). What would prevent the current problems from arising if those debts had to be restructured (events which, unfortunately, are especially likely to occur in the context of an anemic global economy)?

Debt issued under the old terms could in principle be exchanged for securities that incorporate the new terms. But what would rule out holdout behavior if such a proposal were carried out? The vultures would have an incentive not to exchange existing bonds for these new bonds. There is no solution to this quandary within the improved contractual approach.

INTERCREDITOR FAIRNESS

There are complicated bargaining problems among classes of creditors. A supermajority voting does not solve them all.

A simple supermajority rule could lead to a situation wherein junior creditors vote to have themselves treated equally with more senior creditors and can impose their position through a supermajority.[27] This would make the senior status conditional on the outcome of the bargaining process. Indeed, if senior creditors were sufficiently small relative to the junior creditors, there is a presumption that their seniority would not be fully taken into account, and under the proposed arrangements, there is nothing they could do about it. Senior creditors would anticipate this possibility and would react by demanding different contract terms ex ante (for instance, an early senior creditor might limit the amount of junior creditor bonds that could be issued so as not to dilute voting interests, but that would have a deleterious effect on growth; alternatively, he or she could demand a higher interest rate[28]).

When countries issue debt under different jurisdictions, establishing priority of claims could be a daunting task, with multiple contradictions. Contracts could become inconsistent in crisis times. For example, the terms of a bond issued under the jurisdiction A could state that the holder of that bond has priority over all the other claims. But at the same time another bond issued under the jurisdiction B could state the same. If it were not possible to satisfy both claims at the same time, how would priority be determined? Who would ultimately judge over it? It might be impossible to ensure the consistency of rulings from judges of different jurisdictions.[29]

The same bargaining problems may arise when a default is accompanied by a currency crisis, and the country issues debt under multiple currencies. How should debts that mature in the future be valued in the present in the event of a default? What nominal exchange rate should be used? The holders of debt denominated in a currency that is rapidly depreciating would claim that they should be weighed for purposes both of settlement and voting on the basis of a "normal" (i.e., strong) exchange rate, while the holders of debt denominated in the other currencies would argue the opposite, as each party attempts to maximize what he or she receives. It would be unfair to effectively deprive domestic bondholders of their voting rights in the event of a temporary currency crisis; and if that happened, opportunistic bondholders in foreign denominated bonds would have an incentive to seize the opportunity to effectively discriminate against the domestic bondholders.

Finally, how should the informal claimants (such as workers and pensioners) be treated? Under CACs, they would have no voting rights. A solution to this problem within the contractual approach is not easy. Governments could decide to give full creditor rights to social security claimants. But then government agencies would be fiduciary for those claimants, which might "drown out" traditional creditors—an issue that would be anticipated and that would also be reflected in the interest rates and the contract terms.

Under a decentralized private contractual approach, anticipating all of these possibilities would result in highly complex contracts, and solving the disputes would require intricate and lengthy negotiations, with complex legal questions, and would almost surely cast a pall of uncertainty over what might happen in the event of the need for a restructuring.

SIGNALING EQUILIBRIUM

In the presence of imperfect information, debtors try to show that they are of a "good type" by using costly signals.

In the context of sovereign debt, debtors may choose excessively "tough" jurisdictions to signal they are unlikely to default—jurisdictions that will make an eventual restructuring very difficult. Other debtors, by acting differently, would signal that they are more likely to restructure.

Hence, the net payoff of deviating to a more reasonable jurisdiction would be negative. The result is an inefficient global equilibrium.[30]

Besides, bargaining models with imperfect information often result in excessive delay—delay itself is a costly signal—again leading to an inefficient global equilibrium.

POLITICAL ECONOMY ISSUES

As described earlier, sovereign lending markets are featured by important political economy tensions both on the debtor and the creditor side. A purely market-based approach for debt crisis resolution would only exacerbate these tensions, leading to inefficient solutions.

On the debtor side, a free-market solution will not internalize the negative externalities of an incumbent government willing to take actions that result in short-run benefits (like giving up on sovereign immunity to receive better financing conditions), leaving succeeding governments to pay the costs. The frameworks for SDR should recognize these perverse incentives and should consequently make it impossible to sign away sovereign immunity.

On the creditor side, a decentralized negotiation would face the opposition of investors who use sovereign bonds as collateral and, in a world of less than perfect corporate governance, will oppose the devaluation of the bonds in the short term, even if not writing debt off leads to more sustainability problems and larger haircuts in a longer term.

POSSIBLE FURTHER IMPROVEMENTS TO
THE CONTRACTUAL APPROACH

There are other modifications to the standard contract that could improve the workings of the market-based approach. They entail regulations on contracts, changes in domestic legislation, and the inclusion of clauses that make debt payments contingent on the economic situation of the debtor.

REGULATION OF SOVEREIGN CREDIT DEFAULT SWAPS (SCDSS)

CDSs have been advertised as helping to complete markets.[31] But they have failed to do so and instead have made matters worse. The use of SCDSs distorts incentives.

SCDSs distort incentives when they are used for insurance purposes (as noted earlier). But third parties can also demand SCDSs for speculation purposes. This would not necessarily be a problem if there were no connections between the actions of the buyers and the interests of the sovereign. But the lack of transparency of these markets makes the connections possible (and profitable).[32]

To avoid conflicts of interest that could undermine the success of restructurings, and considering that the opacity of CDSs markets makes regulation too difficult, all CDS positions of parties involved in the restructuring negotiations should be fully disclosed.[33]

REINSTATING VARIANTS OF THE CHAMPERTY DEFENSE

If investors who purchase debt in default were willing to settle under "reasonable" conditions, they would just provide a liquidity service in the markets for defaulted debt and could thus contribute to avoiding an even larger depression in bond prices in such circumstances. But that is not what vulture funds do. Reinstating variants of the champerty defense that prohibit the purchase of defaulted debt with the intent of litigating against the issuer, together with a clarification of the pari passu clause, would undermine the vultures' business, correcting the many inefficiencies associated with their behavior that we have identified.[34]

GDP-INDEXED BONDS

With GDP-indexed bonds, the principal is indexed to the nominal GDP of the country. The contingent element in the contract improves debt sustainability, as it makes debt obligations less burdensome when debt repayment is more difficult and vice versa. Creditors also benefit from a lower probability of default.

These securities may also be an effective part of SDR. Exchanging fixed-coupon bonds with GDP-indexed bonds would be akin to a debt-equity swap. The inclusion of this contingency clause would align the incentives of the debtor and the creditors, as each would benefit from the faster growth of the country. (Similar benefits might be achieved through the issuance of ordinary bonds, which automatically convert to GDP-linked bonds in the extreme events associated with crises.)

The capacity for countercyclical fiscal policies would also improve. The numbers may be significant: Bank of England economists (Barr, Bush, and Pienkowski, 2014) estimate that GDP-linked bonds can increase fiscal space, that is, they can increase the level of what is called "sustainable debt."[35] (It must be noted, however, that "debt limit" is a subjective concept whose quantification requires taking a stance on the expectations about the government's capacity for generating revenues—a complicated issue over which it is relatively easy to make wrong assumptions, especially in the most volatile economies, which are the ones more likely to need restructurings. The IMF itself has been systematically overestimating the speed of recovery of economies in crises and the multipliers in response to the conditionalities imposed on the bailed-out countries. See Guzman, 2014).

Even if these proposals were incorporated, the contractual approach would be insufficient. The approach needs to be complemented by a multinational legal framework—the object of analysis of the next section.

A MULTINATIONAL LEGAL FRAMEWORK FOR SDR

A majority of countries have become convinced both by experience and the force of the arguments of the previous sections that the private contractual approach, no matter how improved, will not solve the basic problem of SDR. These countries are advocating for institutionalizing a multinational statutory solution, as reflected in Resolution 68/304, passed by the General Assembly of the United Nations on September 9, 2014.

GUIDELINES FOR THE FRAMEWORK

The framework must recognize the limitations of the private contractual approach. It needs to solve the "too little, too late" syndrome and the possibility that restructuring would take too long. It also needs to ensure a reasonably fair treatment of all parties.

Any framework for SDR must take account of the primacy of the functions of the state, its obligations to its citizens, and the "social contract" the state has with its citizens (Stiglitz et al., 2015).

Although there are differences between sovereign debt and corporate debt restructurings, there are also important analogies. Thus, some of the provisions of Chapters 9 and 11 of the U.S. Bankruptcy Code should be considered (Stiglitz, 2002a, 2010a).[36]

DEADLINES

The sovereign should initiate the restructuring in a timely way. The framework should provide the right incentives for avoiding delays in the initiation and in the finalization of the restructuring. Therefore, it must set specific deadlines for the different stages of the process. This would make the whole process more predictable.

LENDING INTO ARREARS

The framework must recognize the macroeconomic externalities associated with debt crisis resolution. Thus, it should facilitate countercyclical macroeconomic policies. Provisions of lending into arrears, according to which creditors who lend while the restructuring process is being carried on would receive senior treatment, should be contemplated.

STAYS

Litigation induces costly delays. As previously described, it also creates a moral hazard problem, as it negatively affects creditors' incentives to enter into restructurings. Therefore, the framework should incorporate clauses of stays for litigation, which would prohibit litigation in courts between the initiation and the finalization of the restructuring process.

Litigations could still occur in jurisdictions that do not endorse the framework, remaining a problem, as a large proportion of debts will still be issued under those jurisdictions. However, judges of nonparticipating jurisdictions could consider the multinational framework as a reference on what good practice in SDR looks like.

HARD LAW VERSUS SOFT LAW

The design of the framework must consider what constitutes the set of principles on which all the parties involved would agree. One possibility could be to follow a "hard law" approach, in which countries adhere to an international bankruptcy court. If the rulings of the court were enforceable, countries would be giving up on sovereign immunity. Of course, any international treaty entails giving up on sovereignty and compromising sovereign immunity. The benefit would be a more orderly restructuring. But countries would, at least initially, worry about the fairness of the tribunal. Besides, geopolitical problems would be intense: How would the members of the international court be appointed? What interests would they represent? Indeed, it might even be difficult, at least initially, to define the principles that should guide restructuring. The intense debates within countries over the design of bankruptcy law should make it clear that resolving these issues internationally might be difficult. The creditor countries would push for creditor-friendly principles, with the debtor countries advocating for the converse.

There is a single principle countries could agree to that would restore a semblance of order to the global sovereign debt market: the restoration of sovereign immunity. More precisely: there is a consensus that there should be restrictions on what counts as acceptable contracts. Individuals cannot sell themselves into slavery. Many countries do not allow certain kinds of perpetuities. There should be a global agreement that no country can surrender its sovereign immunity (even voluntarily). Such a restriction is particularly important given the political economy problems discussed earlier. It is too easy for a government today to surrender the sovereign immunity of some government in the future, in return for money that would enhance its popularity and the wealth of its supporters.

To this should be added a framework that would facilitate restructuring. This would occur through what might be called a "soft law" approach, with the creation of an oversight commission with the mission of mediating and supervising the restructuring process. The commission would also maintain a registry of the debt stocks. The members of the commission would be countries that endorse the multinational framework. The commission would not rule over different alternatives. Instead, the sovereign would finalize the process with a final proposal and the commission would produce statements about the reasonability of the process and the final proposal. This approach would serve to legitimate the restructuring or, alternatively, to legitimate positions that speak of illegitimate restructurings.[37]

CONCLUSIONS

Restructuring is not a zero-sum game. The mechanisms in place can have large effects on the overall economic performance of the countries involved. The existing institutional arrangements make the sum too negative, as they delay the initiation of restructurings and lead to "solutions" that do not promote economic recovery—making recessions more severe and persistent overall. Deficiencies in the restructuring process also get reflected ex ante in the terms and volumes transacted in sovereign debt markets.

The world of debt restructuring needs to move to a different equilibrium. There is consensus on the necessity of this, but there are different views on how to move forward.[38] On the one hand, the business community and the IMF advocate for tweaking the terms of contracts. Although the suggested new terms (aggregation of CACs and clarification of the pari passu clause) are improvements over the old terms (terms that clearly did not work), they still leave a legacy of problems unaddressed. There are further improvements that can be implemented, as we discussed earlier.

But with incomplete contracts, even with all those improvements, a variety of problems will remain. In times of default, debt contracts will need to be rewritten. Under a market-based approach for restructurings, outcomes will be more determined by bargaining power than by considerations of efficiency and equity. Particularly disturbing is the fact that most countries that are entering debt restructurings are in particularly weak positions and are therefore particularly vulnerable to pressure from creditors to agree to terms that are adverse to their long-term interests. And the knowledge that this is so gives rise itself to bad lending practices, especially in the context of the political economy problems we discussed earlier: creditors encourage more lending than is socially efficient, in the knowledge that they can use their market power to extract a favorable outcome for themselves in the event of a crisis. At least in the past, practices of the IMF, which provided funds to the government to bail out the creditors—ensuring that they were paid in full—only exacerbated the problem.[39]

A comprehensive solution requires the implementation of a statutory approach at the multinational level—an approach that helps "complete" contracts. The framework needs to address the limitations of the current approach. It needs to redefine the balance among the parties involved in the negotiation. It should be built respecting the principles on which the different actors involved would agree.

For now, the single most important change over which there is the possibility of getting agreement is the restoration of sovereign immunity and the recognition that no government can sign away sovereign immunity for itself or for successor governments.

We believe a soft law approach that entails a more active role for a quasi judiciary can mitigate some, perhaps many, of the inefficiencies and inequities noted earlier. While this approach is not a panacea, we believe it represents a substantial step forward—and a substantial step beyond the private contractual approach.

NOTES

We are indebted to Sebastian Ceria, Richard Conn, Juan José Cruces, Anna Gelpern, Matthias Goldman, Barry Herman, Daniel Heymann, Brett House, Charles Mooney, Kunibert Raffer, Wouter Schmit Jongbloed, and Sebastian Soler; the participants of the Conference on "Frameworks for Sovereign Debt Restructuring" at Columbia University, the ECON 2014 Forum at University of Buenos Aires, the RIDGE Forum on Financial Crises at Central Bank of Uruguay, and the First Session of the Ad Hoc Committee of the United Nations General Assembly on a Multilateral Legal Framework for Sovereign Debt Restructuring; the seminar participants at Javeriana University (Bogota), the Central Bank of Argentina, the UNCTAD Conference on "Legal Framework for Debt Restructuring Processes: Options and Elements" at Columbia University, the INET Annual Conference at OECD, the Research Consortium for Systemic Risk Meeting at MIT, and the International Institute of Social Studies in The Hague; the Academia Nacional de Ciencias Económicas (Argentina), the CIGI-IPD Conference on Sovereign Debt Restructuring at Columbia University, the Central Bank of Colombia, FLACSO (Argentina), the RIDGE workshop on International Macroeconomics (Montevideo, 2015), the RIDGE workshop on Sovereign Debt at University of Buenos Aires, and three anonymous reviewers for useful comments, discussions, and suggestions. We are grateful to the Ford and MacArthur foundations for support to the Roosevelt-IPD Inequality Project; the Institute for New Economic Thinking for financial support; and Debarati Ghosh and Ines Lee for research assistance. A previous version of this chapter was circulated with the title "Fixing Sovereign Debt Restructuring."

1. It is not high debt per se that is bad for economic growth or full employment, as careless studies that were influential in the policy debate have suggested (Reinhart and Rogoff, 2010; see, in particular, the important critique of Herndon, Ash, and Pollin, 2014). Indeed, standard general equilibrium theory argues that there is a full-employment equilibrium regardless of the level of debt (Stiglitz, 2014). Instead, it is the difficulty of running expansionary macro policies when primary surpluses are allocated to debt payments in times of recessions (which are indeed often associated with high debt) that makes debt a constraint for economic recovery.

Note, too, that even then it is not only the economic constraints that matter, but those arising out of political economy—a political economy which itself is affected by the largely ideological research referred to in the previous paragraph.

In particular, for countries like the United States, which can borrow even now at a negative real interest rate—and borrowed at very low real interest rates even when its debt to GDP ratio was in excess of 130 percent—borrowing for public investments that yield significantly higher returns than the cost of capital can improve the nation's balance sheet.

2. The only situation in which the temporary assistance (bailout) might make sense is if there is a liquidity crisis, e.g., markets are irrationally pessimistic about the country's prospects, with the evidence that they are wrong expected to be revealed in the not too distant future. But it is ironic that those in the financial market who normally profess such faith in markets suddenly abandon that faith when markets turn skeptical on them; and that at that point, they seem willing to rely on the judgment of a government bureaucrat or an international civil servant over that of the market. There are other irrationalities implicit in these arguments: it is sometimes suggested that if the intervention stabilizes, say, the exchange rate, that will restore confidence and prevent contagion. But if it is known that the reason that the exchange rate has been stabilized is that there has been IMF intervention, why should the stabilization of the exchange rate change beliefs, and especially so if the intervention is announced to be short term? And if there are reasons to believe that the IMF would not intervene in other countries (e.g., because they are less systematically important or less politically connected), then why should the intervention in one country change beliefs about the equilibrium exchange rate in the others? It is even possible that it could have adverse effects (Stiglitz, 1998).

3. Even if the funds were offered without such conditions, to the extent that the funds are not used for addressing the fundamental problems that make debts unsustainable, the country would be worse off over the long run, unless there was commitment to provide these funds indefinitely—which is in effect equivalent to a debt write-off.

4. Since bonds replaced loans, nearly 40 percent of restructurings ended in re-default or another restructuring within five years (Gelpern, 2015).

5. And when they do not take too long, they may not achieve the objectives of restructuring that we define in the section on the objectives of restructuring. This is the case of the Greek debt restructuring in 2012. The deal was mostly a socialization of banks' debts that was not conducive to the recovery of the economy. Three years later, the country is still suffering, with an more deeply depressed economy: GDP has fallen by 25 percent since the beginning of the recession, and the unemployment rate was above 25 percent in January 2015 (as reported by the Hellenic Statistical Authority Labor Force Survey, 2015).

6. Where an American court seemingly has taken an action affecting payments on Argentinean bonds issued in other jurisdictions, such as the United Kingdom, and a British court has ruled that they cannot do so (England and Wales High Court (Chancery Division) Decisions, Case No.: HC-2014-000704).

7. This is not the first attempt to implement a framework of this nature. The IMF had called for the implementation of a sovereign debt restructuring mechanism (Krueger, 2001; although the IMF executive board would have determined sustainability and judged on the adequacy of the debtor's economic policies, a task in which it has not excelled in recent times (see Guzman and Heymann, 2015)), and the report of

the International Commission of Experts of the International Monetary and Financial System appointed by the president of the General Assembly of the United Nations had pointed out the necessity of exploring enhanced approaches for the restructuring of sovereign debt (Stiglitz et al., 2010).

8. We will explain some of the reasons for the growth of vulture funds later in the chapter.

9. In private debt markets, other considerations relating to adverse selection and moral hazard also militate for at least some reliance on debt. See, e.g., Stiglitz (1985). The problems of costly state enforcement for sovereign debt markets have, we think, been greatly exaggerated, and there have been several important proposals for such bonds. (Argentina actually introduced GDP-linked bonds as part of its debt restructuring.)

10. This would be true even if lenders were risk averse and markets highly competitive. Under these assumptions, each lender would receive the certainty equivalent return from each of his or her investments. Though such an assumption dominates within the finance literature, there are reasons to be skeptical. Still, the conclusion holds that forcing the borrower to absorb all the risk is not efficient.

11. Importantly, it also depends on the discrepancy between the expectations on the future capacity of repayment and the realizations that determine the actual capacity of repayment. See Guzman (2014).

12. The nature of the distress also depends on actions of the creditors, i.e., their willingness to roll over.

13. There is some controversy over whether there is a stigma that makes it more difficult for the borrower to borrow after the resolution of the debt. There is theory (and some evidence) that markets are forward looking, infer that the cost of bankruptcy is sufficiently high that few if any countries go into default if they can avoid it—and that therefore there is no inference of a flawed "character trait" that can be made from a default; as a result of the cleaning of balance sheets, at least following a deep restructuring, there will be more access to credit markets. Russia's 1998 default falls into this model. See Stiglitz (2010b).

14. That is, there are both macro-inefficiencies and micro-inefficiencies. In the chaos surrounding disorderly debt distress situations, assets typically do not get used in the most efficient way, and complementary investments to those assets are not undertaken.

15. It is important to realize that the normal presumption that markets on their own are efficient fails in this context for a large number of reasons: there are imperfections and asymmetries and incomplete risk markets (and in such situations, there is a strong presumption that markets are not efficient). Moreover, the context with which we are most concerned—in which there is significant underutilization of resources—is again one in which there is a presumption of market inefficiency. Finally, the bargaining that surrounds debt resolution is itself evidence of the absence of perfect competition, another essential assumption if markets are to be efficient. See, e.g., Greenwald and Stiglitz (1986).

16. The judge's decision was peculiar in other ways: it forced the trust bank into which funds were deposited to enforce his decision, i.e., the trustee was forbidden from distributing funds that it had received on behalf of the restructured bonds. Thus,

to enforce one contract, it had to break other contractual arrangements. There seemed to be little rationale for the court's decision about which contracts to respect and which to abrogate. Thus, the decision was not (as it has sometimes been put) about the sanctity of contracts (see chap. 4 by Sergio Chodos in this volume).

17. The upshot is that vulture funds are poised to get returns on their "investments" more than five times greater than the holders of the exchange bonds.

18. In the 1990s, bonds issued in the London market under the English law contained CACs, while bonds issued in the New York market under the law of the state of New York did not (Eichengreen and Mody, 2003). Mexico was the first country to put these clauses in its contracts under the jurisdiction of the state of New York in 2003.

19. In a world of globalization, the distinction between foreign and domestic bonds may not be clear. Moreover, the rules of the game would be expected to change the mix.

20. This is especially true when there are large macro-economic disturbances. See Miller and Stiglitz (1999, 2010).

21. See Elliott Assocs. v. Republic of Peru, 961 F. Supp. 82, 86-87 (S.D.N.Y. 1997), and 194 F.3d 363 (2d Cir. 1998).

22. Even with marked to market, there is always a chance that the country will recover and the bonds will pay off. If the write-down is greater than the expected loss (recall that if there is not a restructuring now, there is a chance, even a likelihood, that matters will get even worse, and the necessary write-down will be even greater), then the write-down will be associated with a decrease today in the value of the firm.

23. Similar problems arise, of course, with domestic debt, and played an important role in the evolution of the U.S. financial crisis. See Stiglitz (2010b).

24. See Gelpern, Heller, and Setser (2016) for a description of the ICMA's proposal.

25. There is still a problem when debt is issued in different currencies and there are marked changes in exchange rates (as in the East Asian crisis). Depending on the rules, it may be relatively easy for a vulture fund to buy enough bonds to block a restructuring or to obtain a settlement that advantages it over other claimants (the issue is more extensively analyzed in the section analyzing the limitations of the ICMA-IMF solution). Similar problems can arise when there are different maturities: long-dated bonds might, for instance, sell at a marked discount relative to principal values.

26. That is, if the country had issued only one set of bonds, there would be a clear meaning to equity: repayments should be proportional to the face value of the bonds. This is not so if, as is the case in practice, there are many different kinds of bonds.

27. In the world of sovereign bonds, bondholders are on an equal foot. However, some creditors (the IMF for instance) are de facto treated as senior creditors. But nothing prevents the possibility that in the future there could be unsubordinated debt not only de facto to official creditors but also de jure to other bondholders. Indeed, the legal literature suggests that this is feasible (cf. Chatterjee and Eyigungor (2015) for a concrete proposal). A comprehensive solution must also address this concerns (Mooney, 2015).

28. Moreover, the set of contracts in the market will respond endogenously to the rules of the game. For instance, the senior debt contract could have a provision that in the event of a default, the face value of what is owed is multiplied such that, under the aggregation clause, those bondholders have sufficient votes to block any proposal by junior creditors.

29. See Guzman and Stiglitz (2015b) for a description of the interplay between legal jurisdictions in the case of Argentina's restructuring after the 2001 crisis.

30. This is a standard result in the theory of adverse selection and signaling.

31. Arrow and Debreu have established that only if there were a complete set of risk markets would competitive markets be efficient. Some in the financial market therefore argued that introducing new securities (such as CDSs) helps complete the market and thus improves societal welfare. But that conclusion ignores the basic insights of the theory of the second best, which demonstrates that in the presence of multiple market failures, reducing the scope of one could actually (and under plausible conditions often would) lead to a decrease in societal welfare. Thus, Newbery and Stiglitz (1982) showed that eliminating barriers to trade, in the presence of imperfections in risk markets, could lead all individuals in all countries to be worse off.

In this context, Guzman and Stiglitz (2014a, 2015a, 2015d) have shown that introducing these new instruments for betting may actually increase economic volatility and lower output permanently.

32. The recent case of Argentine debt restructuring illustrates how perverse incentives can turn. In the aftermath of Judge Griesa's injunction that blocked the payments of the country to its bondholders, the International Swaps and Derivatives Association (ISDA) classified the credit event as a default. Interestingly, one of the members of ISDA committee was Elliott Management, the same vulture fund that was litigating against the country. (The debt contract only specified that Argentina turn over the requisite funds to the "agent"—which Argentina did. Argentina was thus not in breach of the contracts it had signed in the process of restructuring. Indeed, Argentina had even warned investors in its contract of the possibility of these difficulties. That is why the so-called default has been labeled a Griesafault, to distinguish it from a normal default, wherein a party actually breaches a key contract provision. See Guzman and Stiglitz [2014b]).

33. Some have suggested going further: banning the purchase of SCDSs by third parties (Brooks, Guzman, Lombardi, and Stiglitz, 2015).

34. One could even imagine some variant of such a clause being inserted into the contract: that no secondary purchasers of the bond could make a claim in court for an amount greater than the price at which he or she had purchased the bond. While such a provision arguably might lower the price of the bond at issuance (requiring the sovereign borrower to pay a higher interest rate), the effect is likely to be minimal: few buy a bond on the expectation that it will go into default.

35. When debt becomes too high, then, depending on the rate of growth of the economy and the rate of interest, the ratio of debt to GDP increases without bound. Barr, Bush, and Pienkowski (2014) argue that switching to GDP-linked bonds increases the critical threshold by some 45 percent.

36. Raffer (1990, 2015) explains that the essential points of the special insolvency procedure for municipalities in the United States (Chapter 9, Title 11, U.S.C.) can be easily applied to sovereigns.

37. For an analysis of the international-law elements on which a multinational formal framework could be drawn, see Howse (2016).

38. The different chapters in this volume reflect both the consensus and the differences in views on how to move forward. See, for example, Conn (2016),

Herman (2016), Howse (2016), Kaiser (2016), Ocampo (2016), and Raffer (2016). See also Brooks and Lombardi (2015), Gelpern (2015), and Guzman and Stiglitz (2015c).

39. For a more extensive discussion of this problem, see Stiglitz (2002b).

REFERENCES

Barr, David, Oliver Bush, and Alex Pienkowski. 2014. "GDP-linked Bonds and Sovereign Default." Working Paper No. 484, Bank of England, London.

Blackman, Jonathan I., and Rahul Mukhi. 2010. "The Evolution of Modern Sovereign Debt Litigation: Vultures, Alter Egos, and Other Legal Fauna." *Law & Contemporary Problems* 73: 47.

Brooks, Skylar, Martin Guzman, Domenico Lombardi, and Joseph E. Stiglitz. January 2015. "Identifying and Resolving Inter-Creditor and Debtor-Creditor Equity Issues in Sovereign Debt Restructuring." Center for International Governance Innovation Policy Brief No. 53.

Brooks, Skylar, and Domenico Lombardi. 2015. "Governing Sovereign Debt Restructuring Through Regulatory Standards." Paper presented at the Initiative for Policy Dialogue–Center for International Governance Innovation Conference on Sovereign Debt Restructuring at Columbia University, New York, September 22.

———. 2016. "Private Creditor Power and the Politics of Sovereign Debt Governance." In *Too Little, Too Late: The Quest to Resolve Sovereign Debt Crises*, ed. Martin Guzman, José Antonio Ocampo, and Joseph E. Stiglitz, chapter 3. New York: Columbia University Press.

Chatterjee, Satyajit and Burcu Eyigungor. 2015. "A Seniority Arrangement for Sovereign Debt." *American Economic Review* 105 (no. 12): 3740–3765.

Chodos, Sergio. 2016. "From the Pari Passu Discussion to the 'Illegality' of Making Payments." In *Too Little, Too Late: The Quest to Resolve Sovereign Debt Crises*, ed. Martin Guzman, José Antonio Ocampo, and Joseph E. Stiglitz, chapter 4. New York: Columbia University Press.

Conn, Richard A., Jr. 2016. "Perspectives on a Sovereign Debt Restructuring Framework: Less Is More." In *Too Little, Too Late: The Quest to Resolve Sovereign Debt Crises*, ed. Martin Guzman, José Antonio Ocampo, and Joseph E. Stiglitz, chapter 13. New York: Columbia University Press.

Eichengreen, Barry, and Ashoka Mody. 2003. "Is Aggregation a Problem for Sovereign Debt Restructuring?" *American Economic Review* 93 (no. 2): 80–84.

Gelpern, Anna. 2015. "What Is Wrong with Sovereign Debt Restructuring and How to Fix It." Paper presented at the Initiative for Policy Dialogue–Center for International Governance Innovation Conference on Sovereign Debt Restructuring at Columbia University, New York, September 22.

Gelpern, Anna, Ben Heller, and Brad Setser. 2015. "Count the Limbs: Designing Robust Aggregation Clauses in Sovereign Bonds." Paper presented at the Initiative for Policy Dialogue–Center for International Governance Innovation Conference on Sovereign Debt Restructuring at Columbia University, New York, September 22.

Greenwald, Bruce C., and Joseph E. Stiglitz. 1986. "Externalities in Economies with Imperfect Information and Incomplete Markets." *Quarterly Journal of Economics* 101 (no. 2): 229–264.

Guzman, Martin. November 2014. "Understanding the Relationship Between Output Growth Expectations and Financial Crises." Columbia University Initiative for Policy Dialogue Working Paper, New York.

Guzman, Martin, and Joseph E. Stiglitz. 2014a. "Pseudo-wealth and Consumption Fluctuations." Columbia University Working Paper, New York.

——. 2014b. "Argentina's Griesafault." *Project Syndicate*, August 7.

——. 2014c. "Debeaking the Vultures." *Project Syndicate*, October 1.

——. 2015a. "Pseudo-wealth Fluctuations and Aggregate Demand Effects." Columbia University Working Paper, New York.

——. 2015b. "A Fair Hearing for Sovereign Debt." *Project Syndicate*, March 5.

——. 2015c. "A Rule of Law for Sovereign Debt." *Project Syndicate*, June 15.

——. 2015d. "A Theory of Pseudo-Wealth." In *Contemporary Issues in Macroeconomics: Lessons from the Crisis and Beyond*, ed. J. E. Stiglitz and M. Guzman, chap. 1. Palgrave, London.

Hellenic Statistical Authority Labor Force Survey. 2015. Press release. www.statistics.gr/portal/page/portal/ESYE/BUCKET/A0101/PressReleases/A0101_SJO02_DT_MM_01_2015_01_F_EN.pdf.

Herndon, Thomas, Michael Ash, and Robert Pollin. 2014. "Does High Public Debt Consistently Stifle Economic Growth? A Critique of Reinhart and Rogoff." *Cambridge Journal of Economics* 38 (no. 2): 257–279.

Herman, Barry. "Toward a Multilateral Framework for Recovery from Sovereign Insolvency." In *Too Little, Too Late: The Quest to Resolve Sovereign Debt Crises*, ed. Martin Guzman, José Antonio Ocampo, and Joseph E. Stiglitz, chapter 11. New York: Columbia University Press.

Howse, Robert. "Toward a Framework for Sovereign Debt Restructuring: What Can Public International Law Contribute?" In *Too Little, Too Late: The Quest to Resolve Sovereign Debt Crises*, ed. Martin Guzman, José Antonio Ocampo, and Joseph E. Stiglitz, chapter 14. New York: Columbia University Press.

International Capital Markets Association. 2014. "Standard Collective Action and Pari Passu Clauses for the Terms and Conditions of Sovereign Notes." http://www.icmagroup.org/resources/Sovereign-Debt-Information/

International Monetary Fund, October 2014. "Strengthening the Contractual Framework to Address Collective Action Problems in Sovereign Debt Restructuring." https://www.imf.org/external/np/pp/eng/2014/090214.pdf

Jordà, Òscar, Moritz H. P. Schularick, and Alan M. Taylor. 2013. "Sovereigns Versus Banks: Credit, Crises, and Consequences." Working Paper No. 19506, Cambridge, Mass.: National Bureau of Economic Research.

Kaiser, Jürgen. 2016. "Making a Legal Framework for Sovereign Debt Restructuring Operational." In *Too Little, Too Late: The Quest to Resolve Sovereign Debt Crises*, ed. Martin Guzman, José Antonio Ocampo, and Joseph E. Stiglitz, chapter 12. New York: Columbia University Press.

Krueger, Anne. 2001. "International Financial Architecture for 2002: A New Approach to Sovereign Debt Restructuring." American Enterprise Institute, Washington, D.C., November 26.

Li, Yuefen. 2016. "The Long March Towards an International Legal Framework for Sovereign Debt Restructuring." Forthcoming, *Journal of Globalization and Development*.

Miller, Marcus, and J. E. Stiglitz. 1999. "Bankruptcy Protection Against Macroeconomic Shocks: The Case for a 'Super Chapter 11.'" World Bank Conference on Capital Flows, Financial Crises, and Policies, Washington, D.C., April 15.

——. 2010. "Leverage and Asset Bubbles: Averting Armageddon with Chapter 11?" *Economic Journal* 120 (no. 544): 500–518.

Mooney, Charles W. Jr. 2015. "A Framework for a Formal Sovereign Debt Restructuring Mechanism: The KISS (Keep It Simple, Stupid) Principle and Other Guiding Principles." 37 *Michigan Journal of International Law* 37.

Newbery, David MG, and Joseph E. Stiglitz. 1982. "The choice of techniques and the optimality of market equilibrium with rational expectations." *Journal of Political Economy* 90 (no. 2): 223–246.

Ocampo, José Antonio. 2016. "A Brief History of Sovereign Debt Resolution and a Proposal for a Multilateral Instrument." In *Too Little, Too Late: The Quest to Resolve Sovereign Debt Crises*, ed. Martin Guzman, José Antonio Ocampo, and Joseph E. Stiglitz, chapter 10. New York: Columbia University Press.

Orszag, Peter, and Joseph Stiglitz. 2002. "Optimal Fire Departments: Evaluating Public Policy in the Face of Externalities." Brookings Institution, Washington, D.C., January 4.

Raffer, Kunibert. 1990. "Applying Chapter 9 Insolvency to International Debts: An Economically Efficient Solution with a Human Face." *World Development* 18 (no. 2): 301–313.

——. 2015. "Debts, Human Rights, and the Rule of Law: Advocating a Fair and Efficient Sovereign Insolvency Model." Columbia University Initiative for Policy Dialogue Working Paper, New York.

——. 2016. "Debts, Human Rights, and the Rule of Law: Advocating a Fair and Efficient Sovereign Insolvency Model." In *Too Little, Too Late: The Quest to Resolve Sovereign Debt Crises*, ed. Martin Guzman, José Antonio Ocampo, and Joseph E. Stiglitz, chapter 15. New York: Columbia University Press.

Reinhart, Carmen M., and Kenneth S. Rogoff. 2010. "Growth in a Time of Debt (Digest Summary)." *American Economic Review* 100 (no. 2): 573–578.

Schumacher, Julian, Christoph Trebesch, and Henrik Enderlein. 2014. "Sovereign Defaults in Court." http://papers.ssrn.com/sol3/papers.cfm?abstract_id=2189997.

Stiglitz, Joseph E. 1985. "Information and Economic Analysis: A Perspective." *Economic Journal* 95 (Supplement): 21–41.

——. 1998. "Knowledge for Development: Economic Science, Economic Policy, and Economic Advice." In *Annual World Bank Conference on Development Economics*, ed. B. Pleskovic and J. Stiglitz, 9–58. Washington, D.C.: World Bank.

——. 2002a. "Sovereign Debt: Notes on Theoretical Frameworks and Policy Analyses." Columbia University Initiative for Policy Dialogue Working Paper Series, New York.

——. 2002b. *Globalization and Its Discontents.* New York: Norton.

——. 2006. *Making Globalization Work.* New York: Norton.

——. 2010a "Sovereign Debt: Notes on Theoretical Frameworks and Policy Analyses." In *Overcoming Developing Country Debt Crises*, ed. B. Herman, J. A. Ocampo, and S. Spiegel, 35–69. Oxford: Oxford University Press.

——. 2010b. *Freefall: America, Free Markets, and the Sinking of the World Economy*, New York: Norton.

——. 2014. "Crises: Principles and Policies: With an Application to the Eurozone Crisis." In *Life After Debt: The Origins and Resolutions of Debt Crisis*, ed. Joseph E. Stiglitz and Daniel Heymann, 43–79. Houndmills, UK.

Stiglitz, Joseph E., Martin Guzman, Domenico Lombardi, José Antonio Ocampo, and Jan Svejnar. 2015. "Frameworks for Sovereign Debt Restructuring." Columbia Initiative for Policy Dialogue-Center for International Governance Innovation-Center on Global Economic Governance Policy Brief, January 26.

Stiglitz, Joseph E., et al. 2010. *The Stiglitz Report: Reforming the International Monetary and Financial Systems in the Wake of the Global Crisis*, with Members of the Commission of Experts on Reforms of the International Monetary and Financial System appointed by the President of the United Nations General Assembly, New York: New Press.

Townsend, Robert M. 1979. "Optimal contracts and competitive markets with costly state verification." *Journal of Economic Theory* 21 (no. 2): 265–293.

CHAPTER 2

Sovereign Debt of Developing Countries

OVERVIEW OF TRENDS AND POLICY PERSPECTIVES

Marilou Uy and Shichao Zhou

Recent trends in public indebtedness of developing countries are encouraging: public debt and debt service burdens have been declining on average relative to gross domestic product (GDP). Developing countries are increasingly tapping financial markets to finance their development needs. In the process, they face new creditors—sovereign and private—who have been increasing their exposure to developing countries. These trends promise improved access to external financing; at the same time, they could also raise risks for borrower countries. Understanding these new sources of risk should inform countries' debt management policies and motivate the global community to further strengthen mechanisms for sovereign debt resolution. The objective of this paper is to provide an overview of the public debt trends of developing countries, especially over the past decade; to examine the challenges of debt management that some groups of countries face; and to discuss the different perspectives within the global community on how to strengthen the system of sovereign debt resolution.

While accelerated growth and deeper fiscal adjustments have contributed to improved debt burdens in developing countries on average, some groups of countries confront distinct challenges in managing sustainable debt levels due to unique vulnerabilities and enormous development needs. Increasing recourse to debt financing from financial markets expands access but might also lead to new sources of risk with the potential for serious consequences for some sovereign borrowers. Countries have a strong role to play in managing their debt relative to their ability to pay, but the global community has complementary responsibilities, for example, in facilitating an effective system for the resolution of sovereign debt issues that arise. Yet there is currently no clear global consensus on what such a system should involve. Even among developing countries, including G-24[1] members, there is a variety of views on how to improve the system for sovereign debt resolution. Further stakeholder consultations will be necessary to understand how best to proceed with this.

The first section of this paper discusses the trends in public debt in emerging markets and developing countries and the changing composition of lenders to sovereigns. The second and third sections discuss, respectively, the debt management challenges of some groups of countries and the diverse and evolving perspectives of countries, especially G-24 members, on options to strengthen mechanisms for sovereign debt resolution, should the need arise. A concluding section wraps up this overview.

TRENDS IN PUBLIC DEBT IN EMERGING MARKETS AND DEVELOPING COUNTRIES

In the last decade, public debt ratios of emerging markets and developing countries (EMDCs) have improved by international historical standards, while those of advanced countries have broadly weakened (figures 2.1 and 2.2). A remarkable feature of this trend is the decline in debt ratios of low-income countries (LICs),[2] a subset of the EMDCs, especially those of heavily indebted poor countries (HIPCs),[3] which dropped considerably. External indebtedness ratios of EMDCs also lessened significantly over the past two decades. Fewer of these countries were classified as severely indebted in 2012 compared with 2000, and the number of countries classified as having low indebtedness[4] more than doubled during the same period.[5] Furthermore, the EMDCs' debt service burden also declined relative to exports of goods and services (figure 2.3).

The improved debt position of EMDCs has been driven by strong growth and debt relief programs adopted by major creditors under the HIPC initiative. From 2004 to 2014, the output level of EMDCs increased, with growth rates averaging 6.13 percent, thanks to higher levels of investment made possible by an easier external financing environment and abundant global savings. LICs registered average growth of 5.2 percent, while advanced countries as a group grew by only 1.45 percent.[6] By the end of 2012, the total amount of debt relief committed under the HIPC initiative had reached nearly US\$57.5 billion for 36 countries (United Nations, 2012). This saw the average share

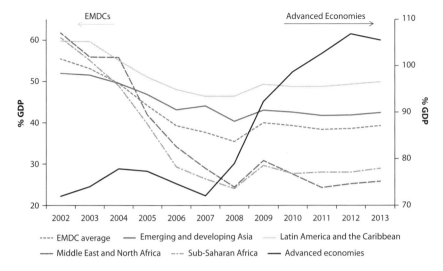

Figure 2.1   Gross government debt as percentage of GDP for advanced countries and EMDCs.

Source: IMF WEO, 2015, April.

Note: Gross government debt refers to all liabilities that require payment or payments of interest and/or principal by the debtor to the creditor at a date or dates in the future. This includes debt liabilities in the form of SDRs, currency and deposits, debt securities, loans, insurance, pensions and standardized guarantee schemes, and other accounts payable (Government Finance Statistics Manual, 2001).

of the external debt stock of all HIPCs decline to less than 30 percent of GDP.

Fiscal adjustment served to improve the debt positions of developing countries as well. Broad public sector reforms were adopted in many EMDCs, including tax policy reforms, rationalization of the public sector, and containment of contingent liabilities. More specific reforms were aimed at raising tax revenues, for example, by broadening the tax base, reducing public expenditures, and improving their efficiency (Tsibouris et al., 2006). Revenue measures provided additional fiscal space, especially in countries with low initial public revenue-to-GDP ratios, though revenue mobilization from natural resources was underutilized. There was scope for rationalizing public expenditures, although concerns were raised on the sustainability of cutting expenditures on social services such as health and education.

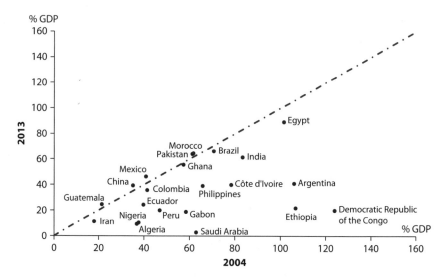

Figure 2.2   Gross government debt as percentage of GDP for G-24 countries.

Source: IMF WEO, 2015, April.

Note: Gross government debt refers to all liabilities that require payment or payments of interest and/or principal by the debtor to the creditor at a date or dates in the future. This includes debt liabilities in the form of SDRs, currency and deposits, debt securities, loans, insurance, pensions and standardized guarantee schemes, and other accounts payable (Government Finance Statistics Manual, 2001).

Better economic performance and a changing international financial landscape have improved developing countries' access to international financial markets. Over the past decade, developing countries' long-term debt[7] to the international financial market has quadrupled (G20, 2013). Financing through bonds has significantly increased: the ratio of bond financing to GDP in developing countries on average is now considerably more than that of bank financing (figure 2.4). Between 2006 and 2013, 22 developing countries issued bonds for the first time or returned to the market after a long absence (Guscina, Pedras, and Presciuttini, 2014). Some bond issues were substantial compared to a country's size and in a few instances amounted to almost 20 percent of GDP (Guscina, Pedras, and Presciuttini, 2014). This trend has also been evident, to a lesser extent, in LICs, which are increasingly turning to bond markets to support their development needs.[8]

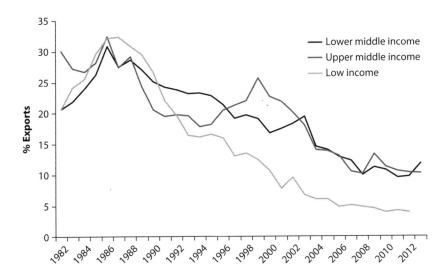

Figure 2.3   Debt service as percentage of exports.

Source: World Bank International Debt Statistics (2015).

Note: Debt service refers to total debt service to exports of goods, services, and primary income. Total debt service is the sum of principal repayments and interest actually paid in currency, goods, or services on long-term debt; interest paid on short-term debt; and repayments (repurchases and charges) to the IMF.

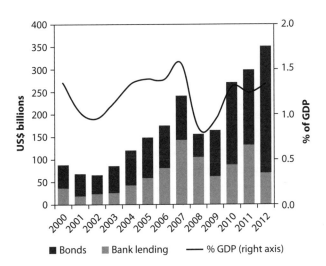

Figure 2.4   International long-term private debt versus bank lending to developing countries.

Source: G20 (2013).

Developments in domestic financial sectors have also led to the strong growth of local currency bond markets, notably in emerging countries in Asia following the financial crisis of 1997–1998. By 2010, the value of outstanding local currency bonds, most of which were sovereign bonds, had risen to 64 percent of GDP in East Asian developing countries,[9] which far exceeded the share of local currency bond financing in other regions (Baek and Kim, 2014).[10] This coincided with a strong increase in foreign investors' investment in emerging market local currency bonds. For the mutual fund sector in particular, the share of local currency–denominated bonds purchased by foreign investors in the emerging economies has risen from almost 0 percent of total cross-border inflows to nearly half by 2012 (figure 2.5; Miyajima, Mohanty, and Chan, 2012).

The mix of global investors in emerging and developing countries has changed over the past fifteen years with the rise of local-currency bond finance. Compared with official creditors and commercial banks, foreign non-banks have significantly increased their stake in emerging-market sovereign debt. An analysis of developments in the investor base of emerging markets shows that between 2010 and 2012 approximately half of foreign investor inflows went toward purchasing government debt issued in both foreign and local currencies (Arslanalp and Tsuda, 2014). By the end of 2012, it was estimated that foreign non-banks[11] held about 80 percent of the total US$1 trillion worth of government debt owned by nonresidents of emerging markets (Arslanalp and Tsuda, 2014).[12] Indeed, in emerging and developing countries in general, non-residents hold an increasingly important share of government debt.

The changing investor base is a source of both opportunity and new risks. As the creditors become more diversified in terms of country origin and risk tolerance, international risk sharing can be more easily achieved (Stulz, 1999; Sill, 2001). Empirical studies have also shown that the increasing importance of foreign investors is associated with lower financing cost (Warnock and Warnock, 2009; Andritzky, 2012). However, at the same time, countries become more vulnerable to changes in global risk aversion (Calvo and Talvi, 2005) and the "sudden stops or reversals" of financial flows, as well as exchange rate depreciation, which could eventually pose challenges to the stability of local financial markets (International Monetary Fund [IMF], 2014a). Moreover, the diversified investor base has significant implications for negotiations between debtors and creditors during stress episodes. Specifically, under the current system of market-based, ad hoc debt negotiation, the growing presence of varied—and

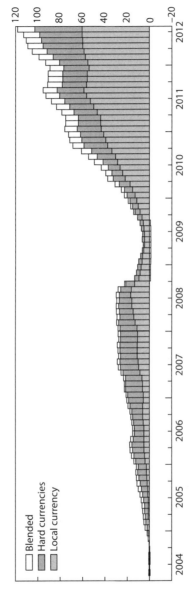

Figure 2.5 Cumulative net inflows to mutual funds dedicated to emerging-market bonds.

Source: Miyajima, Mohanty, and Chan (2012).

The figure legend shows:
- Blended
- Hard currencies
- Local currency

sometimes conflicting—interests can prolong discussions between parties and make resolution more complicated (Pitchford and Wright, 2010).

Finally, it is also worth highlighting that the corporate sector in emerging countries increased their borrowing in financial markets. Corporate debt of non-financial firms across major emerging countries grew from $4 trillion to $18 trillion between 2004 and 2014 (IMF, 2015c).[13] In the same period, the average corporate debt to GDP of emerging market rose to more than 70 percent in 2014, although the extent of the increases varied notably across countries (IMF, 2015c). The growth in corporate debt was accompanied by increased reliance on bond issuance, in addition to cross-border lending (IMF, 2015c; Brookings, 2015). These trends have been driven largely by firms taking advantage of the highly favorable global financial market conditions during this period (IMF, 2015c). Greater corporate leverage raises concerns if financial market conditions tighten[14], a lesson learned from previous financial crises in emerging countries that were preceded by rapid growth in credit and corporate leverage. Overall, both governments and firms face risks associated with increased and accelerated access to volatile financial markets.

DEBT MANAGEMENT CHALLENGES: A LOOK AT TWO COUNTRY GROUPINGS

The broadly favorable aggregate public debt trends of developing countries do not reflect the significant challenges that some countries face in managing the sustainability of their debt levels. This section discusses these challenges in two specific groups— LICs and the middle-income countries of the Caribbean.

LOW-INCOME COUNTRIES

LICs historically have had limited access to external financing and have relied mostly on official flows. Achieving debt sustainability, therefore, has depended largely on the willingness of official creditors and donors to provide positive net transfers for new financing. In the 1970s and 1980s, confronted by external debt levels that exceeded their ability to pay and that were exacerbated by vulnerability to external shocks, many LICs turned to internationally agreed debt restructuring and relief mechanisms through the HIPC and the Multilateral Debt Relief Initiative (MDRI)[15] mechanisms to regain sustainable debt levels. Most of the debt was owed to multilateral institutions and bilateral lenders of the Paris Club.[16] Debt restructuring, therefore, took place mainly through these multilateral and bilateral channels. Smaller levels of private debt were restructured through debt swaps and buybacks through the London Club, composed of commercial banks (Brooks and Lombardi, 2014).

As already noted, LICs, broadly speaking, have achieved robust economic growth and stronger debt positions over the last two decades, and many have begun to seek out more diverse sources of financing. Maintaining higher levels of growth will require greater access to financing that is not readily available from traditional, concessional financing sources.[17] In recent years, a number of countries have turned to new country creditors, such as China. In sub-Saharan Africa, for example, China's share of Africa's infrastructure financing is estimated to have tripled from 2007 to 2012 (figure 2.6), while the region's overall spending on infrastructure doubled in the same period (IMF, 2014b). Policy banks, such as the China Development Bank and Export-Import Bank of China, as well as commercial banks, "committed around US$132 billion of financing to African and Latin American governments between 2003 and 2011" (Brautigam and Gallagher, 2014), in addition to grants and interest-free loans made by the Chinese government.[18]

Some LICs have also started to take on higher-cost, nonconcessional debt from financial markets (figure 2.7). Debt levels have been rising in many LICs, with external borrowing accounting for most of the increase, although most of these countries remain at a low or moderate risk of external debt distress.[19] A worrisome trend is that about one-third of LICs have high debt levels that are increasing significantly (IMF, 2014f). To manage their debt sustainably, these countries must ensure that borrowed funds are used in projects with appropriate levels of return and must manage challenges associated with the use of private, market-based financing, such as the bunching of repayments and rollover risk (IMF, 2014c).

MIDDLE-INCOME CARIBBEAN COUNTRIES

Middle-income Caribbean countries have unique debt challenges that are difficult to address with traditional policy prescriptions. Public debt levels in these economies are high and continue to rise, with debt burdens well above most major middle-income countries.[20] Despite their middle-income status, a number of macroeconomic characteristics stemming from size make Caribbean economies uniquely vulnerable to growth

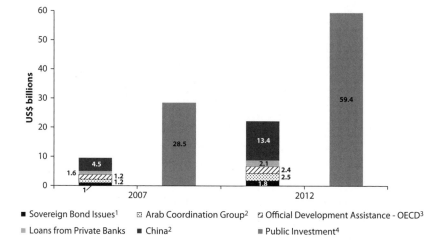

Figure 2.6   Sub-Saharan Africa: Public investment and external financing.

Source: IMF, Regional Economic Outlook, Sub-Saharan Africa: Staying the Course, October 2014b.

Notes: 1. Sovereign bonds were issued by sub-Saharan African countries between 2007 and 2012 for financing infrastructure (column 2007 equals the sum of bonds issued by Ghana in 2007 and Senegal in 2009, and column 2012 equals the sum of bonds issued by Senegal in 2011, Namibia in 2011, and Zambia in 2012).

2. Commitments reported by the Infrastructure Consortium of Africa from 2008 to 2012. Members of the Arab Coordination Group: Arab Fund for Economic and Social Development, Islamic Development Bank, Kuwait Fund for Arab Economic Development, Abu Dhabi Fund for Development, OPEC Fund for International Development, Arab Bank for Economic Development in Africa, and Saudi Fund for Development.

3. Estimated disbursement based on the annual share of the commitments for economic infrastructure and services.

4. 75 percent of total public investment is assumed to be allocated to infrastructure each year.

volatility and debt accumulation, including narrow production bases, higher terms-of-trade volatility, diseconomies of scale, susceptibility to natural disasters and, for some, underdeveloped financial sectors (G-24, 2014). Furthermore, their growth performance was undermined by the global economic and financial crises, and remains below that of other regions. The protracted global recovery also poses substantial risks to their future growth.

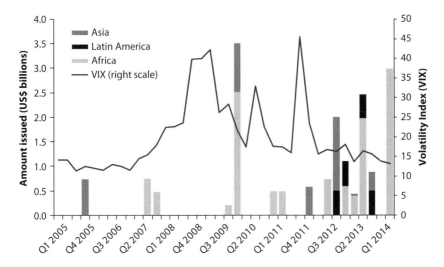

Figure 2.7   Low-income countries: International bond issues.

Source: IMF Fiscal Monitor, 2014, October.

Note: The Volatility Index (VIX) is a popular measure of market's expectations of short-term volatility. It is published by the Chicago Board Options Exchange.

Notwithstanding these considerable challenges, the middle-income status of these countries excludes them from accessing concessional lending facilities that are typically available to LICs facing debt difficulties. Therefore, these countries clearly need to explore other avenues for achieving debt sustainability. As a last resort, an effective debt restructuring mechanism would be an important option for relieving debt distress.

While this discussion has focused on the debt management challenges confronting LICs and middle-income Caribbean countries, these groups are not the only ones vulnerable to debt distress (Roubini and Setser, 2004; Reinhart and Rogoff, 2013). As mentioned earlier, developing countries have gained increased access to international financial markets, and their broad challenge is to ensure that their debt levels are sustainable and that borrowed funds are used in ways that increase productivity and stimulate growth. In addition, financial markets and business models are evolving in ways that give rise to new sources of risk that could make a growing number of EMDCs vulnerable to debt distress, especially in light of a much more volatile international global financial landscape.

Moreover, in times of sovereign debt distress, coordinating a wider range of traditional and new creditors will pose further challenges to existing global mechanisms for sovereign debt resolution that could harm the effectiveness and timeliness of debt workouts. Countries in general have a stake in improving their frameworks for sovereign debt management and in participating in global efforts to improve mechanisms for sovereign debt restructuring.

PERSPECTIVES ON APPROACHES TOWARD SOVEREIGN DEBT RESOLUTION

While there is strong agreement on the importance of sound debt management and crisis prevention at the country level, there are diverse views on how to move forward on improving the global system for sovereign debt resolution. Within the broader international finance community, there is recognition that the existing system for sovereign debt resolution has shortcomings: collective action among creditors has been difficult to achieve, and debt restructurings have often been "too little, too late" (IMF, 2013). Recent developments in the case of *NML Capital, Ltd. v. Republic of Argentina* in the U.S. courts have heightened concerns about incentives that exacerbate holdout behavior, which undermine orderly sovereign debt restructuring. Reforming the system for sovereign debt resolution has been an area of long-standing debate in the international arena. It has been difficult to strike a balance between solutions that are acceptable to creditor interests and solutions that will ensure that the value of the underlying asset—that is, the prospects for economic recovery and eventual debt sustainability of the country undergoing debt restructuring—is maintained.

The different views on how to improve sovereign debt restructuring processes are reflected in the deliberations and positions taken in intergovernmental discussions on the reform of the international financial system. The key debate has revolved around the efficacy of market-based contractual approaches versus the need for complementary statutory sovereign resolution mechanisms. These discussions have evolved significantly since they began in 2002. Initially, there was broad support for focusing primarily on market-based contractual approaches that aimed to ensure more effective coordination of creditors during debt stress episodes and sought to prevent holdouts from derailing debt restructuring efforts. In their 2002 communiqué, G-24 ministers and governors expressed a preference for "voluntary, country-specific and market-friendly approaches," noting that any proposed system for sovereign debt restructuring should not impair developing countries' access to financial markets (G-24, 2002). The G20 subsequently supported this stance and encouraged discussions among home countries of major creditors and sovereign issuers toward a voluntary code of conduct for sovereign debt restructuring (Martinez-Diaz, 2007). In 2004, the G20 endorsed the Principles for Stable Capital Flows and Fair Debt Restructuring in Emerging Markets, which outlined a voluntary, market-based approach to sovereign debt restructuring between private creditors and sovereign debtors (G20, 2004).

The G20 further encouraged more widespread use of "collective action clauses" (CACs)[21] in sovereign bond contracts issued in foreign jurisdictions (G20, 2003). Supported by the U.S. Treasury (Drage and Hovaguimian, 2004), CACs were encouraged in bonds issued in New York, with Mexico being the first issuer to include them, followed subsequently by a majority of other emerging countries that issued bonds in the New York market. This widened the usage of CACs, which was already a long-standing feature in bonds issued in the London market (Helleiner, 2009). Debtors' initial concerns that creditors would seek additional risk premiums because of perceived vulnerability if CACs were used have been generally dispelled (Eichengreen and Mody, 2000). The International Capital Market Association/IMF-led improvements of the CACs and clarifications of the pari passu agreements reached in 2014[22] have been broadly welcomed by developing countries and the G20.[23]

Nevertheless, the shortcomings of the contractual approach are widely acknowledged (United Nations, 2009; IMF, 2014d): they do not address the existing stock of debt, except through gradual reissuance of bonds to introduce CACs; they have not stopped holdout behavior among creditors in some cases of debt restructuring, including the recent experience in resolving Greek bonds that have built-in CACs. Furthermore, difficulties have arisen from differences in court rulings and interpretations on debt restructuring cases across different jurisdictions (for example, the U.S. court's ruling on Argentina[24] and the decision by the Australian courts upholding the principle of sovereignty vis-à-vis Nauru's debt servicing of its bonds[25]) that indicate an absence, at the global level, of a consistent set of principles necessary for a functional system of sovereign debt resolution. Against this backdrop, more recent views expressed by the G-24 showed renewed concerns about holdout behavior and the losses that result from prolonged sovereign debt workouts, and there was a call for exploring further options to improve the global system of sovereign debt restructuring (G-24, 2014, 2015). The G20, on the other hand, has not in recent years aired its views on the calls for further reform in global governance of sovereign debt restructuring, beyond its support for the strengthened CACs and pari passu clauses. It has, however, hosted joint discussions with the Paris Club, engaging nontraditional official creditors and private sector representatives to foster a continuous dialogue on the future of sovereign debt restructuring mechanisms.[26]

Discussions on addressing the shortcomings of the existing sovereign debt resolution system have gained momentum among developing countries in recent years. A notable development was the passage of a UN resolution to start negotiations toward a multilateral legal framework for sovereign debt restructuring[27] that was sponsored by the G-77 and China, and supported by most developing countries.[28] In this context, the G-24 welcomed as a positive development the creation of the UN Ad Hoc Committee on Sovereign Debt Restructuring Processes (G-24, 2015) but also called for substantive discussions on the content and nature of possible proposals. The engagement of the United Nations has been viewed as a signal of greater interest from developing countries to address the shortcomings of the existing sovereign debt restructuring regimes and broadens consultations beyond the traditional intergovernmental processes through which sovereign debt resolutions issues have been discussed.

While the role of the United Nations in broadening consultations on possible options to improve sovereign debt resolution is recognized, its role as a potential arbiter of a multilateral statutory sovereign debt resolution system is controversial. Many view the IMF as an effective arbiter in cases of debt distress, given its expertise and continuous involvement in assessing countries' debt sustainability in the context of its lending framework. Others express concern over potential conflicts of interest, since the IMF is itself also a creditor to sovereigns (Stiglitz, 2006) and instead favor a more prominent role for the United Nations as a neutral entity to provide the oversight and management of a global sovereign debt resolution system.

Approaches discussed within a proposed multilateral statutory framework address critical issues of sovereign debt restructuring that contractual approaches have not resolved. As previously noted, countries' issuance of bond in various jurisdictions, as well as in hard and local currencies, coupled with the increasing diversity in the investor base of sovereign bonds, will give rise to a multitude of complicated issues, such as bargaining between investors who have bought instruments in different markets and currencies and with different seniorities (see Guzman and Stiglitz, 2016). An independent and universal arbiter would be better positioned to achieve a fair, consistent allocation of debt repayment, thus preventing debt restructuring from becoming a zero-sum, or even negative-sum, game (see chap. 1). The statutory framework proposals also include provisions to approve payment standstills, providing the time needed to bring creditors together in order to agree on possible debt restructuring solutions (Krueger, 2001; Schneider, 2012). In addition, they address incentives to obtain new financing from private creditors when countries are still in arrears. These features contribute significantly to maximize growth prospects and financial stability of developing countries (Roubini and Setser, 2004), even during times of debt distress, and prevent a debt crisis from becoming an economic crisis (Chodos, 2012).

Despite the reopening of discussions on a multilateral legal framework for sovereign debt resolution, its feasibility remains questionable without the support of major financial centers from which most of the sovereign debt has been issued. In this context, proposals for less formal solutions have emerged as pathways to effect meaningful change.[29] They are classified as "soft law" approaches, whose definition ranges from informal solutions to those that indicate weak obligations (Brummer, 2011). One of the earlier proposals, for example, is the sovereign debt forum (SDF), the objective of which is to bring together creditors, debtors, and other stakeholders so that early, proactive consultations can be made when cases of sovereign debt distress emerge (Gitlin and House, 2014). Equipped with research capacity, the forum would document best practices in sovereign debt restructuring and inform continuous discussions on how to advance reforms in the system of sovereign debt resolution that has historically elicited periodic interest in the international setting. A clear advantage of the SDF is that it could be implemented within existing legal frameworks and would not compete with any of the existing institutions. In conceptualizing the SDF, Gitlin and House (2014) drew lessons from the experience in domestic corporate bankruptcy reforms and other nonpublic forums, such as the Paris and London Clubs, the Extractive Industries Transparency Initiative, and the Asia-Pacific Economic Cooperation, which rely more on coordination mechanisms as a means of fostering resolution.[30] Similarly, the success of the SDF will depend on its ability to engage key stakeholders, including all creditors, in ways that would lead to orderly debt resolution.

In the discussions related to the recent 2014 UN-led resolution, options being considered include mechanisms to put into practice sound principles of a sovereign debt workout within a global setting governed by national legislation and in which coordination mechanisms are the norm (United Nations Conference on Trade and Development, 2015). The role of national legislation is gaining more attention, following the UK's initiative to protect HIPCs permanently from the pursuit of debt enforcement by so-called vulture funds (Government of United Kingdom, 2011) and the Belgian Parliament's recent proposal to prevent vulture funds from seeking full repayment on defaulting sovereign bonds in Belgium (*Wall Street Journal*, 2015). Institutional arrangements that facilitate consensual sovereign debt workouts, such as mediation and arbitration, are also being proposed, and further discussion will be required on how to make these operational. These elements of sovereign debt workouts based on coordination and soft law are not mutually exclusive but could collectively serve as building blocks of a workable, principles-based system for sovereign debt workouts.

Although these proposals fall short of a legally binding multilateral agreement, they present meaningful opportunities for more concrete action to improve existing sovereign debt resolution mechanisms. Further consultations with a wide range of stakeholders will clearly be necessary. Among sovereigns, intergovernmental forums such as the G-24, which is composed of developing countries, and the G20, which includes advanced and emerging countries, will broaden consultations among national authorities. While the United Nations primarily engages foreign ministries, the G-24 and the G20—forums consisting of finance ministers and central bank governors—have the standing and expertise for developing and implementing policies for sovereign debt management and resolution. Such involvement would be enormously helpful in defining options and reaching any eventual agreement on approaches to sovereign debt resolution.

In addition, more could be done within intergovernmental forums to engage a wider group of emerging and developing countries to broaden the constituency for reform within the international financial community. While countries have divergent views in the polarized debate over a contractual versus statutory/multilateral sovereign debt resolution system, they may find common ground in defining the global principles for governing sovereign debt workouts and in identifying the institutional mechanisms for effectively achieving orderly and timely resolution.

CONCLUSION

The changing landscape of financing within developing countries has been characterized by improving trends in public debt burdens, increased access to international financial markets, and the rise of nontraditional official creditors. These new sources of borrowing present opportunities for more and better development financing, but they also introduce new sources of risk and consequent challenges to debt management at the country level. In addition, if and when sovereigns encounter episodes of debt distress, coordination between a greater and more varied range of borrowers could further complicate sovereign workout processes. Countries have a stake in addressing the shortcomings of the existing global system of sovereign debt resolution so that it can facilitate debt workout processes that will enable countries to subsequently embark on a path of economic recovery and eventual debt sustainability.

Advanced and developing countries have diverse opinions on how best to reform the global system of sovereign debt resolution. Debate has centered on whether or not there is a need for a multilateral statutory system to complement existing contractual approaches to sovereign debt resolution. In face of the evident shortcomings of existing global systems of sovereign debt resolution, developing countries have called for improvements to the system. In view of the lack of support for multilateral statutory approaches by major financial centers, options along the lines of putting in place the institutions needed to improve coordination during sovereign debt workouts and national legislation in financial centers have come to the fore. By broadening consultations between policy makers and countries, intergovernmental groups will have an important role to play in moving away from a polarized debate and finding common ground on concrete ways to improve future sovereign debt workout mechanisms.

NOTES

1. The Intergovernmental Group of Twenty-Four on International Monetary Affairs and Development (G-24) was established in 1971 as a representative grouping of developing countries across Asia, Africa, Latin America, and the Caribbean. The purpose of the group is to coordinate the position of developing countries on monetary

and development issues in order to enhance the effectiveness of their participation in discussions of monetary, financial, and development issues at the Bretton Woods institutions and other forums.

2. Based on the World Bank's definition of LICs. LICs now comprise 60 countries whose per capita income is below US$2,500; they are not viewed as emerging markets.

3. Thirty-nine countries were eligible for support from the HIPC initiative of the World Bank and the IMF (IMF, 2015a).

4. These are countries whose outstanding external debt is below 40 percent of their gross national income.

5. G-24 calculations based on data from the International Debt Statistics database (2013).

6. G-24 calculations based on data from World Economic Outlook, April 2015 (IMF, 2015b).

7. This comprises bonds and internationally syndicated bank lending with at least five years of maturity.

8. This is discussed further later in the chapter.

9. Government bonds had risen to 40 percent of GDP by 2010.

10. The countries sampled by the authors include China, Hong Kong SAR, Indonesia, Malaysia, Philippines, Republic of Korea, Singapore, and Thailand.

11. A non-bank financial institution (NBFI) is a financial institution that does not have a full banking license or is not supervised by a national or international banking regulatory agency. NBFIs facilitate bank-related financial services, such as investment, risk pooling, contractual savings, and market brokering (Carmichael and Pomerleano, 2002).

12. The countries sampled by the authors include China, India, Indonesia, Malaysia, Philippines, Thailand, Argentina, Brazil, Chile, Colombia, Mexico, Peru, Uruguay, Bulgaria, Hungary, Latvia, Lithuania, Poland, Romania, Russia, Ukraine, Egypt, Turkey, and South Africa.

13. The Bank of International Settlements (2015) publishes data that consolidates the debt of non-financial firms in some emerging economies in http://www.bis.org/statistics/totcredit.htm?m=6%7C326.

14. See also Shin (2013).

15. The MDRI provided countries that reached the completion point under the HIPC initiative with 100 percent relief on eligible debt from three multilateral institutions: the International Development Association, the African Development Fund, and the IMF (International Development Association, 2005).

16. The Paris Club is a voluntary, informal group of official creditors that holds meetings throughout the year to discuss the renegotiation of debts they hold on sovereign debtors. The members of the Paris Club are: Australia, Austria, Belgium, Canada, Denmark, Finland, France, Germany, Ireland, Israel, Italy, Japan, the Netherlands, Norway, the Russian Federation, Spain, Sweden, Switzerland, the United Kingdom, and the United States.

17. This is especially the case for infrastructure investments.

18. Information from the Office of the State Council, People's Republic of China (2010 and 2014).

19. Based on IMF/World Bank Debt Sustainability Assessments.

20. G-24 Secretariat calculations based on IMF World Economic Outlook (October 2013).

21. The CACs were designed to provide the ability to amend key financial terms by the vote of a qualified majority in a debt restructuring (IMF, 2002). Features of CACs include the creation of a creditors meeting when the need for restructuring arises, the selection criteria of creditor representatives, the prevention of holdout actions that would lead to court disputes, and the decision on number of majority bondholders needed to accept contractual changes. (Weidemaier and Gulati, 2013)

22. IMF, 2014d.

23. G20, 2014.

24. In July 2014, U.S. federal court judge Thomas Griesa ruled that Argentina was required to repay the full value of the bonds that were not covered by the restructuring that followed its 2001 default. These bonds were bought after the default for fractions of their original value by a hedge fund that intended to litigate for full repayment and thus refused to participate in any restructuring efforts. Judge Griesa's ruling in favor of these holdouts froze Argentina's assets in New York and prevented the country from continuing to repay the creditors who had participated in and agreed to the restructuring. Subsequently, a UK court found that interest payments to holders of Euro-denominated bonds were not subject to the U.S. court rulings but rather were covered by UK law. These disconnects between the debt negotiations in Argentina, the ruling in the U.S. federal court, and the contradictory decision of the British court reflects the lack of clarity and significant scope for chaos in the current debt system. See Guzman and Stiglitz (2015) for a detailed discussion. U.S. case: NML Capital, Ltd. v. Republic of Argentina, 727 F.3d 230 (2d Cir. 2013). UK case: Knighthead Master Fund Lp & Ors v. The Bank of New York Mellon & Anor, [2014] EWHC 3662 (Ch) (06 November 2014).

25. In Firebird Global Master Fund II Ltd v. Republic of Nauru [2014] NSWCA 360, the New South Wales Supreme Court's Court of Appeal considered the issue of enforcing a foreign judgment against a nation-state in the Australian jurisdiction. It held that Firebird Management had failed to properly served summons on Nauru in seeking to register the judgment in Australia and that the registration of the Japanese judgment should be set aside under the Foreign States Immunities Act 1985 (Cth). The original judgment, made in Japanese courts, held Nauru liable to pay AU$31 million to New York–based Firebird Management for defaulted bonds that were issued on the Japanese stock exchange in the 1980s.

26. The G20 and the Paris Club have been hosting the Paris Forum of Sovereign Creditors and Debtors on an annual basis since 2013. See also Morris (2013).

27. The full resolution can be found at: www.un.org/ga/search/view_doc.asp ?symbol=A/RES/68/304&Lang=E.

28. It should be noted that most advanced economies abstained from voting or objected.

29. See also the Center for International Governance Innovation presentation at the G-24 Technical Group Meeting, Beirut, in March 2015 (Lombardi, 2015) and deliberations associated with the UN Ad Hoc Committee on Sovereign Debt Restructuring at www.un.org.

30. The Paris and London Clubs, for example, do not have international legal identities (Gelpern, 2012).

REFERENCES

Andritzky, J. R. 2012. "Government Bonds and Their Investors: What Are the Facts and Do They Matter?" International Monetary Fund Working Paper 12/158, Washington, D.C.

Arslanalp, S., and T. Tsuda. 2014. "Tracking Global Demand for Emerging Market Sovereign Debt." International Monetary Fund Working Paper, Washington, D.C.

Baek, S., and P. K. Kim. 2014. "Determinants of Bond Market Development in Asia." In *Asian Capital Market Development and Integration: Challenges and Opportunities*, ed. Asian Development Bank and Korea Capital Market Institute, 286–316. India: Oxford University Press.

Brautigam, D., and K. P. Gallagher. 2014. "Bartering Globalization: China's Commodity-backed Finance in Africa and Latin America." *Global Policy* 5 (no. 3): 346–352.

Brookings Institution. 2015. "Corporate Debt in Emerging Economies: A Threat to Financial Stability." Washington, D.C.

Brooks, S., and D. Lombardi. 2014. "Sovereign Debt Restructuring: A Backgrounder." Waterloo, ON: Centre for International Governance Innovation.

Brummer, C. 2011. *Soft Law and the Global Financial System: Rule Making in the 21st Century.* New York: Cambridge University Press.

Calvo, G. A., and E. Talvi. 2005. "Sudden Stop, Financial Factors and Economic Collapse in Latin America: Learning from Argentina and Chile." Working Paper 11153, Cambridge, Mass.: National Bureau of Economic Research.

Carmichael, J., and Pomerleano, M. 2002. "The Development and Regulation of Non-Bank Financial Institutions." World Bank Group, Washington, D.C.

Chodos, S. 2012. "The Argentina Experience on Debt Restructuring." Presented at the G-24 Technical Group meeting in Washington, D.C., September 14, 2012. http:// 173.254.126.101/~gtwofouo/wp-content/uploads/2014/03/Session-5_3.pdf (accessed July 2015).

Drage, J., and C. Hovaguimian. 2004. "An Analysis of Provisions Included in Recent Sovereign Bond Issues." Bank of England, London. http://webarchive.nation-alarchives.gov.uk/20100710141234/http://www.bankofengland.co.uk/publications /fsr/2004/fsrfull0412.pdf

Eichengreen, B., and A. Mody. 2000. "Would Collective Action Clauses Raise Borrowing Costs?" Working Paper 7458, Cambridge, Mass.: National Bureau of Economic Research.

G20. 2003. Communiqué, October 27. G20 Information Centre. www.g20.utoronto .ca/2003/2003Communiqué.html (accessed July 2015).

———. 2013. "Long-Term Investment Financing for Growth and Development."

———. 2014, Communiqué, November 16. G20 Leaders' Brisbane Summit, November 2014. https://g20.org/wp-content/uploads/2014/12/brisbane_g20_leaders_summit _Communiqué1.pdf (accessed July 2015).

G-24. 2002. Communiqué, September 27. Intergovernmental Group of Twenty-Four. http://173.254.126.101/~gtwofouo/wp-content/uploads/2014/03/G-24_Comm -Sept27–02.pdf (accessed July 2015).

———. 2014. Communiqué, October. Intergovernmental Group of Twenty-Four. http://g24.org/wp-content/uploads/2014/03/English2.pdf (accessed July 2015).

———. 2015. Communiqué, April. Intergovernmental Group of Twenty-Four. http://g24.org/wp-content/uploads/2014/03/ENGLISH-G-24-Communiqué-April-2015-Final.pdf (accessed July 2015).

Gelpern, A. 2012. "Hard, Soft, and Embedded: Implementing Principles on Promoting Responsible Sovereign Lending and Borrowing." Geneva: UNCTAD.

Gitlin, R., and B. House. 2014a. "A Blueprint for a Sovereign Debt Forum." CIGI Working Paper 27. Waterloo, ON: Centre for International Governance Innovation.

———. 2014b. "The Sovereign Debt Forum: A Snapshot." G-24 Policy Brief.

Government of the United Kingdom. 2011, May 16. "Government Acts to Halt Profiteering on Third World Debt Within the UK." www.gov.uk/government/news/government-acts-to-halt-profiteering-on-third-world-debt-within-the-uk (accessed July 2015).

Guscina, A., G. Pedras, and G. Presciuttini. 2014. "First-Time International Bond Issuance—New Opportunities and Emerging Risks." International Monetary Fund Working Paper 14/127, Washington, D.C.

Guzman, M., and J. E. Stiglitz. 2015. "A Fair Hearing for Sovereign Debt." *Project Syndicate*. March 5.

———. 2016. "Creating a Framework for Sovereign Debt Restructuring That Works." In *Too Little, Too Late: The Quest to Resolve Sovereign Debt Crises*, ed. Martin Guzman, José Antonio Ocampo, and Joseph E. Stiglitz, chapter 1. New York: Columbia University Press.

Helleiner, E. 2009. "Filling a Hole in Global Financial Governance? The Politics of Regulating Sovereign Debt Restructuring." In *The Politics of Global Regulation*, ed. N. Woods and W. Mattli, 89–120. Princeton, N.J.: Princeton University Press.

International Monetary Fund. 2001. "Government Finance Statistics Manual." Washington, D.C.

———. 2002. "Collective Action Clauses in Sovereign Bond Contracts—Encouraging Greater Use." Washington, D.C.

——— 2013. "Sovereign Debt Restructuring-Recent Developments and Implications for the Fund's Legal and Policy Framework." Washington, D.C.

——— 2014a. "Global Financial Stability Report: Moving from Liquidity- to Growth-Driven Markets." Washington, D.C.

——— 2014b. "Regional Economic Outlook, Sub-Saharan Africa: Staying the Course." Washington, D.C.

——— 2014c. "Reform of the Policy on Public Debt Limits in Fund-Supported Programs." Washington, D.C.

——— 2014d. "Strengthening the Contractual Framework to Address Collective Action Problems in Sovereign Debt Restructuring." Washington, D.C.

——— 2014e. "Fiscal Monitor: Back To Work: How Fiscal Policy Can Help." Washington, D.C.

———2014f. "Macroeconomic Developments in Low-Income Developing Countries." Washington, D.C.

—— 2015a. "Debt Relief Under the Heavily Indebted Poor Countries (HIPC) Initiative." Washington, D.C.

—— 2015b, April. "World Economic Outlook Database." www.imf.org/external/pubs /ft/weo/2015/01/weodata/index.aspx (accessed May 2015).

——2015c. October. "Global Financial Stability Report: Vulnerabilities, Legacies, and Policy Challenges." Washington, D.C.

International Development Association. 2005. "The Multilateral Debt Relief Initiative: Implementation Modalities for IDA." Washington, D.C.: World Bank Group.

Krueger, A. 2001. "International Financial Architecture for 2002: A New Approach to Sovereign Debt Restructuring." Address to the National Economists' Club annual members' dinner hosted by the American Enterprise Institute, Washington, D.C.

Lombardi, D. 2015. "Sovereign Debt Restructuring: Current Challenges, Future Pathways." Presented at the G-24 Technical Group meeting in Beirut, March 2, 2015. http://g24.org/wp-content/uploads/2014/03/G-24-TGM-March-2015-Domenico -Lombardi-Sovereign-Debt-Restructuring-Current-Challenges-Future-Pathways .pdf (accessed July 2015).

Martinez-Diaz, L. 2007. "The G20 After Eight Years: How Effective a Vehicle for Developing Country Influence?" Global Economy and Development Working Paper 12, Brookings Institution, Washington, D.C.

Miyajima, K., M. S. Mohanty, and T. Chan. 2012. "Emerging Market Local Currency Bonds: Diversification and Stability." BIS Working Paper 391.

Morris, S. 2013. "The Paris Club Is Trying to Be Less Clubby and Maybe Just in Time." Center for Global Development, Washington, D.C.

People's Republic of China, Information Office of the State Council. 2010 and 2014. "China's Foreign Aid." www.scio.gov.cn/zxbd/tt/Document/1374895/1374895.htm (accessed July 2015).

Pitchford, R., and M. L. Wright. 2010. "Holdouts in Sovereign Debt Restructuring: A Theory of Negotiation in a Weak Contractual Environment." Working Paper 16632, Cambridge, Mass.: National Bureau of Economic Research.

Reinhart, C. M., and K. S. Rogoff. 2013. "Financial and Sovereign Debt Crises: Some Lessons Learned and Those Forgotten." International Monetary Fund Working Paper 13/266, Washington, D.C.

Roubini, N., and B. Setser. 2004. "New Nature of Emerging Market Crises." In *Bailouts or Bail-Ins? Responding to Financial Crises in Emerging Economies.* Washington, D.C.: Peterson Institute for International Economics, 70.

Schneider, B. 2012. Perspectives on Sovereign Debt Restructuring. G-24 Technical Group Meeting in Washington, D.C.: http://173.254.126.101/~gtwofouo/wp -content/uploads/2014/03/Session-5_1.pdf (accessed July 2015).

Shin, H.S. 2013 November 3-5. "The Second Phase of Global Liquidity and Its Impact on Emerging Economies." Keynote Address at the Federal Reserve Bank of San Francisco Asia Economic Policy Conference.

Sill, K. 2001. "The Gains from International Risk Sharing." *Quarterly Business Review*: 23–32. Federal Reserve Bank of Philadelphia, Penn.

Stiglitz, J. 2006. *Making Globalization Work.* New York: Norton.

Stulz, R. M. 1999. "International Portfolio Flows and Security Markets." Working Paper 99-3, Cambridge, Mass.: National Bureau of Economic Research.

Tsibouris, G. C., M. A. Horton, M. J. Flanagan, and W. S. Maliszewski. 2006. "Experience with Large Fiscal Adjustments." International Monetary Fund Occasional Paper 246, Washington, D.C.

United Nations. 2012. "Millennium Development Goals Indicators." http://mdgs .un.org/unsd/mdg/Search.aspx?q=debt (accessed 16 June 2015).

—— 2009. "Report of the Commission of Experts of the President of the United Nations General Assembly on Reforms of the International Monetary and Financial System." New York.

United Nations Conference on Trade and Development. April 2015. "Sovereign Debt Workouts: Going Forward, Roadmap and Guide." http://unctad.org/en /PublicationsLibrary/gdsddf2015misc1_en.pdf (accessed July 2015).

Wall Street Journal. 2015, June 9. "Belgium to Block 'Vulture' Funds from Profiting on Government Debt." www.wsj.com/articles/belgium-to-prevent-hedge-funds-from -seizing-indebted-nations-assets-1433884810 (accessed July 2015).

Warnock, F. E., and V. C. Warnock. 2009. "International Capital Flows and US Interest Rates." *Journal of International Money and Finance* 28 (6): 903–919.

Weidemaier, W. M., and M. Gulati. 2013. "A People's History of Collective Action Clauses." *Virginia Journal of International Law* 54: 1.

World Bank Group. 2014. "International Debt Statistics." Washington, D.C.

World Bank Group. 2015. "International Debt Statistics." Washington, D.C.

CHAPTER 3

Private Creditor Power and the Politics of Sovereign Debt Governance

Skylar Brooks and Domenico Lombardi

In 2001, then International Monetary Fund (IMF) deputy managing director Anne Krueger described the absence of an international mechanism for restructuring sovereign debt as a "gaping hole" in the global financial architecture (Krueger 2001). More than a decade later, it is clear that not enough has been done to fill this hole, which remains a significant challenge to effective economic governance. Recent events—notably the 2012 Greek debt restructuring and the 2014 New York court ruling in favor of Argentina's holdout creditors (Stocker and Rathbone 2014)—provide clear lessons that reinforce the long-standing need for some sort of international bankruptcy framework for sovereigns (Buchheit et al., 2013). To be sure, governments and international organizations have tried, and continue to try, to create such a framework, but to no avail.[1] This outcome is puzzling, given not only the high-profile attempts to establish a formal debt restructuring arrangement but also the increasingly widespread recognition that the absence of such an arrangement generates large economic and social costs, arguably for both debtor countries and their creditors (Buchheit et al., 2013).[2]

To explain this outcome, we briefly review two efforts to reform debt restructuring practices in the 1930s and 1970s before embarking on a more in-depth examination of the IMF's attempt to establish a Sovereign Debt Restructuring Mechanism (SDRM) in 2001–2003. The SDRM initiative remains a highly instructive historical case. It gained considerable attention and momentum and yet failed to materialize despite strong support from G7 governments and top officials within the IMF and the U.S. Treasury.

Existing explanations of the failure to create an SDRM in the early 2000s point to collective action problems, distributional concerns, and opposition from private creditors, large sovereign borrowers, and important actors within the U.S. government (Gelpern and Gulati, 2004; Hagan, 2005; Soederberg, 2005a; Setser, 2008; Helleiner, 2008, 2009).[3] These accounts effectively illustrate the coordination problems that exacerbate individual crises and the distributional issues that lead to divergent preferences over how best to resolve sovereign debt crises more generally. They also do a good job of identifying the mechanisms through which government preferences are translated into concrete international policy outcomes. For example, these analyses correctly point out that without U.S. support, reforms that require amendment to the IMF's Articles of Agreement (which the SDRM would have) stand no chance because of U.S. veto power within the IMF voting structure.[4] Where existing explanations fall short, however, is in their treatment of private creditor influence. While they all note the importance of private creditor opposition to the SDRM, they struggle to identify any specific mechanisms through which this opposition affected the ultimate outcome. We therefore direct attention toward the less transparent, though no less important, mechanisms through which private creditor preferences influence government decisions and shape public policy considerations and outcomes.

We argue that the power and preferences of private creditors helps to further explain the failure to create a sovereign debt restructuring framework.[5] Although this has been suggested elsewhere (Soederberg, 2005a), there have not yet been sufficient attempts to uncover the causal mechanisms at work or formalize our understanding of private creditor power more generally. Drawing on insights from international political economy, we begin to develop a theoretical framework for understanding how private creditor preferences shape outcomes through two distinct but overlapping forms of power: relational and structural.[6] Relationally, creditors lobby policy makers in advanced and emerging market economies and promote strategic reforms to preempt more far-reaching measures. Structurally, creditor preferences are *internalized* by states with systemically important financial markets and states that rely on international markets for their borrowing.

Few observers have seriously considered the role of private power and interests in obstructing the emergence of a sovereign debt restructuring framework. One reason for this may be the fact that the preferences of private creditors and governments often appear to be fairly aligned. But ignoring power relations because of common preferences overlooks the source of actor preferences. Structural power can have the effect of transforming the preferences of one actor or set of actors in ways that align with the interests of those who possess such power (i.e., getting others to want what you want them to want).

THE THEORETICAL FOUNDATIONS OF PRIVATE CREDITOR POWER

For our purposes, "power" refers simply to the ability of actors to successfully pursue desired political objectives (Fuchs, 2005). As mentioned, power can be divided into two subcategories: relational and structural. Relational power refers to the ability of actor A to get actor B to do something that B would otherwise not do (Dahl, 1957). When private financial actors influence decision makers through lobbying and campaign/party finance, they are exercising relational power. This power is relational in the sense that it is exercised by one actor in direct, one-to-one relation to another. It is therefore targeted and intentional.

If relational power in this context is the ability to influence legislators, regulators, and policy makers through direct contact, structural power is the ability to influence or shape the broader systemic environment within which legislative, regulatory, and policy-making processes take place. Put differently, relational power derives from the ability to influence actors within a given system, while structural power derives from the ability to influence or control the system itself. By influencing or controlling the systems within which others must operate, those with structural power are able to alter incentives and transform others' interests in ways that reflect and align with their own (Kirshner, 2014). While structural power is harder to detect than its relational counterpart, the ability to shape incentive structures and, in doing so, prevent certain options from gaining political traction or even surfacing in the first place also makes structural power far more potent than its more conspicuous cousin.[7]

RELATIONAL POWER

Private creditors exercise relational power (the two left quadrants in the matrix shown in table 3.1) when they successfully use financial resources and market expertise to influence regulatory outcomes (Tsingou, 2008; Underhill and Zhang, 2008; Igan, Mishra, and Tressel, 2009; Johnson

Table 3.1   A taxonomy of private creditor power

Types of state	Types of creditor power	
	Relational power	Structural power
Creditor-hosting	Lobbying; regulatory capture	Systemic stability concerns
Sovereign debtor	Lobbying; bargaining in debt negotiations	Creditworthiness concerns

and Kwak, 2010; Baker, 2010). Although it is difficult to measure this type of lobbying and assess its impact on policy outcomes, a number of scholars emphasize the formidable resources at the disposal of financial firms and associations. A common argument is that the concentration of wealth in the financial sector is used to buy better access to policy makers or to shield the industry from regulatory costs (Pagliari and Young, 2014).

Private information and technical expertise are also considered key assets to be used in influencing public policy. In the highly technical area of financial regulation, rule-making authority is often delegated to those with the most intimate knowledge of financial markets (Cerny, 1994). Despite the conflict of interest, this role is often given to market participants themselves. Some scholars also link the effectiveness of lobbying to the institutional context in which public policy is designed and implemented. As Pagliari and Young (2014: 3) note, a number of scholars believe that the "formal independence of financial regulatory agencies in most jurisdictions disguises the privileged access to regulators enjoyed by the financial industry they regulate and oversee," increasing opportunities for "regulatory capture." In sum, by deploying money and expertise in relatively opaque and closed institutional settings, private creditors are sometimes able to directly influence public policy outcomes.

Relational power works largely the same way regardless of the type of state creditors are looking to influence. There is a slight difference, however, between some of the forums in which advanced economy states and developing country debtors are lobbied or pressured by creditors. While private creditors certainly lobby debtor country policy makers directly, they also interact at the negotiating table during debt restructuring negotiations. In this setting, creditors can exercise collective bargaining power through the committees or "cartels" they form.

STRUCTURAL POWER

Private creditors derive structural power from their control of the credit system—the main lubricant of all economic activity. Susan Strange (1988) recognized as much when she remarked that structural power lies with those who control, inter alia, the supply and distribution of credit. Here, it is useful to think of creditor structural power in terms of how it affects two generic types of state: creditor-hosting states and sovereign debtor states. Although these two categories are not mutually exclusive, they serve to highlight a basic distinction between the states most often afflicted by debt crises, on one hand, and the states in which the majority of important international lenders are located, on the other. Creditor structural power vis-à-vis creditor-hosting states typically manifests itself in "systemic stability concerns," while such power over sovereign debtor states finds expression in "creditworthiness concerns."

SYSTEMIC STABILITY CONCERNS

Private creditors derive structural power over the states in which they are located (the top right quadrant in table 3.1) from two features of the credit system: its importance to the broader economy and its proneness to crises. This simultaneous importance and fragility means that in addition to having to support failing financial institutions, the governments of financially advanced countries will typically avoid taking actions that might destabilize financial markets and in turn undermine the workings of the credit system.

In this sense, creditor-hosting states *internalize* the interests of their private creditors. Take the example of bailouts. Even if governments would like to see creditors punished for making risky bets, bailing out banks and other financial actors is usually a safer short-term political and economic choice. Anastasia Nesvetailova (2014: 560) captures the power this importance-fragility duality implies when she states: "Finance is powerful not only because it can create wealth and precipitate certain shifts or political actions, but also because it can destroy things."

The power this relationship entails for creditors is structural in the sense that it derives not from acts of coercion or persuasion but from their systemic location within advanced capitalist economies (Hacker and Pierson, 2002; Bell and Hindmoor, 2013). Furthermore, if the financial sector expects the government to act as a backstop when things go wrong, it may be tempted to take greater risks. Commonly referred to as "moral hazard," this phenomenon is an example of structural power being harnessed in an intentional manner to shift risk from the private to the public sector while keeping returns in the former.

CREDITWORTHINESS CONCERNS

Private creditors have structural power over developing and emerging market borrowers (the bottom right quadrant in table 3.1) to the extent that they can set the terms on which these countries borrow from international markets. By controlling the resources that governments and entire economies require and rely on, creditors are able to shape the range of viable policy choices available to governments without appearing to put direct pressure on them. The power to grant or deny access to (affordable) credit, and thus punish or reward countries for their policy choices, need not be exercised in an intentionally disciplinary manner, but it does need to have the effect of discouraging/encouraging policies that harm/serve private creditor interests (Soederberg, 2005b).

The globalization of financial flows is said to have cemented this power by creating an international environment in which developing and emerging market governments compete with one another for capital (Gill and Law, 1989). In such an environment, creditors quite reasonably lend on the most favorable terms to governments whose policies are considered economically sound (i.e., fiscally responsible, growth enhancing, and so on) and offer less favorable terms or deny credit to governments whose policies pose a risk to the safety or profitability of their investment. Karl Polanyi's depiction of the influence of finance over debtor governments during nineteenth-century globalization fits nicely with the version of structural power developed here:

> Finance . . . acted as a powerful moderator in the councils and policies of a number of smaller sovereign states. Loans, and the renewal of loans, hinged upon credit, and credit upon good behavior. Since . . . behavior is reflected in the budget and the external value of the currency cannot be detached from the appreciation of the budget, debtor governments were well advised to watch their exchanges carefully and to avoid policies which might reflect upon the soundness of the budgetary position. (Polanyi, 1944: 14)

From a different angle, reputational theories of sovereign debt also implicitly support the structural power interpretation (Eaton and Gersovitz, 1981; Eaton, Gersovitz, and Stiglitz, 1986; Tomz, 2007). According to this view, private creditors base their lending decisions—including whether or not to lend and on what terms—largely on a sovereign debtor's reputation for repayment (i.e., on perceptions of a debtor's creditworthiness based on its historical track record; Tomz, 2007). When governments default on their external debt obligations, especially during good economic times, their reputation is sullied and their ability to access international credit is consequently circumscribed. Thus, to establish and maintain access to affordable international finance, sovereign debtors must constantly concern themselves with how their actions might affect their perceived creditworthiness among foreign creditors.

Some readers might accuse our framework of treating creditors as a homogeneous group. To be sure, we recognize that creditors do not all have identical interests or act in identical ways, and that in reality, they are a relatively heterogeneous group (Brooks et al., 2015; Lienau, 2014). And yet it is a truism of finance that as a borrower becomes a greater credit risk, its borrowing costs increase. Different creditors may have different interests and investment strategies, but virtually all creditors want to be compensated for the risks they take. It is only this basic commonality that must hold for our framework to remain credible.

It is also worth noting that our discussion of structural power is in no way meant to downplay the importance of agency. In our view, structures constrain but do not determine the behavior of agents. When agents act in accordance with the constraints of certain structures, they reinforce and reify them. But there is always room for agents to defy structures and/or reshape them through collective action. Structure and agent are thus coconstitutive.

CREDITOR POWER AND THE POLITICS OF THE SDRM

In this section we examine the politics surrounding the SDRM proposal in the early 2000s. This was not the first attempt to establish a formal international framework for sovereign debt restructuring. Such attempts were made in the 1930s, 1940s, 1970s, and 1990s. Efforts made in the 1930s and 1970s are particularly important to our analysis. While a full exploration of these two episodes is beyond this paper's scope (for this, see Helleiner, 2008), a few stylized facts illustrate salient similarities and differences between these episodes and our main case study.

THE 1930S PROPOSAL

The first substantive proposal for a mechanism to govern sovereign debt restructuring was made in December 1933 at the Pan-American Conference in Montevideo, Uruguay. The idea was put forward by Mexican foreign minister José Manuel Puig, who called on conference participants to explore "the possibility of establishing public international organizations to take care of debt negotiations and agreements, in order to exclude thereby the intervention of Bankers' Committees and to look for the interest of both debtors and creditors" (quoted in Helleiner, 2008: 95). Intended to strengthen the bargaining power of debtors vis-à-vis their private creditors, such a mechanism was of particular interest to Latin American governments, almost all of which had defaulted on their foreign debts in the early 1930s (Eichengreen and Lindhert, 1989). The proposal was supported by several Latin American governments, including those of El Salvador, Nicaragua, and Colombia. A number of others, however, strongly opposed the idea. Argentina, Haiti, Honduras, and Chile all feared that their support for a debt restructuring mechanism would send the wrong signals to foreign investors, undermining their perceived creditworthiness and curtailing their access to affordable international credit (Helleiner, 2008). The stark divide between debtors who supported and opposed the Mexican proposal prevented it from gaining widespread support.

This episode offers an important lesson that remains relevant today: even though a formal debt restructuring mechanism would benefit sovereign debtors *in the event of a crisis*, many debtor governments refuse to support initiatives that they fear could raise their international borrowing costs during normal times. Guzman and Stiglitz (chap. 1 in this volume) observe a similar dynamic when they note that political economy incentives that lead sovereigns to try to minimize their borrowing costs over the short term—for example, by giving up their sovereign immunity—make it more difficult and costly for current or future governments to restructure their debts in the event of a sovereign debt crisis. In the case of the 1930s, some debtors shied away from supporting the Mexican proposal for fear that their support alone would cast doubt on their creditworthiness. Beyond this concern, debtors feared that with a sovereign debt restructuring arrangement in place, private creditors would view the risk of sovereign default (and the potential losses from any such default) as higher than before and thus charge higher interest

rates when lending to foreign governments. This was not the only factor that prevented the Mexican proposal from gaining momentum, but
it was undoubtedly an important one. In addition to creditworthiness
concerns and the divisions they created between Latin American governments, the U.S. government also refused to support the call for a new
organization to handle debt negotiations. U.S. opposition, admittedly,
was a large obstacle in its own right.

THE 1970S PROPOSAL

Similar dynamics were at play in the late 1970s, when a debtor-driven
proposal for a debt restructuring arrangement appeared again. In October
1978, the United Nations Conference on Trade and Development
Secretariat called for the creation of an "independent international forum
to facilitate the restructuring of sovereign debts owed to both private and
official creditors" (Helleiner, 2008: 104). The idea was then picked up
by the G-77, which in 1979 proposed the creation of an "International
Debt Commission" made up of "imminent public figures with recognized
knowledge and expertise of debt problems and economic development"
(Rogoff and Zettelmeyer, 2002: 472). The G-77's aim was to increase
their members' bargaining power vis-à-vis creditors by creating a more
debtor-friendly forum for sovereign debt negotiations—that is, more
debtor-friendly than the creditor-led Paris and London Clubs (Rogoff
and Zettelmeyer, 2002).

Since it was championed by the G-77, not an individual country, the
proposal appeared to have the backing of a large and united group of
countries. Unlike the Mexican proposal of the 1930s, which was from the
outset hamstrung by divisions among debtors, the appearance of debtor
cohesion in the late 1970s likely gave the initiative a reasonable degree of
credibility.

Fearing that a more institutionalized debt restructuring mechanism
"might encourage more applications for debt relief and, more importantly, shift the terms of bargaining in favor of debtor countries," Western
banks and their governments emerged as vocal opponents of the proposal
(Soederberg, 2005a: 935). It seems likely that such opposition weakened
the G-77's resolve, as debtor support for the initiative began to erode.
As in the 1930s, many debtors feared that supporting debt restructuring
would undermine their creditworthiness in the eyes of foreign investors,
raising their borrowing costs and limiting their access to foreign credit.

As Helleiner (2008: 105) reports, "a number of the wealthier developing countries expressed concerns that the endorsement of debt restructuring and debt relief might discourage future capital flows to the developing world." Unable to forge a strong pro-change coalition, the G-77 stopped supporting the idea of an international debt commission by October 1980 (Rieffel, 2003).

One of the key points to be taken from these episodes is that for sovereign debtors, the policy choice of whether to create or support a sovereign debt restructuring framework has been looked at not in terms of how it might stabilize economies and produce more efficient and equitable outcomes in the event of sovereign default, but in terms of how private foreign creditors would interpret and react to it. By controlling the availability and price of the credit that developing countries so desperately need, private creditors have been able to influence policy outcomes in ways that preserve their interests without having to engage in large lobbying efforts or, in some cases, even voice their concerns. This speaks to the structural power of private creditors vis-à-vis sovereign debtors, whose concern with maintaining creditworthiness has helped prevent the emergence of a formal debt restructuring framework (see table 3.2).

THE CASE OF THE SDRM

In the early 2000s, the idea of creating a formal framework for sovereign debt restructuring made a major comeback. This time, it came not from sovereign debtors but from the upper echelons of the global economic policy-making elite.

The demand for a new framework was primarily a response to two factors: (1) a series of large-scale emerging market crises with *systemic* effects and (2) an increasingly widespread belief that the international community lacked the proper tools for resolving such crises in a fair and effective manner. IMF bailouts, which often had the effect of socializing

Table 3.2   Private creditor power in the 1930s and 1970s

Types of state	Types of creditor power	
	Relational power	Structural power
Creditor-hosting		
Sovereign debtor		Creditworthiness concerns

private losses, were increasingly seen not only as unjust but also as setting the stage for future crises by encouraging moral hazard—something U.S. Treasury Secretary Paul O'Neill worried deeply about.

In September 2001 (just prior to the Argentine default), O'Neill approached the IMF's senior management and the U.S. Congress to urge serious consideration of the idea of an international bankruptcy regime for sovereign debtors (Hagan, 2005). Two months later, Anne Krueger, then deputy managing director of the IMF, formally proposed a "Sovereign Debt Restructuring Mechanism." Housed in the IMF, the SDRM would be a legal mechanism designed to approve payment standstills for states experiencing severe debt-servicing difficulties and, if necessary, facilitate deeper debt restructurings (Fischer, 2003). It would arguably address the moral hazard problem by minimizing private sector bailouts, and by establishing a more orderly way of resolving sovereign debt crises, it would provide benefits to both debtors and creditors.[8]

Spanning the period 2001 to 2003, the SDRM initiative was the closest such an arrangement had ever come to being made a reality. Its advancement reflected not just the world's recent experience with crises but also the new coalition of supporters. Whereas the proposals of the 1930s and 1970s came straight from sovereign debtors and failed to gain support outside that group (or even sufficient support within it), the SDRM proposal came from one of the highest-ranking officials within the IMF. That Krueger was an American and seemed to have support from the U.S. administration via the secretary of the treasury gave the proposal additional weight by signaling American interest in the SDRM. This was significant, because creating the SDRM would mean amending the IMF's Articles of Agreement, which could only be done with American approval.

The SDRM also enjoyed the support of G7 countries. European officials had become strong critics of large IMF bailouts, which they saw as benefiting primarily *American* financiers, and they wanted to limit discretionary lending. Germany called for hard lending limits, as did the Bank of England and Bank of Canada jointly. In general, European officials wanted "firm crisis management rules" and the "SDRM was their chance" (Gelpern and Gulati, 2004: 16). Moreover, "Europe's over-representation in the IMF Board made its support impossible to ignore" (Gelpern and Gulati, 2004: 16).

While the U.S. secretary of the treasury, the G7 countries, and a significant segment of IMF staff all supported the creation of an SDRM, the private creditor community quickly lashed out at the proposal, a reaction that Gelpern and Gulati (2004: 12) describe as "scathing." Private creditors did not like the SDRM for several reasons, but their overriding concerns seemed to be that it would enhance the bargaining position of sovereign debtors during restructuring negotiations and shift the burden of the risk of sovereign default from the sovereign debtors and the IMF to banks and bondholders (Dickerson, 2004; Setser, 2008).[9] For creditors, "even the very idea of an official endorsement of sovereign default through the creation of a formal mechanism would tilt the balance too far in favor of debtors" (Helleiner, 2009: 10). They also worried about IMF control over the SDRM, since the organization is an interested party with its own exposure to debtors (Dickerson, 2004).

Nonetheless, the strength and source of SDRM support meant that private creditors could not ignore the initiative, nor would their structural power over debtors have the same effect it did during the 1930s and 1970s. They thus had to make their interests and concerns heard through active lobbying (i.e., relational power). As Sean Hagan (2005: 391), director of the IMF's legal department, recalls: "A number of leading financial industry associations joined forces to lobby against the SDRM proposal."[10] The creditor community lobbied key officials within creditor-hosting and debtor states on the grounds that the SDRM was an inappropriate solution to the problems of debt crisis management. But that line of reasoning implied that *some* solution was indeed needed. Strategically, private creditors likely understood that the best way to undercut the SDRM would be to present a "more appropriate" solution. They therefore played a leading role in developing and promoting an alternative, more market-friendly approach to debt restructuring: collective action clauses (CACs).[11] If CACs were implemented and worked, they would render the SDRM unnecessary.[12]

One example of the financial sector's lobbying efforts against the SDRM is documented by Soederberg (2005a), who describes the writing campaign to key policy makers led by the directors of the world's top financial sector associations. In a letter to O'Neill, the directors of these associations made clear their position on the proposed SDRM:

> We believe that a market-based approach to strengthening crisis management holds the only promise for success. Consequently, we have taken the lead in developing marketable collective action clauses (CACs) that could command the support of both investors and issuers . . . the active

pursuit of an SDRM has eroded the support for these efforts. (quoted in
Soederberg 2005a: 945)

Interviews conducted by Gelpern and Gulati (2004: 10) "confirm[ed]
that industry representatives tried more than once to trade their acceptance of CACs for the official sector's commitment to 'drop' SDRM."
For creditors, a key upside of the CAC approach was that it would
allow them to remain in control of their loans to debtors during crises
(Soederberg, 2005a).

The nature of this alternative solution shifted focus back to the interests and behavior of debtor states. As a set of provisions that could be
written into a sovereign's bond contracts, CACs could not be implemented in a top-down manner like the SDRM. CACs had to be accepted
and adopted by key sovereign debtors to emerge as a viable alternative
to the SDRM. But sovereign debtors worried that the adoption of CACs
would be interpreted as an intention to default and thus raise their borrowing costs. Almost ironically, the logic of borrowing costs—and the
structural power at its core—was so strong that it made many sovereign borrowers (especially larger, wealthier ones) want to distance themselves from anything and everything associated with debt restructuring,[13]
including the more market-friendly approach promoted by their private
creditors.

To help overcome debtor reluctance, the U.S. Treasury (now under the
leadership of John Snow) and key members of the creditor community
planned to meet with a group of important sovereign debtors (such as
Mexico, Korea, Poland, and South Africa) in February 2003. As Gelpern
and Gulati (2004: 28) report: "The objective was to have large investors
reassure the countries that they were willing to buy their debt with CACs
and did not expect to charge a penalty." This objective illustrates a high
level of awareness of private creditor structural power and the difficulty of
overcoming it, even by the creditors themselves.

Private creditor lobbying also targeted individual debtors, especially the
sympathetic and systemically important Mexico. On December 3, 2002,
Robert Gray, director of the International Primary Market Association,
traveled to Mexico City to convince Augustin Carstens, Mexico's under-
secretary of finance and public credit, to adopt CACs (Gopinath, 2003).
Carstens continued to worry that CACs would increase Mexico's borrowing costs. A few months later, though, in March 2003, Mexico became
the first emerging-market economy to include CACs in its international

bonds. Shortly thereafter, Brazil, Uruguay, and other key sovereign debt-ors followed suit (Setser, 2008).

Having interviewed more than 100 people directly or closely involved in the SDRM debate, Gelpern and Gulati (2004: 38) conclude that "the investment community and Mexico deployed CACs to pre-empt official initiatives, notably SDRM" (see also Blustein, 2005: 230). In the words of then Mexican central bank president Guillermo Ortiz: "We were worried because it [the SDRM] would increase our financing costs. The truth is we did it [issued CACs] because it was a way to get rid of the SDRM" (quoted in Helleiner, 2009: 14).[14] In emphasizing his concern over how the SDRM would affect Mexico's borrowing costs, Ortiz's statement high-lights the systemic importance of private international creditors and, with it, their structural power over sovereign debtors.

WHAT DOES THE EVIDENCE TELL US?

Interpreted through the theoretical framework outlined earlier, the evi-dence indicates that private creditor power, especially the structural kind, has been an important force behind the more widespread opposition to a sovereign debt restructuring mechanism.

Although difficult to measure, it is likely the lobbying power of private creditors over both creditor-hosting states and sovereign debtor states was underpinned by an implicit understanding of their structural importance within the global economic system. In other words, the relational power of private creditors was bolstered by their structural power. This struc-tural power ensured that in the cases examined earlier, sovereign debtor states *internalized* the preferences of their private creditors. Hagan's (2005: 391–392) observation clearly illustrates this internalization: "Opposition to the SDRM proposal by financial industry associations was, of course, also an important reason why a number of emerging-market countries also opposed the SDRM proposal. The private sector consistently warned that the SDRM, if adopted, would adversely affect the volume and price of capital to these countries." The cases examined earlier have thus shown the relational power of private creditors over both types of state and their structural power over sovereign debtors (see table 3.3). Although, as we mentioned earlier, creditors are a diverse group with different—some-times divergent or conflictive—interests, we have found no evidence to suggest that any significant private creditor supports the idea of an SDRM. In addition to the reasons given earlier, this is perhaps partly

Table 3.3   Private creditor power in the early 2000s

Types of state	Types of creditor power	
	Relational power	Structural power
Creditor-hosting	Lobbying	
Sovereign debtor	Lobbying	Creditworthiness concerns

out of fear that an SDRM, in embodying the idea that debt restructuring is sometimes necessary and acceptable, would challenge the deeply entrenched norm that sovereign debts must always be repaid.[15]

CONCLUSION

When the theoretical framework developed in this paper is applied to the relevant empirical cases, it helps shed additional light on the power and politics surrounding sovereign debt governance. Mainly, it shows that previous attempts to create a formal sovereign debt restructuring framework have met significant resistance from private creditors, whose relational and, more significantly, structural power has weakened governmental support for such initiatives. In the 1930s, Mexico's proposal for a new debt restructuring arrangement was largely undercut by opposition from several Latin American debtors who worried that merely supporting such a proposal would negatively affect perceptions of their creditworthiness and thus raise their international borrowing costs. Similar dynamics were at play during the late 1970s, leading to the downfall of the G-77's proposal for an "International Debt Commission." In both cases, the failure to create a debt restructuring arrangement can in important ways be linked back to the structural power that private creditors derive from their control over international credit and their attendant ability to reward or punish debtor countries for their policy choices.

The SDRM proposal of the early 2000s came not from sovereign debtors but from within creditor-hosting states, which meant that structural power over sovereign debtors would not be sufficient to thwart the initiative. Private creditors therefore deployed relational power by lobbying key U.S. officials to abandon the SDRM, knowing that American opposition alone could prevent the proposal from advancing within the IMF. As part of their case against the SDRM, private creditors promoted the adoption of a more market-friendly alternative: CACs. But CACs could only succeed in preempting the SDRM if sovereign debtors accepted them. In the end, it was a combination of lobbying (relational power), backed up by the threat of punishment if the SDRM were to be implemented (structural power), that convinced Mexico to embrace CACs, effectively killing the SDRM. In the cases examined in this paper, the international policy choice of whether to create or support a sovereign debt restructuring framework has been viewed not in terms of its potential for public good but largely in terms of how private creditors might react to and be affected by it.

Although we have not discussed the European experience since the outbreak of the eurozone crisis in 2009, we would argue that it illustrates state-led attempts to avoid debt restructuring—and any mechanism that in principle supports it—largely for systemic stability reasons (i.e., the remaining aspect of private creditor structural power we have not discussed). Due to space constraints, however, this more recent European case will have to be put aside for the moment.

When it comes to sovereign debt governance, the power of private creditors is telling, but not the whole story. Governmental power, especially that of the United States and other great powers, is also a key factor, as mentioned by Richard Conn (chap. 13 in this volume) and others. So too are ideas and the broader normative context in which policy choices are given meaning and gain (or lose) support. For the sake of analytical tractability, however, we have chosen to exclude these factors and focus on the highly important yet underexplored issue of private creditor power. As we have shown, such power plays a critical role in the politics of sovereign debt governance. This insight is not revolutionary, but it should be taken seriously. Only after identifying the source and nature of power and (status quo) preferences can we meaningfully appraise, politically and strategically, the best ways to advance humanity's collective interests.

NOTES

1. Current efforts mainly center on the UN General Assembly resolution, passed on September 9, 2014, that calls for "the establishment of a multilateral legal framework for sovereign debt restructuring processes" (www.un.org/press/en/2014/ga11542.doc.htm).

2. Guzman and Stiglitz (chap. 1 in this volume) also note the significant weaknesses in the international financial architecture generated by the lack of an international legal framework to facilitate necessary sovereign debt restructurings.

3. See also Conn (chap. 13 in this volume), who argues that the SDRM was voted down because "countries, including the United States, did not wish to cede the power necessary to the IMF or other multilateral bodies to allow the SDRM to function."

4. Likewise, the amendment of sovereign bond contracts can only be done directly by the sovereigns that issue such bonds. In both cases, the mechanisms through which government preferences lead to particular outcomes are clear.

5. In general, creditors seem to oppose a formal sovereign debt restructuring arrangement, because they fear it would enhance the bargaining position of sovereign debtors during restructuring negotiations and, to an extent, would shift the risk of default from the official creditors to banks and bondholders (Dickerson, 2004; Setser, 2008).

6. This distinction was famously made by Susan Strange (1988).

7. It is also worth noting that structural power can operate independent of intentionality or it can be exploited to bolster relational power.

8. As an institution, the IMF also had bureaucratic reasons to support this idea.

9. For a discussion of how the current system broadly favors creditors by encouraging creditor moral hazard and socializing private sector losses during crisis resolution efforts, see Ocampo (chap. 10 in this volume). Guzman and Stiglitz (chap. 1 in this volume) also point out that the current system tends to place the onus for the buildup of unsustainable sovereign debt squarely on debtor countries.

10. Among these associations were the Institute of International Finance, the Emerging Market Traders Association, the International Primary Market Association, the Bond Market Association, the Securities Industry Association, the International Securities Market Association, and the Emerging Market Creditors Association

11. CACs are not the type of formal sovereign debt restructuring mechanism or arrangement that this paper is interested in. For an overview of CACs and how they differ from approaches like the SDRM, see Eichengreen (2006).

12. To be sure, as Haley (chap. 9 in this volume) rightly notes, CACs are an important step in the right direction, but they are no panacea when it comes to solving the myriad problems that Guzman and Stiglitz (chap. 1 in this volume) point to. This is true of both the first-generation CACs referred to in this chapter and the newer CACs introduced by the International Capital Market Association in 2014.

13. Within the IMF's executive board, the fiercest critics of the SDRM had been Mexico and Brazil.

14. As Helleiner (2009: 14) explains: "The timing of the Mexican move was very significant in this respect; it was announced shortly before the April 2003 meeting of the IMFC that was to decide the fate of the SDRM. If the bond issue was successful, it would take some of the wind out of the sails of the SDRM proposal by highlighting the viability of the CAC alternative."

15. For a discussion of this norm, see Lienau (2014).

REFERENCES

Baker, Andrew. 2010. "Restraining Regulatory Capture? Anglo-America, Crisis Politics and Trajectories of Change in Global Financial Governance." *International Affairs* 86 (no. 3): 647–663.

Bell, Stephen, and Andrew Hindmoor. 2013. "The Structural Power of Business and the Power of Ideas: The Strange Case of the Australian Mining Tax." *New Political Economy* 19 (no. 3): 470–486.

Blustein, Paul. 2005. *And the Money Kept Rolling In (And Out)*. New York: Public Affairs.

Brooks, Skylar, Martin Guzman, Domenico Lombardi, and Joseph E. Stiglitz. 2015. "Identifying and Resolving Inter-creditor and Debtor-Creditor Equity Issues in Sovereign Debt Restructuring." CIGI Policy Brief No. 53, Waterloo, Ont.

Buchheit, Lee C., Anna Gelpern, Mitu Gulati, Ugo Panizza, Beatrice Weder di Mauro, and Jeromin Zettelmeyer. 2013. "Revisiting Sovereign Bankruptcy." Committee on International Economic Policy and Reform. Brookings Institution. October.

Cerny, Philip. 1994. "The Dynamics of Financial Globalization: Technology, Market Structure, and Policy Response." *Policy Sciences* 27: 317–342.

Dahl, Robert A. 1957. "The Concept of Power." *Behavioral Science* 2 (no. 3): 201–215.

Dickerson, A. Mechele. 2004. "A Politically Viable Approach to Sovereign Debt Restructuring." William & Mary Law School Scholarship Repository, Faculty Publications, Williamsburg, Va.

Eaton, Jonathan, and Mark Gersovitz. 1981. "Debt with Potential Repudiation: Theoretical and Empirical Analysis." *Review of Economic Studies* 48: 289–309.

Eaton, Jonathan, Mark Gersovitz, and Joseph E. Stiglitz. 1986. "The Pure Theory of Country Risk." NBER Working Paper No. 1894, Cambridge, Mass.

Eichengreen, Barry. 2006. "Assessing Contractual and Statutory Approaches: Policy Proposals for Restructuring Unsustainable Sovereign Debt." In *The New Public Finance*, ed. Inge Kaul and Pedro Conceicao, 433–452. Oxford University Press.

Eichengreen, Barry, and Lindert, Peter. 1989. "Overview." In *The International Debt Crisis in Historical Perspective*, ed. Barry Eichengreen and Peter Lindert, 1–11. Cambridge, Mass.: MIT Press.

Fischer, Stanley. 2003. "Globalization and Its Challenges." *American Economic Review* 93: 1–30.

Fuchs, Doris. 2005. "Commanding Heights? The Strength and Fragility of Business Power in Global Politics." *Millennium—Journal of International Studies* 33: 771–801.

Gelpern, Anna, and Mitu Gulati. 2004. "How CACs Became Boilerplate, or the Politics of Contract Change." Working Paper Series, IPD Task Force on Debt Restructuring and Sovereign Bankruptcy. Columbia University Academic Commons. New York, NY.

Gill, Stephen and Law, David. 1989. "Global Hegemony and the Structural Power of Capital." *International Studies Quarterly* 33 (no. 4): 475–499.

Gopinath, Deepak. 2003. "Avoiding Bankruptcy: Bankers and Investors Say the Plan to Let Emerging Markets Declare Bankruptcy Stinks. Their Bid to Defeat It Got a Boost from O'Neill's Ouster, but the Scheme Isn't Dead Yet." *Institutional Investor*, January 1. http://business.highbeam.com/435607/article-1G1-96893340/avoiding-bankruptcy-bankers-and-investors-say-plan.

Hacker, J., and P. Pierson. 2002. "Business Power and Social Policy: Employers and the Formation of the American Welfare State." *Politics and Society* 30: 277–325.Hagan, Sean. 2005. "Designing a Legal Framework to Restructure Sovereign Debt," *Georgetown Journal of International Law* 36: 299–402.

Helleiner, Eric. 2008. "The Mystery of the Missing Sovereign Debt Restructuring Mechanism." *Contributions to Political Economy* 27: 91–113.

———. 2009. "Filling a Hole in Global Financial Governance? The Politics of Regulating Sovereign Debt Restructuring." In *The Politics of Global Regulation*, ed. Ngaire Woods and Walter Mattli, 89–120. Princeton, N.J.: Princeton University Press.

Igan, Deniz, Prachi Mishra, and Thierry Tressel. 2009. "A Fistful of Dollars: Lobbying and the Financial Crisis." Paper presented at the 10th Jacques Polak Annual Research Conference, hosted by the International Monetary Fund in Washington, D.C., November 5–6.

Johnson, Simon, and James Kwak. 2010. *13 Bankers*. New York: Pantheon.

Kirshner, Jonathan. 2014. *American Power After the Financial Crisis*. Ithaca, N.Y.: Cornell University Press.

Krueger, Anne. 2001. "International Financial Architecture for 2002: A New Approach to Sovereign Debt Restructuring." Speech given at the National Economists' Club Annual Members' Dinner. American Enterprise Institute, Washington, D.C. November 26.

Lienau, Odette. 2014. *Rethinking Sovereign Debt: Politics, Reputation, and Legitimacy in Modern Finance*. Cambridge, Mass.: Harvard University Press.

Nesvetailova, Anastasia. 2014. "Innovations, Fragility and Complexity: Understanding the Power of Finance." *Government and Opposition* 49 (no. 3): 542–568.

Pagliari, Stefano, and Kevin Young. 2013. "Leveraged Interests: Financial Industry Power and the Role of Private Sector Coalitions." *Review of International Political Economy* 21 (no. 3): 575–610.

Polanyi, Karl. 1944. *The Great Transformation*. New York: Farrar and Rinehart.

Rieffel, Lex. 2003. *Restructuring Sovereign Debt: The Case for Ad Hoc Machinery*. Washington, D.C.: Brookings Institution Press.

Rogoff, Kenneth, and Jeromin Zettelmeyer. 2002. "Bankruptcy Procedures for Sovereigns: A History of Ideas, 1976–2001." *IMF Staff Papers* 49 (no. 3): 470–507.

Setser, Brad. 2008. "The Political Economy of the SDRM." IPD Task Force on Sovereign Debt. Columbia University. New York, NY.

Soederberg, Susanne. 2005a. "The Transnational Debt Architecture and Emerging Markets: The Politics of Paradoxes and Punishment." *Third World Quarterly* 26 (no. 6): 927–949.

———. 2005b. *The Politics of the New International Financial Architecture: Reimposing Neoliberal Domination in the Global South*. London: Zed.

Strange, Susan. 1988. *States and Markets*. London: Continuum.

Stocker, Ed, and John Paul Rathbone. 2014. "US Supreme Court Ruling Leaves Argentina in a Quandary." *Financial Times*, June 17.

Tomz, Michael. 2007. *Reputation and International Cooperation: Sovereign Debt Across Three Centuries*. Princeton, N.J.: Princeton University Press.

Tsingou, Eleni. 2008. "Transnational Private Governance and the Basel Process: Banking Regulation, Private Interests and Basel II." In *Transnational Private Governance and Its Limits*, ed. Andreas Nolke and Jean-Christophe Graz, 58–68. London: Routledge.

Underhill, Geoffrey, and Xiaoke, Zhang. 2008. "Setting the Rules: Private Power, Political Underpinnings, and Legitimacy in Global Monetary and Financial Governance." *International Affairs* 84 (no. 3): 535–554.

PART II

Two Case Studies
Argentina and Greece

CHAPTER 4

From the Pari Passu Discussion to the "Illegality" of Making Payments

THE CASE OF ARGENTINA[1]

Sergio Chodos

The Argentine debt discussion and saga are by now relatively well known. Obscure Latin expressions like "pari passu" are now normal terms of art, and their novel interpretation and meaning are relatively widespread.

As is also known, U.S. Federal District Judge Thomas Griesa decided that Argentina breached a boilerplate pari passu clause included in sovereign bond issuances and created a novel "equitable remedy" that basically signified, from a practical perspective, a prohibition to Argentina to continue to pay restructured debt until holdout creditors (vulture funds) had been paid in advance in full. This decision, which was confirmed by the Court of Appeals of the Second Circuit in October 2012, became operational after the U.S. Supreme Court denied in June 2014 a petition for certiorari.

This decision dramatically affected the sovereign debt restructuring realm. It shattered equilibriums, understandings, and assumptions.

For more than thirty years before this game-changing decision came into force, there existed an ongoing and profuse debate and dialogue over the problems relating to the absence of a framework for sovereign debt restructuring. The debate ranged from the convenience of crafting a global statutory framework of some sort, to the advocates of pure market solutions, to those who felt there was not even a problem. This dialogue had relative peaks of intensity, such as the IMF's Sovereign Debt Restructuring Mechanism proposal discussion of 2001, but overall it flowed with a sense of importance, not urgency.

The purpose of this paper is to argue that the Argentine decision constituted a game changer that affected sovereign debt restructuring to a point where the problems generated by the absence of a fair, effective, and efficient mechanism to deal with sovereign debt restructuring needs can no longer be neglected. I also argue that one of the main consequences of such decision is to render untenable the so-called market-based approach.

THE PARI PASSU CLAUSE

The pari passu clause is a contractual provision that aims to ensure the relevant obligation will maintain its equal ranking in payment rights vis-à-vis all the borrower's other unsubordinated debts (including any future debt). As Lee Buchheit and Jeremiah Pam eloquently discuss in their seminal article on pari passu clauses in sovereign debt instruments (written before the 2012 Second Circuit Court of Appeals decision upholding District Judge Griesa's decision), the international financial markets long understood the clause to protect a lender against the risk of legal subordination in favor of another creditor.[2]

So, basically the whole idea of pari passu clauses was related to the concept of "rank." However, as Bucheit and Pam explain, another interpretation of the clause was advanced in 2000, trying to establish that the clause meant that "judgment creditors" of sovereigns were entitled, as per the clause, to ratable payments from the payments made to other (current) creditors.

So, in a nutshell, there was a consensus on the "rank" nature of the pari passu clause, then a "novel" and far-fetched interpretation of the clause that linked it to "payment" or "ratable payment" rather than "rank," and then—upon analysis—an understanding that "payment" interpretation of the pari passu clause was a "fallacy."[3]

It is interesting to read, then, what the relevant pari passu clause of the Argentine Bonds subject to by now known litigation said in the 1994 Fiscal Agency Agreement.

SECTION 1(C)

The Securities will constitute (except as provided in Section 11 below) direct, unconditional, unsecured and unsubordinated obligations of the Republic and shall at all times rank pari passu and without any preference among themselves. The payment obligations of the Republic under the Securities shall at all times rank at least equally with all its other present and future unsecured and unsubordinated External Indebtedness (as defined in this Agreement).[4]

The language is fairly straightforward with respect to "rank" and clearly falls within the analysis of Bucheit and Pam, as well as other academics such as Mitu Gulati. More importantly, or more sticking for some, is the fact that District Judge Griesa himself characterized in 2004 the "payment or ratable payment" interpretation of the pari passu clause as "very odd."[5]

In fact, the whole issue in 2004 transpired around the request by Argentina to have certainty as the meaning of the clause. The holdouts insisted that there was no case, because no attempts to apply the "payment" interpretation of the clause was being made. Hence, there was no "actual controversy."[6] It was obvious that the holdouts then intended to project a potential use of the clause as a threat but were unwilling to undergo a legal analysis of its implications and understanding. They would revisit it and try again several years later.

In December 2011, District Judge Griesa decided that, effectively, Argentina had violated the pari passu obligation when it made payments due of restructured debt (as per the exchanges of 2005 and 2010) while "persisting" in its refusal to satisfy its payment obligations due to the holdout plaintiffs, and when it enacted the Lock Law and the Lock Law suspension.[7]

This decision, later upheld in October 2012 and August 2013 by the Second Circuit Court of Appeals, makes evident—apart from an extraterritorial erroneous reading of an Argentine law, applicable in Argentina— the shift toward an understanding of the pari passu clause as entailing "payment" rather than "rank"

This decision, consecrating the "payment" interpretation of the pari passu clause, changed not only established understanding over the meaning of the clause but also dramatically affected the natural equilibrium in sovereign debt.

In effect, for more than thirty years the absence of a specific legal framework for sovereign debt had resulted in an equilibrium, the main elements of which were that while recalcitrant creditors were not able to easily attach assets (other than commercial assets held abroad by the relevant sovereign), sovereigns knew that persistent access to international capital markets depended upon their ability to service international debt.

THE REMEDY

However, much more relevant than the pari passu decision, was the crafting of the "remedy." In effect, Judge Griesa decided to order an "equitable remedy" in the form of an injunction that consisted in making it illegal for Argentina to pay its restructured debt unless and until it paid the holdout plaintiffs in advance.

It is paradoxical at least that the "remedy" be a construction at "equity," that is, it is a remedy originated in the judge's consideration on equity and thus based neither in law nor in contract.

This aspect, the invasion of third-party rights (bona fide creditors, financial institutions, custodians, etc.) and of a sovereign's right to pay, is what constitutes the real game changer of the Argentine debt restructuring saga and is the cornerstone of the huge windfall of bargaining power benefiting sovereign holdout creditors everywhere. Preventing the flow of payments from reaching creditors defies the very concept of what being a sovereign entails.

All the more striking is the fact that as new petitions and judicial proceedings went forward, it became clearer that the main point of the judicial decisions was the extraterritorial application of the "injunction" so as to impede both the right of the sovereign to pay and the applicable law of other jurisdictions (the United Kingdom).

Even the pari passu specifics lost some of their importance. In effect, between 2012 and 2013 the district court and the court of appeals went back and forth over the correct "formula" or application of the ratable payment concept. But ultimately, when Judge Griesa was faced with a request by some holdout plaintiffs (not the ones obtaining the big windfall) to apply the pari passu ratable payment formula over monies held by Bank of New York in Argentina as trustee for the exchange bondholders, he decided against the request, because the funds were in Argentina.

So what transpires is that the whole construction of the pari passu clause as a payment obligation was construed to find that Argentina had breached the contractual obligation (in addition to the obvious default and its plain vanilla subsequent "summary judgment"), and that breach warranted a special and new remedy at equity that pretends to prevent a sovereign from paying and prevents and affects bona fide third parties not party to the holdout litigation from receiving their monies.

This construction is what is the real threat and what encourages holding out. Ultimately it is an issue about judicial "equity" remedies that bring about the most inequitable possible outcome.

THE CONSEQUENCES

The evolution of the Argentine litigation and the effects of the "remedy" show that the most important issue is not so much the redefinition of the pari passu, clarifying that what is meant is not "payment" but rather "rank."

This is so for a number of reasons.[8] The first one is that the initiative on new collective action clauses (CACs) is forward looking. There is a significant stock of sovereign bonds in the international markets without new aggregate-version CACs. This stock of around US$915 billion will not completely mature in fifteen years. Moreover, the initiative encouraging countries to issue with new enhanced CACs is going well but is not reducing the stock of nonenhanced CACs. In fact, since the initiative started, some countries continue to issue without the new enhanced framework. As a result, the stock is increasing. So the new contractual approach will not solve the issue, at least not for the next fifteen years.

But there are other shortcomings. For many countries—and this is especially troublesome for small countries—old pari passu clauses subject to the novel Griesa interpretation are inserted in commercial contracts that can easily be assigned and end up in the hands of recalcitrant holdouts or vultures. There is no way to recraft commercial contracts.

But ultimately, the real risk is of the "remedy" repeating itself: if a judge were to decide in the future that a sovereign breached its bonds or contractual provisions in a way that warrants an "equitable" remedy of the sort granted to the holdout plaintiffs.

Such a risk is what the new "framework" after the Argentine decisions brings. One that the old "equilibrium" of uncertainty between sovereigns and creditors entailed. Now the balance has been tilted toward avoiding restructuring at all costs, because there is an enhanced premium in holding out. Not only could holding out mean being granted an unwarranted privilege; it could also entail being able to block the payment stream to participating creditors. This signifies that the assumption upon which any "market" solution rests is no longer available. This is because the essential "precedent" element of the Argentine decision is the dislodging between risk and yield. If remedies of the type granted to Argentine plaintiffs is an available alternative for Sovereign Debt litigation, then there is no counterpart for exorbitant and unwarranted returns. The equilibrium of balanced uncertainties is gone.

As a result, equilibrium can at this stage only be restored through a statutory approach to sovereign debt restructuring.[9]

NOTES

1. The views expressed herein are exclusively the author's, and not necessarily those of the IMF or the government of Argentina.

2. See Lee C. Bucheit and Jeremiah S. Pam. "The *Pari Passu* Clause in Sovereign Debt Instruments," *Emory Law Journal* 53, special edition (2004): 869–922.

3. See Bucheit and Pam, "Pari Passu Clause," 870.

4. For purposes of clarity, the 1994 Fiscal Agency Agreement describes the relevant defined terms as follows.

> "External Indebtedness" means obligations (other than the Securities) for borrowed money or evidenced by securities, debentures, notes or other similar instruments denominated or payable, or which at the option of the holder thereof may be payable, in a currency other than the lawful currency at the Republic provided that no Domestic Foreign Currency Indebtedness, as defined below, shall constitute External Indebtedness.

> "Public External Indebtedness" means, with respect to the Republic, any External Indebtedness of, or guaranteed by the Republic which (i) is publicly offered or privately placed in securities markets, (ii) is in the form of, or represented by, securities notes or other securities or any guarantees thereof and (iii) is, or was intended at the time of issue to be, quoted, listed or traded on any stock exchange, automated trading system or over-the-counter or other securities market (including, without prejudice to the generality of the foregoing, securities eligible for PORTAL or a similar market for the trading of securities eligible for sale pursuant to Rule 144A under the U.S. Securities Act of 1933 (or any successor law or regulation of similar effect).

> "Domestic Foreign Currency Indebtedness" means (i) the following indebtedness (i) [list of Argentine law securities]; (ii) any indebtedness issued in exchange, or as replacement, for the indebtedness referred to in (i) above; and (iii) any other indebtedness payable by its terms, or which at the option of the holder thereof may be payable, in a currency other than the lawful currency of the Republic of Argentina which is (a) offered exclusively within the Republic of Argentina or (b) issued in payment, exchange, substitution, discharge or replacement of indebtedness payable in the lawful currency of the Republic of Argentine; provided that in no event shall the following indebtedness be deemed to constitute "Domestic Foreign Currency Indebtedness: (1) Bonos Externos de la República Argentina issued under law No. 19,686 enacted on June 15, 1972 and (2) any indebtedness issued by the Republic in exchange, or as replacement, for any indebtedness referred to (1) above."

5. See transcript of Allan Applestein, Trustee FBO D.C.A. Grantor Trust v. The Republic of Argentina and Province of Buenos Aires, No. 02 Civ. 1773 (TPG) 6-10 (S.D.N.Y. Jan. 15, 2004), p. 14.

6. On January 15, 2004, the district court (Judge Griesa) ruled that the issue was not ripe for adjudication. However, holdouts were required to give the court thirty days prior notice if they intended to use the clause. See Bucheit and Pam (2004): 920.

7. The Lock Law (Law 26,017) was an internal Argentine law passed by the Argentine Congress that merely prevented the executive branch from reopening the sovereign debt exchange in terms more favorable to holdouts. It was later suspended, and in any event, was utterly misread and misconstrued by Judge Griesa.

8. For an extensive analysis of the deficiencies of this approach, see Guzman, M. and J. E. Stiglitz (2015). "Creating a Framework for Sovereign Debt Restructuring that

Works," in *Too Little, Too Late: The Quest for Resolving Sovereign Debt Crises*, chapter 1. New York: Columbia University Press.

9. This volume discusses different proposals on how to move forward. See Guzman and Stiglitz (2016), Conn (2016), Herman (2016), Howse (2016), and Raffer (2016).

REFERENCES

Bucheit, Lee C., and Jeremiah S. Pam. 2004. "The Pari Passu Clause in Sovereign Debt Instruments," *Emory Law Journal* 53 (2004).

Conn, Richard A., Jr. 2016. "Perspectives on a Sovereign Debt Restructuring Framework: Less Is More." In *Too Little, Too Late: The Quest to Resolve Sovereign Debt Crises*, chapter 13. New York: Columbia University Press.

Guzman, Martin and Joseph E. Stiglitz. 2016. "Creating a Framework for Sovereign Debt Restructuring That Works." In *Too Little, Too Late: The Quest to Resolve Sovereign Debt Crises*, chapter 1. New York: Columbia University Press.

Herman, Barry. 2016. "Toward a Multilateral Framework for Recovery from Sovereign Insolvency." In *Too Little, Too Late: The Quest to Resolve Sovereign Debt Crises*, chapter 11. New York: Columbia University Press.

Howse, Robert. 2016. "Towards a Framework for Sovereign Debt Restructuring: What Can Public International Law Contribute?" In *Too Little, Too Late: The Quest to Resolve Sovereign Debt Crises*, chapter 14. New York: Columbia University Press.

Raffer, Kunibert. 2016. "Debts, Human Rights, and the Rule of Law: Advocating a Fair and Efficient Sovereign Insolvency Model." In *Too Little, Too Late: The Quest to Resolve Sovereign Debt Crises*, chapter 15. New York: Columbia University Press.

CHAPTER 5

Greek Debt Denial

A MODEST DEBT RESTRUCTURING PROPOSAL AND WHY IT WAS IGNORED

Yanis Varoufakis

THERAPEUTIC VERSUS LETHAL DEBT WRITEDOWNS

The point of restructuring debt is to reduce the volume of new loans needed to salvage an insolvent entity. Creditors offer debt relief to get more value back and to extend as little new finance to the insolvent entity as possible.[1]

Sequence and speed are of the essence. General Motors recovered after 2009 because its debts were restructured deeply and speedily *before* the company's new business plan was implemented and certainly before new credit lines were granted. Had the admission of its insolvency been postponed, with debt relief deferred to an unspecified future date, GM would have failed and a total debt writeoff would have followed. So while it is true that an unsustainable debt *will* be written down, a debt restructure delayed generates avoidable deadweight losses.

Where Greek debt is concerned, a clear pattern has emerged since 2010. This pattern remains unbroken to this day.

A BRIEF HISTORY OF THE GREEK STATE'S INSOLVENCY

Greek public debt became unserviceable in 2009, following the 2008 international financial crisis. Between 2008 and 2009, Greece's nominal gross domestic product (GDP) growth subsided by a massive 18.25 percent,[2] while the interest rates investors demanded to refinance the government's more than 120 percent of debt-to-GDP ratio jumped from 4.4 percent in 2008 to 5.6 percent in 2009, exceeding 8 percent in the spring of 2010.

It took powerful political motives to deny the obvious unsustainability of Greek public debt caused by this violent transition from high (low-interest loan-fueled) growth to a deep recession that came hand in hand with a capital exodus and a domestic credit crunch. Against this bleak background, in May 2010 official Europe and the International Monetary Fund extended loans to the insolvent Greek state equal to 44 percent of the country's shrinking GDP. The very mention of debt restructuring was considered inadmissible and a cause for ridicule, indeed vilification, hurled at those of us who dared suggest its inevitability.[3] Moreover, the gigantic new loan, the largest in history (in absolute terms), came attached with the largest fiscal consolidation target during peacetime. The combination of this target's "announcement effect" with (1) the ongoing credit crunch, (2) the capital exodus, and (3) the private sector's deleveraging conspired to shed a devastating 29.63 percent off Greece's nominal GDP; the very income from which the new and legacy public debts would have to be repaid.

The inevitability of a debt writedown broke through the veil of official denial in 2012 after the debt-to-GDP ratio skyrocketed from just under 120 percent to 171.3 percent. The same politicians, and economic commentators, who were remonstrating that a debt restructure was neither necessary nor useful, announced the largest haircut in history. With key German and French banks already taken care of between 2010 and 2012,[4] Greece's remaining private creditors (the public pension funds being the worst hit) were served a substantial haircut. In net present-value terms, the size of that haircut, which excluded the post-2010 official sector loans, reached 90 percent,[5] equivalent to 34 percent of the nominal stock of Greece's public debt.

Despite this substantial haircut, the largest in economic history, Greece's public debt remained deeply unsustainable, presenting itself as a splendid case study of how debt restructuring can be "too little" when it is "too late." The reasons were threefold:

(1) Debt that had been taken on the books of the ECB (as part of the 2010/1 SMP bond purchase program) was excluded from the haircut. Moreover, the fact that this part of Greece's debt had the shortest maturity undermined debt sustainability further.[6]

(2) Greek banks, who had lost much of their capital due to the haircut of government bonds, were to be recapitalized by a new loan tranche of €50 billion, ensuring that written old debt was immediately replaced

with new debt. In sum, the new loans of the second bailout (that accompanied the 2012 haircut) came to a whopping 63 percent of GDP.

(3) The austerian conditionalities attached to the new loans, the wildly optimistic privatization revenue targets, and the complete lack of a strategy to deal with the banks' nonperforming loans caused serious investors (who correctly predicted another sequence of spectacular misses of the troika's medium term fiscal targets) to continue their investment "strike," convinced that the troika would return shortly with even more austerian demands, condemning the Greek economy to yet more recession. This ensured that, despite the large haircut, the debt to GDP ratio continued to rise beyond control.[7]

A few months later, in November 2012, in a muted recognition that Greece's public debt remained unsustainable despite the 2012 haircut, the Eurogroup (comprising eurozone members' finance ministers) indicated that debt relief would be finalized by December 2014, once the 2012 program was "successfully" completed and the Greek government's budget had attained a primary surplus. Alas, even though a small primary surplus was achieved during 2014, the troika of Greece's lenders refused the government of Antonis Samaras the promised debt relief, insisting instead on further austerity measures that the government could not deliver, having lost the Greek electorate's approval and the support of a majority of members of Parliament. In a desperate bid to secure a new mandate, the Samaras government brought the general election forward by at least a few months. And so it was that in January 2015 the left-wing Syriza party became the governing party and I became Greece's finance minister.

Our government's top priority was, naturally, to renegotiate the terms of our loan agreement, together with the medium-term fiscal plan and the administrative, tax, product market, and social reform agenda that had to be rethought in view of the economic implosion and the humanitarian crisis that the previous five years had engendered.

From the first day of our government, it was clear that our lenders were utterly divided. International Monetary Fund officials were keen to place debt relief in the right sequence. Indeed, I could even go as far as to say that they were even more "militant" than I was regarding the importance of a straight writedown (including in terms of net present *and* face values). On the other hand, the European Stability Mechanism,[8] the European Central Bank (ECB), and finance ministers of the surplus nations were opposed even to a discussion on possible debt relief.

This is not the place to recount the negotiations in which I was involved. However, it might be useful to present my ministry's proposals regarding the debt restructure we put forth. Given the well-orchestrated public relations exercise by which most well-meaning commentators were convinced that our government had no credible proposals to offer, it is important to present those proposals here, so the reader can make up his or her own mind. Were our proposals' credible? If they were, why were they ignored, causing a six-month impasse that led to bank closures and to a new loan agreement that defers to the future both debt restructuring and, remarkably, the presentation of a growth strategy for Greece?

THE GREEK FINANCE MINISTRY'S ANALYSIS

An ex ante debt restructure was my ministry's priority, because it would provide the "optimism shock" necessary to energize investment in Greece's private sector. In contrast, the troika program we inherited was always going to fail, because its logic was deeply flawed and, for this reason, guaranteed to deter investment. It was a logic (see below) based on incoherent backward induction, reflecting political expediency's triumph over sound macroeconomic thinking.

Figure 5.1 captures the logic of the "program" we inherited and were elected to renegotiate. The program's authors began by setting 2019 as their horizon and chose as their main target the reduction of Greece's ratio of nominal debt to national income from 177.1 percent in 2014 to 139.4 percent in 2019; the underlying assumption being that money markets would start lending to the Greek state again once they were convinced that the debt ratio could be pushed below the psychological threshold of 120 percent by 2020.

To achieve the 2019 target, the total debt consolidation had to reach an astounding 62.8 percent of the nation's GDP for the 2015–2019 period, as the Greek government was committed to debt repayments amounting to 25.1 percent of cumulative GDP during that same period. Where would that 62.8 percent of the 2015–2019 period's GDP be found to bring about the desired consolidation? To answer this question, the troika's analysts employed a series of sequential assumptions.

First, they valued public assets to be privatized at 7 percent of that period's GDP, as if their value were exogenous. Then, with this figure as a given, they assumed that nominal GDP would grow by a total of 27.3 percent and that, in addition, deflation would turn into a mild inflation

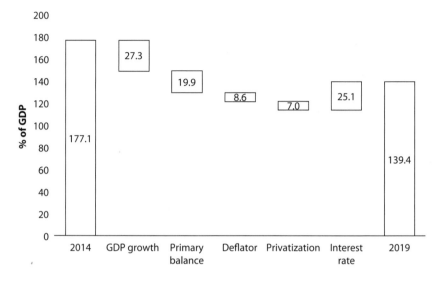

Figure 5.1   Austerity versus nominal GDP growth 2009–2014.

that would, through the economy's deflator, shave off another 8.6 percent of the country' debt-to-GDP ratio. With these assumptions in place, the "residual" portion of the debt reduction target came to 19.9 percent of the period's GDP—the amount the troika decided was to be paid for by the government's cumulative primary surplus. Thus, the absurd primary surplus targets of 3.5 percent for 2015, rising to 4.5 percent of GDP in 2016 and in every year henceforth, ad infinitum.

It is not difficult to see that the logical foundations of this program were flimsy. The value of public assets was taken as independent of the economy's growth rate. Moreover, while the primary surplus target was dependent on the troika's assumption regarding the growth rate, the negative impact of an absurd primary target on investment and aggregate demand was simply assumed away.

Was this faulty backward induction the result of poor macroeconomic models? My colleagues at the Greek finance ministry and I did not think so. The incoherent analysis was, at least in our estimation, the price Greece and Europe had to pay so the troika would maintain the politically motivated illusion that Greek debt restructuring could be left for "later."

In practical terms, the result of this method, whatever its motivation might have been, was an "austerity trap." When fiscal consolidation turns on a predetermined debt ratio to be achieved at a predetermined point in the future, the primary surpluses needed to hit those targets are such that the effect on the private sector undermines the assumed growth rates and thus derails the planned fiscal path. Indeed, this is precisely why previous fiscal-consolidation plans for Greece missed their targets so spectacularly (see figure 5.2).

Based on this analysis, my proposals to our European and international creditors were based on a simple idea: instead of backward induction we should map out a forward-looking plan based on reasonable assumptions about the primary surpluses consistent with the rates of output growth, net investment, and export expansion that could stabilize Greece's economy and debt ratio. If that meant that the 2020 debt-to-GDP ratio would be higher than 120 percent, we would need to devise smart ways to rationalize, reprofile, or restructure the debt—keeping in mind the aim of maximizing the effective present value to be returned to Greece's creditors.

In this context, I presented the following debt restructuring proposal to key finance ministers and officials of the European Commission, the International Monetary Fund (IMF), and the ECB in April 2015.

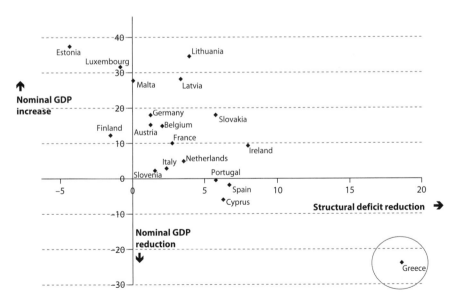

Figure 5.2   The "austerity trap" for Greece.

THE GREEK FINANCE MINISTRY'S MODEST DEBT
RESTRUCTURING PROPOSAL (APRIL 2015)

The actual April 2015 non-paper is reproduced in this section, with minor redactions to enhance readability.[9] Its purpose was to illustrate that it was in Greece's creditors' interest to agree to a substantial easing of austerity (i.e., a primary surplus target of around 1.5 percent) and to a debt restructure that did not need to involve a politically "difficult" haircut of the debt's face value. The said non-paper follows:

PREAMBLE

The current 178 percent debt-to-GDP ratio raises concerns amongst investors and the public that debt remains an obstacle to a sustainable recovery. In turn, these concerns viz. Greece's solvency hinder the country's growth prospects (as investors are hesitant about committing resources to a country that could default) and thwart a return to the market.

The new Greek government believes that a primary surplus of 1.5 percent is an appropriate target for the medium term and could be boosted further as long as recovery has pushed nominal GDP growth above 4.5 percent for a number of years. Such low but significant primary surpluses, together with measures for restructuring Greece's debt repayments, should put the country on the path of solvency, strictly defined as the ability to lower the debt-to-GDP ratio asymptotically.

A sequence of debt swaps that will return Greece to solvency and, thus, to the markets, is explored below:

THE DEBT OVERHANG

DEBT SUSTAINABILITY: SOME BASIC PRINCIPLES

Debt sustainability is about keeping the debt-to-GDP ratio under control. This typically requires that the deficit is low enough to guarantee that, given the growth rate, the debt ratio is constant or falling. An economy with zero (nominal) growth needs a balanced budget. Negative nominal growth, which has been Greece's case since 2009, requires an increasing primary surplus just to keep the debt-to-GDP rate constant. However, with positive nominal growth, some deficit is consistent with solvency; all that it takes is for the debt to grow less rapidly than nominal GDP.

In the case of Greece, where the debt-to-GDP ratio stands at 178 percent while nominal GDP is shrinking, the most pressing need is for a return to nominal GDP growth. Allowing for a medium-term, conservative, nominal GDP growth rate of 3 percent the government budget deficit above which the debt continues to grow in proportion to GDP is 5.25 percent of GDP (= 3% × 1.75).[10] But this deficit target has already been achieved,[11] which means that Greece's debt needs only a small primary budget surplus rate to be stabilized.

In other words, a 3 percent deficit is well within the boundaries of debt sustainability as conventionally defined. Given the interest bill, about 4.5 percent of GDP, a primary surplus of 1.5 percent is fully consistent with the stabilization of Greece's debt-to-GDP ratio at the current levels.

Our debt-sustainability analysis (DSA) exercises (such as shown in figure 1 and table 1) reveal, based on methods that the IMF has been utilizing, that maintaining the current cyclically adjusted primary surplus at around 1 percent to 1.5 percent until the effective primary surplus reaches 2.5 percent, and maintaining this level constant forever after is clearly sufficient to restore Greece's solvency over the long run.

Of course, significantly to reduce Greece's debt-to-GDP ratio (and thus propel Greece back to the money markets within months), the effective interest rate reduction must also be significant; from

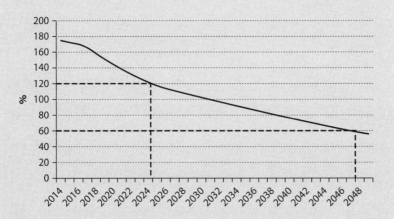

Figure 1   Debt sustainability analysis.

Table 1 Debt sustainability analysis

Year (end of period)	2014	2015	2016	2017	2018	2019	2020	2021	2022	2023	2024
Nominal GDP (€bn)	181.9	178.8	182.4	189.2	197.5	207.1	217.2	228.6	241.1	254.3	267.4
Output gap (% of potential GDP)	-10.30%	-11.5%	-11.1%	-9.6%	-8.2%	-6.8%	-5.4%	-4.0%	-2.6%	-1.1%	0.0%
Potential GDP	202.8	202.1	205.2	209.3	215.2	222.1	229.5	238.1	247.4	257.2	267.3
Real potential GDP growth (%)	—	1.5%	1.5%	1.6%	1.7%	1.9%	1.9%	1.9%	1.9%	1.9%	1.9%
Real GDP growth (%)	—	0.1%	2.0%	3.3%	3.3%	3.5%	3.4%	3.4%	3.4%	3.4%	3.1%
GDP deflator (%)	—	-1.8%	0.0%	0.4%	1.1%	1.3%	1.4%	1.8%	2.0%	2.0%	2.0%
Primary balance (% of GDP)	—	0.8%	1.0%	1.7%	2.4%	2.5%	2.5%	2.5%	2.5%	2.5%	2.5%
Cyclically adjusted primary balance (% of potential GDP)	—	5.7%	5.7%	5.7%	5.7%	5.2%	4.7%	4.1%	3.5%	3.0%	2.5%

4.5 percent to something closer to 1–1.5 percent. A series of smart debt swaps that achieve this at negligible cost to the creditors is presented below.

NET PRESENT VALUE VERSUS FACE VALUE

In an interview in September 2013, European Stability Mechanism president Klaus Regling stated that any DSA undertaken by the IMF is "meaningless." Regling's key argument was that to assess debt sustainability we need to take into account not only the debt's nominal (or face) value but also its net present value (NPV) at every point in time.

Greece currently owes the European Financial Stability Facility (EFSF) €142 billion, bearing an interest rate of 2.5 percent and having a final maturity of 39 years (amortizing from year 8). This high level of concessionality of the EFSF loans is not captured in the nominal debt-to-GDP ratio.

Indeed, if Greece's debt were calculated in NPV terms, for example, with a 5 percent discount factor, the debt-to-GDP ratio would fall to 135 percent instantly.

THE LIABILITY MANAGEMENT DEBATE

LENGTHENING THE MATURITY OF THE DEBT

Official creditors appear to be willing to lengthen the maturities of their claim on Greece and to reduce the interest they charge. Given the current low yields of the sovereign debt of the major creditor countries (Germany and France in particular), extending low interest rates to Greece would create a valuable breathing space.

SMP BONDS

The first "slice" of Greece's public debt that needs to be restructured is the €27 billion of pre-PSI SMP bonds still held by the ECB. These bond holdings by the ECB constitute short-term debt and, in addition, block (as they sit on the ECB's books) Greece's participation in the ECB's quantitative easing (QE) monetary operations. Swapping these bonds for longer-term debt at low interest rates would help deal with Greece's funding gap in two ways: (1) it would remove the need to borrow short term at high rates, and (2) it would push down Greek government bond yields massively, courtesy of allowing new bonds to be purchased by the ECB as part of the latter's QE monetary operations.

Recommendation: Immediate buyback of SMP bonds from the ECB (€27 billion) by means of the following procedure: Greece acquires a new loan from the ESM; Greece then purchases the SMP bonds back from the ECB; and Greece retires these bonds. Finally, the ECB returns to Greece approximately €8 billion (of its own profits from having purchased the SMP Greek government bonds below par). This sum could be deposited in an escrow account to be used only in order to extinguish maturing IMF credits, thus helping Greece meet over the next few years its total remaining IMF debt (of just below €20 billion).

NB: The conditionalities for this new ESM loan can/should be the same as the conditionalities for completing the final review of the ongoing Greek ESM program.

GREEK LOAN FACILITY LOAN SEGMENT

The Greek loan facility (GLF) harks back to the first Greek loan agreement (May 2010). It is a complex, multiple, bilateral loan agreement between Greece and each of the eurozone member states, and it is unique to Greece (unlike the EFSF loans that were also extended to Portugal, Ireland, Spain, and Cyprus).

The GLF slice of Greece's debt would be well suited to restructuring: the interest rate is floating, based on the Euribor 6M, and the creditors could lock the current low rates into much longer maturities.

RESTRUCTURING GLF THROUGH LONGER MATURITIES

Ideally, from the perspective of both Greece and the member states that have lent it GLF monies, the GLF loans should be transformed into a perpetual bond bearing a 2–2.5 percent interest rate. It would be ideal for Greece, because it would avoid any refinancing risk. And it would be ideal for creditor states because of the relatively large interest rate it would bear.

In case a perpetual bond proves difficult politically/legally, an alternative would be to lengthen the GLF debt to 100 years, with minimal principal payable upon maturity. Even a full principal repayment would lighten the load of this GLF debt upon Greece without imposing significant losses on the creditor member states.

RESTRUCTURING GLF THROUGH NOMINAL GDP-INDEXED BONDS

GDP-indexed bonds were already introduced in the PSI debt exchange in 2012. The merit of nominal GDP-indexed bonds is to lower the risk of volatility and ensure that debt sustainability becomes slowdown proof, as debt repayments are reduced procyclically during downturns and accelerated during an upturn.

Two options are available. One is to link the interest payment of the debt to nominal GDP growth rates (NB: This was the approach embedded in the PSI bonds; see box 5.1). Another method could be to index the principal debt redemption to nominal GDP. Debt repayments could be automatically suspended during years following nominal growth rate below a certain (low) threshold. Cumulatively, that would reduce debt repayments if nominal GDP (in absolute terms) failed to reach a certain level by a certain point in time, e.g., 2022). [The reader should note that this proposal of ours ended up being adopted, a few months later, for Ukraine . . .]

GDP-indexed instruments already designed for the PSI

In March 2012, the PSI bonds were issued together with separately tradable warrants providing for certain payments indexed to Greece's real GDP growth as follows. The warrants have an aggregate notional amount ("Notional Amount") equal to the aggregate principal amount of the PSI bonds with which they are issued. The GDP securities were issued as a single instrument.Subject to the conditions below, Greece will make a payment to all holders of outstanding warrants in each year beginning in the year 2015. Starting in 2015 and each year thereafter to and including 2042, Eurostat will publish the nominal GDP in euros and the real rate of growth of GDP (Actual Real Growth Rate) for the preceding calendar year ("Reference Year"). Greece will be obligated to make payments to all holders of warrants (as described below) if and only if each of the two conditions set forth below is satisfied:

1. Nominal GDP for the Reference Year exceeds the "Reference GDP" projected by the EuroWorking Group for that year, and
2. The Actual Real Growth Rate for the Reference Year is positive and exceeds the real growth rate projected by the EuroWorking Group (the "Reference GDP Growth Rate"), provided that for

purposes hereof, beginning with the Reference Year 2021, if the Actual Real Growth Rate for the calendar year preceding the Reference Year is negative, the Actual Real Growth Rate for the Reference Year shall be deemed to be the cumulative (i.e., the sum of) Actual Real Growth Rate for both years.

In the event that conditions 1 and 2 are satisfied, Greece will pay to each holder of outstanding warrants an amount equal to the GDP Index Percentage of the Notional Amount. The GDP Index Percentage shall be an amount (expressed as a percentage) not to exceed 1.00 percent, equal to 1.5 times the amount by which the Actual Real Growth Rate exceeds the Reference GDP Growth Rate.

By way of example, if the Actual Real Growth Rate for calendar year 2020 is −0.3 percent and the real growth rate for the Reference Year 2021 is +2.6 percent, the Actual Real Growth Rate for the Reference Year 2021 shall be deemed to be 2.3 percent (−0.3% + 2.6%), and the payment due in 2022 in respect of the Reference Year 2021 shall be equal to 0.45 percent (1.5 × (2.3% − 2%)) of the Notional Amount.

EFSF LOAN SEGMENT: SPLITTING THE EFSF DEBT IN TWO

The EFSF loans are less flexible than the GLF. To the extent that the EFSF had to borrow on the market the corresponding amounts that it granted to Greece at an average rate of about 2.5 percent, its funding cost is already locked in.

One way to proceed, however, would be to split Greece's debt obligations (except for the part under a cofinancing agreement) into two instruments: half of it would be a 5 percent interest–bearing instrument, and the other half would be a series of non–interest bearing instruments (zero-coupon bonds) that would repay the other 50 percent principal at maturity.

The merit of making explicit the concessionality of the debt is to allow for a wider range of options. The liability management exercise would then focus on the long-term non–interest bearing assets.

Ideally, the creditors should simply cancel, in a phased fashion, the part that carries no coupon. In real economic terms, they would lose little, only the market value of the non–interest bearing bonds and would still cash the amount of interest originally due.

From the creditors' viewpoint this approach would have two merits:

- It would give them time to provision for the EFSF losses, especially if the debt has been initially lengthened to, say, 50 years (in NPV terms, the market loss could amount to 50 percent of face value, or about 25 billion). Here the creditors will be willing to lengthen the maturity as it reduces their losses!

- It keeps Greece under the pressure of honoring a significant (but sustainable) primary surplus, as the debt service remains high.

From Greece's perspective, such a move would reduce significantly (up to 50 percent) the face value of the EFSF debt, further accelerating Greece's return to the money markets.

SUMMARY AND CONCLUSION

The above interventions on the structure of Greece's debts will, upon their very announcement, cause Greece to reenter the markets in a short space of time—especially if combined with policies for boosting investment and carrying out important reforms.

Figure 2 shows what the trajectory of nominal debt would look like under the joint assumptions of a swap against a perpetual for the GLF, a reduction by half of the EFSF loan (as explained earlier), and a swap of ECB bonds against ESM loans with longer maturities.

The result is striking: Greece could lower its debt-to-GDP ratio from more than 175 percent now to 93 percent in 2020 to 60 percent by 2030.

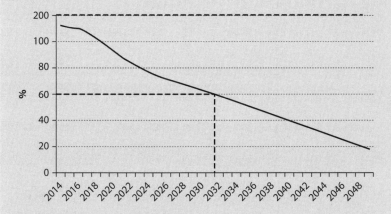

Figure 2   Debt sustainability analysis.

APPENDIX

GREECE'S FUNDING NEEDS
(WITHOUT PROPOSED SWAPS)

2015 funding needs

May	930 million IMF
June	1526 million IMF
July	450 million IMF – 3.49 billion ECB
August	174 million IMF – 3.17 billion ECB
September	1.526 billion IMF
October	450 million IMF
November	153 million IMF
December	1.191 billion IMF

REPOS–Common Bank of Greece Account: previous government raised the sum from 4 billion in August 2014 to 8.5 billion by end of January 2015. Currently at 10.7 billion.

Greek debt repayment schedule

	Principal	Interest	Total
2015	12,384	2,906	15,289
2016	7,190	6,134	13,324
2017	9,621	5,808	15,430
2018	4,531	5,602	10,134
2019	13,523	5,698	19,221
2020	4,947	5,199	10,146
2021	4,992	5,256	10,248
2022	6,728	20,624	27,352
2023	9,062	11,892	20,954
2024	8,937	10,424	19,361
2025	7,429	7,666	15,095

2026	8,058	7,617	15,675
2027	8,062	6,978	15,040
2028	7,469	6,607	14,076
2029	6,892	6,202	13,095
2030	7,247	5,879	13,126
2031	6,723	5,549	12,272
2032	9,523	5,227	14,750
2033	6,760	4,807	11,567
2034	9,520	4,492	14,012
2035	9,248	4,200	13,448
Sum	168,846	144,767	313,615

REJECTION IN THE SERVICE OF DENIAL

The troika did not reject the above debt restructuring proposals.[12] They did not have to reject them, because they never allowed our proposal to be even discussed!

The political will of the Eurogroup, and of the troika that dominates it, was to ignore our proposals, let the negotiations fail, impose an indefinite bank holiday, and force the Greek government to acquiesce on everything—including a massive new loan that is at least double the size Greece would have needed under our proposals.[13]

Once again, Greece's creditors put the cart before the horse by insisting that another new loan be agreed *before* any discussion of debt relief. As a result, the new loan deemed necessary grew inexorably, as it had done in 2010 and 2012.

Our government's surrender was formalized in the Euro Summit agreement of July 12, 2015.[14] That agreement, which is now the blueprint for Greece's relation with the eurozone, perpetuates the five-year-long pattern of placing debt restructuring at the end of a sorry sequence of fiscal tightening, economic contraction, and program failure.

Indeed, the sequence of the new "bailout" agreement envisaged in the agreement of July 12, 2015, predictably started with the adoption of harsh tax measures and medium-term fiscal targets equivalent to another bout of stringent austerity. Then came a midsummer negotiation of another large loan, equivalent to 48 percent of 2014's GDP. Finally, the agreement promises that, after the first review of the new program is completed, "the Eurogroup stands ready to consider, if necessary, possible additional measures . . . aiming at ensuring that gross financing needs remain at a sustainable level."

CONCLUSION: ON THE POLITICAL ECONOMY OF GREEK DEBT DENIAL

In a private conversation Amartya Sen astutely commented that the case of Greek debt is fascinating because it is one of those curious situations in which creditors extend new loans under conditions that guarantee they will not get their money back. Why do Greece's creditors refuse to move on debt restructuring before any new loans are negotiated? And why did they ignore our proposals? What is the reason for preferring a much larger new loan package than necessary?

The answers to these questions cannot be found by discussing sound finance, public or private, for they reside firmly in the realm of power politics. Debt is creditor power; and as Greece has learned the hard way, unsustainable debt turns the creditor into Leviathan. Life under it is becoming nasty, brutish, and for many of my compatriots, short. Be that as it may, it remains crucial to pinpoint the precise political motives behind the dogged rejection of sensible debt restructuring ideas that, if adopted, would have returned more value to Greece's creditors.

The first bailout loan agreement, in May 2010, can be easily explained as a cynical transfer of private losses from the books of French and German banks to the shoulders of Europe's taxpayers. The second loan agreement, in early 2012, had the purpose of underpinning the first agreement through a combination of a large haircut for the less powerful private creditors (e.g., private investors and Greek public pension funds) and another large loan used to "extend-and-pretend" the earlier official loans and to recapitalize the Greek banks. What about the third loan agreement that, according to Prime Minister Tsipras (who acquiesced to it), was imposed upon the Syriza government by a coup d'état?

A number of small-minded political motives are well understood already. For example, if our government were to conclude a viable, mutually advantageous agreement with the troika of creditors, after having opposed its "program," our "success" would have seriously jeopardized the electoral prospects of troika-friendly governing parties in Portugal, Spain, and Ireland. Additionally, the social democratic parties of Germany, France, and Austria that had acquiesced to or even promoted the troika's policies for the previous five years might have faced domestic challenges from their own left-wing opposition (either within or without these parties), invoking the specter of PASOK's (the Greek socialist party) fate.

However, while these considerations were important factors in the perpetuation of the "Greek debt denial," there is a more powerful explanation buried deep in the architectural faults of the eurozone and in the manner in which a significant European politician (1) understands these faults and (2) is planning to resolve them. The politician in question is none other than the German finance minister, Wolfgang Schäuble.

Schäuble understands that the original Maastricht Treaty (the no-bailout clause in particular) and the toxic bailouts that followed the eurozone's first financial crisis were always a poor substitute for political union. "Ideally, Europe would be a political union," he wrote in a joint article with Karl Lamers, the Christian Democratic Union's former foreign affairs chief (*Financial Times*, September 1, 2014).[15]

Schäuble is, of course, right to advocate institutional changes that might provide the eurozone with its missing political mechanisms. Not only because it is impossible otherwise to address the eurozone's current crisis but also for the purpose of preparing Europe's monetary union for the next crisis. The question is: Is his specific plan a good one? Is it one that Europeans should want? Is it realistic?

The Schäuble-Lamers plan rests on two ideas: "Why not have a European budget commissioner with powers to reject national budgets if they do not correspond to the rules we jointly agreed?" asked Schäuble and Lamers. "We also favour," they added "a 'eurozone parliament' comprising the MEPs of eurozone countries to strengthen the democratic legitimacy of decisions affecting the single currency bloc."

The first point to raise about the Schäuble-Lamers plan is that it is at odds with any notion of democratic federalism. A federal democracy, like Germany, the United States, or Australia, is founded on the sovereignty of its citizens as reflected in the *positive* power of their representatives to legislate what must be done on the sovereign people's behalf.

In sharp contrast, the Schäuble-Lamers plan envisages only negative powers: a eurozonal budget overlord (possibly a glorified version of the Eurogroup's president) equipped solely with negative or veto powers over national parliaments. The problem with this is twofold. First, it would not be sufficient to safeguard the eurozone's macroeconomy. Second, it would violate basic principles of Western liberal democracy.

Consider events both prior to the eruption of the euro crisis, in 2010, and afterward. Before the crisis, had Schäuble's fiscal overlord existed, she or he might have been able to veto the Greek government's profligacy but would be in no position to do anything regarding the tsunami of loans flowing from the private banks of Frankfurt and Paris to the periphery's private banks.[16] Those capital outflows underpinned unsustainable debt that unavoidably was transferred back onto the public's shoulders the moment financial markets imploded. Postcrisis, Schäuble's budget Leviathan would be powerless in the face of potential insolvency of several states caused by their bailing out (directly or indirectly) the private banks.

In short, the new high office envisioned by the Schäuble-Lamers plan would have been impotent to prevent the causes of the crisis and to deal with its repercussions. Moreover, every time it did act, by vetoing a national budget, the new high office would be annulling the sovereignty of a European people without having replaced it by a higher-order sovereignty at a federal or supranational level.

Back in May 2015, on the sidelines of yet another Eurogroup meeting, I had had the privilege of a fascinating conversation with Schäuble. We talked extensively both about Greece and the future of the eurozone. Later on that day, the Eurogroup's meeting agenda included an item on future institutional changes to bolster the eurozone. In that conversation, it was abundantly clear that Schäuble's plan was the axis around which the majority of finance ministers were revolving. It was also abundantly clear that the French authorities resisted this plan tooth and nail, fearing (with excellent cause) that it was merely a means of giving a Berlin-friendly appointee complete and unequivocal control over the French national budget.

Though Grexit was not referred to directly in that Eurogroup meeting of nineteen ministers, plus the institutions' leaders, veiled references were most certainly made to it. I heard a colleague say that member states that cannot meet their commitments should not count on the eurozone's indivisibility, since reinforced discipline was of the essence. Some even talked explicitly of the importance of bestowing upon a permanent Eurogroup president the power to veto national budgets. Others discussed the need to convene a Euro chamber of parliamentarians to legitimize her or his authority. Echoes of Schäuble's plan reverberated throughout the room.

Judging from that Eurogroup conversation, and from my discussions with Germany's finance minister, Grexit features in Schäuble's plan as a crucial move that would kickstart the process of its implementation. A controlled escalation of the pain most Greeks have been suffering for more than seven years, intensified by closed banks while ameliorated by some humanitarian aid, was foreshadowed as the harbinger of the new eurozone. On the one hand, the fate of the "prodigal" Greeks would act as a morality tale for the Italian and French governments resisting the transfer of national sovereignty over their budgets to the Eurogroup president. On the other hand, the prospect of (extremely limited) fiscal transfers (e.g., a partially common deposit insurance scheme and a common unemployment benefit pool to kick in when structural unemployment exceeds some threshold) would offer the requisite carrot.

In short, behind the Eurogroup rhetoric and decisions a war is waging between Berlin and Paris over the form of political union that must be introduced to bolster Europe's monetary union. Greek debt will not be restructured until this conflict is resolved. For without the Greek debt's continued unsustainability, Grexit fades, and with it an important weapon that Germany's finance ministry deploys against the French authorities would be disarmed.

The humanitarian crisis caused by the delayed Greek debt restructure is literally nothing more than collateral damage in a conflict that has nothing to do with Greece.

NOTES

Acknowledgments: I wish to thank the many advisers and collaborators for their input to the Greek finance ministry's debt restructuring proposals (reproduced in this chapter). Beginning with my international team, my sincere thanks go to Jeff Sachs (Columbia), Daniel Cohen (Lazard), and Matthieu Pigasse (Lazard). Finally, my heartfelt gratitude goes to my closely knit and dedicated team comprising Natasha Arvaniti, Harinos Micromatis, Daniel Munevar, Elena Pararitis, and Tasos Patokos.

1. The only exceptions are when creditors mistake a case of insolvency for one of illiquidity, or when they have reasons for "pretending and extending," i.e., delaying as much as possible the revelation that loans they had previously granted have now turned "bad."

2. Dropping from 11.27 percent in 2007–2008 to –6.98 percent in 2008–2009 and –9.168 percent in 2009–2010.

3. While it has been widely claimed that the IMF's staff opposed the pretense that Greece's debt remained sustainable, nevertheless the Fund's very definition of sustainable public debt errs on the side of hyper-"optimism," thus adding to the policy makers' "natural" aversion to debt restructuring. See M. Guzman and D. Heymann (2015), *The IMF Debt Sustainability Analysis: Issues and problems*, forthcoming in Journal of Globalization and Development.

4. Through redemptions that were financed either by the May 2010 bailout (i.e., Europe's taxpayers) or through the more than €50 billion the ECB spent buying Greek government bonds in the context of the so-called SMP program.

5. If we take into account the so-called debt buyback of December 2012 that was to follow the spring of 2012 haircut (the so-called PSI, or private sector involvement).

6. The bulk of these bonds, worth approximately €50 billion, matured between 2012 and 2018. Only in July and August of 2015, the Greek government had to redeem approximately €7 billion to the ECB.

7. By means of a recapitalization that was, "curiously," engineered so as to leave banks' private shareholders in full control, despite the fact that the state now owned the crushing majority of the shares.

8. The ESM was created as the permanent bailout fund for eurozone member states. It was the successor institution to the informal, makeshift, private special-purpose vehicle called EFSF (European Financial Stability Facility).

9. That my ministry's proposals were presented in the form of a non-paper reflects the curious practice of Eurogroup negotiations not to admit official proposals. Time and again our government (and I personally) was warned by the Eurogroup's President that any officially tabled proposal would be considered casus *belli*. Meanwhile, the troika's negotiators studiously avoided handing over to our side anything on paper, until on 25th June 2015 we were handed their ultimatum, in the form of a three-part draft agreement (comprising a medium term fiscal plan, a reform agenda, a five month funding plan plus, interestingly, a Debt Sustainability Analysis that the IMF took great pains to disavow as "preliminary" and lacking its seal of approval.).

10. Deficit = (debt-to-GDP ratio) × (nominal growth rate).

11. In 2014, the deficit fell under the Maastricht benchmark of 3 percent. In structural terms, correcting the measure of the deficit for the output gap, Greece is actually engineering a fiscal surplus (up to 1.6 percent of GDP according to the IMF).

12. Indeed, officials close to the troika conceded that our proposals were technically rigorous and legally sound.

13. The third "bailout" agreement, signed in the summer of 2015, provides for up to €85 billion. Our proposal (see previous section) would require no more than €33 billion of new, ESM-sourced financing, none of which would be needed for the Greek state's primary budget.

14. An annotated (by this author) copy of which can be found here: http://yanisvaroufakis.eu/2015/07/15/the-euro-summit-agreement-on-greece-annotated-by-yanis-varoufakis.

15. See www.ft.com/intl/cms/s/0/5565f134-2d48-11e4-8105-00144feabdc0.html?siteedition=intl#axzz3BwDyx9jA.

16. Moreover, if the Greek state had been barred from borrowing by Schäuble's budget commissioner, Greek debt would still have piled up via the private banks—as it did in Ireland and Spain.

REFERENCE

Guzman, Martin, and Daniel Heymann. 2016. "The IMF Debt Sustainability Analysis: Issues and Problems." Forthcoming, *Journal of Globalization and Development.*

PART III

Improvements to the Contractual Approach

CHAPTER 6

Count the Limbs

DESIGNING ROBUST AGGREGATION CLAUSES IN SOVEREIGN BONDS

Anna Gelpern, Ben Heller, and Brad Setser

On August 29, 2014, the International Capital Market Association (ICMA) published new recommended terms for sovereign bond contracts governed by English law (ICMA, 2014b). The change would allow a supermajority of creditors to approve a debtor's restructuring proposal in one vote across multiple bond series. The vote could bind all bondholders, even if one series voted unanimously against restructuring, so long as enough holders in the other series voted for it. This apparently technical change, awkwardly named "single-limb aggregated collective action clauses" promised to eliminate free-riding holdouts for the first time in the history of sovereign bond restructuring. A single vote across different bond issues could also open up new possibilities for abuse.

The markets might have rebelled. Instead, they yawned. On October 7, barely a month after ICMA launched its new collective action clauses (CACs), Kazakhstan became the first to use them in an English-law bond. The issue, Kazakhstan's first in fourteen years, was oversubscribed by a factor of four.[1] Vietnam adapted the mechanism in an unregistered $1 billion New York–law bond within a month with no apparent pushback from investors, despite being well below investment grade (at BB–). In November, investment-grade Mexico inserted a streamlined version of single-limb aggregation in its multi-billion-dollar New York–law bond program. Mexico's size and prominence among emerging-market issuers ensured that its choice of contract terms would be closely watched in the market. During a conference call hosted by Mexico's investment bankers to introduce the new CACs, not one investor objected or asked a question (JPMorgan, 2014). The November issue set the record for the lowest yield and lowest coupon of any ten-year U.S.-dollar bond issued by the

Mexican government (Diaz de Leon, 2016). Half a dozen other countries adopted single-limb aggregation within months; each launch was equally uneventful. The financial press greeted the news with a smattering of articles and editorials, calm in tone and broadly supportive in substance.

Flash back twelve years. The pages of the *Financial Times* and the *Wall Street Journal* sizzled with opinion columns from prominent academics debating proposals to neutralize holdouts. A high-profile contest between contract reforms to empower a supermajority of creditors and a treaty-based Sovereign Debt Restructuring Mechanism (SDRM) fueled a stream of news stories in 2002 and 2003. Back-to-back speeches by Stanford economists Anne Krueger and John Taylor, then number two at the International Monetary Fund (IMF) and the U.S. Treasury, respectively, gave the battle epic academic and policy stature and an air of Beltway intrigue (Krueger, 2002; Taylor, 2002). Investor groups sprang up to resist all official sovereign debt restructuring initiatives as creeping encroachments on creditor rights. Analysts predicted that bond markets would shun sovereigns for deviating from the prevailing contract boilerplate. Emerging-market finance ministers agonized over these predictions and fumed at IMF and G7 officials for sticking their noses into other people's contracts and sowing doubts in the markets about sovereigns' ability and willingness to pay (Setser, 2010). Few if any believed the more extravagant claims made by reform advocates—that majority amendment terms in sovereign bonds would make it possible to scale back IMF lending (Gelpern and Gulati, 2006).

Mexico launched the first SEC-registered bond with majority-amendment CACs in February 2003, departing from the New York custom of giving each bondholder a veto over contract amendments. By all accounts, it did so primarily to recapture its own debt narrative and block SDRM; fighting holdouts was a secondary objective at best (Gelpern and Gulati, 2013). Perhaps as a result, the change looks modest in retrospect: each series of bonds must vote separately, so that any series where objectors held a blocking minority could drop out of the restructuring. Nevertheless, investors on the conference call with Mexico's underwriters were outraged and threatened to boycott the issue.

It turns out that the amplitude of public debate and market resistance are poor proxies for the magnitude of change. The new generation of aggregated CACs goes some way toward bridging the gap between corporate and sovereign bankruptcy. Once widely adopted, single-limb aggregation would introduce—by contract—a basic bankruptcy concept of voting by class, rather than by instrument, in sovereign bonds governed by foreign law (IMF, 2003b). As a result, single-limb aggregated CACs are likely to have a much bigger impact on sovereign restructurings than the series-by-series CACs introduced in New York in 2003 and long customary in the London market.

The relatively smooth introduction of potent contract changes in 2014 has many explanations. Substance and process learning are surely a big part of the story. Substance learning came from over a decade of experience with series-by-series CACs, which helped on the margins in several small restructurings but were hardly revolutionary (Das, Papaioannou, and Trebesch, 2012; Duggar, 2013). "Two-limb" aggregation clauses with both stock-wide and series-by-series polling had been introduced in Uruguay (in 2003), Argentina (in 2005), and most importantly, across euro-area sovereign bonds (in 2013)—although they had not been used in a restructuring (Gelpern and Gulati, 2013). CACs had become mainstream: constructive and inoffensive. On the other hand, the Greek debt restructuring in 2012 and never-ending litigation stemming from Argentina's 2001 default revealed vulnerabilities in series-by-series CACs. In Greece, blocking positions led more than half of all foreign-law bonds to drop out of the restructuring, even though most Greek foreign-law bonds had CACs. These bonds continue to be paid in full (Zettelmeyer, Trebesch, and Gulati, 2013). In the case of Argentina, rulings by U.S. federal courts in favor of holdouts beginning in 2011 effectively blocked payments on restructured bonds unless the government paid the holdout plaintiffs in full, potentially upsetting the delicate balance between risk and reward that drove investor participation in earlier restructurings. As we write, neither the holdouts nor the restructured bondholders in Argentina are getting paid. Judicial rulings inadvertently demonstrated the perils of incomplete restructuring that had preoccupied theoretical literature in the 1990s (Eichengreen and Portes, 1995; Brooks, Guzman, Lombardi and Stiglitz, 2015).

Process learning was at least as important. On the one hand, finance officials on all sides emerged bruised from the battles of 2003 and sought to avoid reviving the standoff between statute and contract, despite pressure from some borrowing governments, academics, and civil society groups.[2] In a sign of the times, the IMF endorsed the new clauses less than a month after they were proposed (IMF, 2014a). A parallel process at the U.N. General Assembly stopped short of a binding treaty and chose for now to articulate broad-based restructuring norms (UN, 2015).

On the other hand, the adoption of CACs beginning in 2003 had created a process playbook, where all stakeholders could coalesce around model contract language without being bound. The words would not be mandatory, and could be adapted to individual country circumstances, but would enjoy a form of "compliance pull" from endorsements by diverse governments, multilateral organizations, and market associations.

ICMA's 2014 model clauses emerged out of a working group convened by Mark Sobel of the U.S. Treasury staff in 2013 to coordinate approaches to contract reform. The group included debt managers from mature and emerging-market countries, IMF officials, lawyers, investors, and investment bankers.[3] The robust discussion inside the working group helped build consensus on the nature of the needed reform and the trade-offs intrinsic in any new voting mechanism. In addition, informal consultations with market participants and other stakeholders took the better part of two years and contributed to the development of the new generation of CACs (for an example of consultation, see ICMA 2014a).

In sum, the prevailing approach to sovereign debt restructuring reform requires agreement on contract design. As a matter of design, moving from unanimity to supermajority approval in New York in 2003 was relatively simple, especially since majority voting had already been the practice in London. Design was a bigger challenge in moving from series-by-series to robust cross-series voting in 2014. The new terms had to preserve the balance of power between debtors and creditors, empower a majority of creditors, neutralize free riders, and protect minorities from abuse. This balancing had to be achieved with out statutory guidance or court oversight, which in bankruptcy help ensure that creditors voting as a class share the same interests. As with most matters in sovereign debt, it was all down to contract.

Contract design is our focus for the remainder of this chapter. We start by briefly reviewing the introduction of series-by-series voting to amend financial terms into New York–law bonds in 2003. We then look at the factors that helped create broad consensus on the need to move beyond series-by-series voting in 2012. Most of the essay is devoted to analyzing the key features of the new generation of aggregated CACs and the considerations that shaped decisions about these features. We conclude with observations on contract reform in sovereign debt restructuring and the challenges ahead.

CACS IN NEW YORK–LAW BONDS: 1996–2003

In 2015, it is hard to make sense of the 1996 to 2003 controversy over arcane boilerplate in New York–law sovereign bond contracts. The terms at the heart of intense public debates were simple and not entirely novel. English-law bonds had long permitted creditor majorities to amend financial terms in sovereign bonds (Weidemaier and Gulati, 2011). New York–law bonds did the same for nonfinancial terms, but required unanimous bondholder consent to change maturity, interest rate, currency, and the like. Mechanically, reforms first proposed in 1996 and ultimately implemented in 2003 could be accomplished by changing a few words in New York boilerplate (G10, 1996; Buchheit, 1998; G22, 1998). English-law contracts did not need to change at all.[4]

The symbolism of shifting from veto power for every bondholder to qualified majority rule offers part of the explanation. For some market participants, unanimity stood for bonds' special immunity from restructuring, with roots in the Brady bonds of the late 1980s and early 1990s. The Brady bonds delivered substantial debt relief in exchange for a special commitment to pay, which ended the cycle of syndicated loan renegotiations and paved the way for emerging-market sovereigns to access the global capital markets (Cline, 1995).

New York–law Brady bonds could only be amended with unanimous consent of all bondholders. As a technical matter, this did not immunize them from restructuring. Instead of amending its bond contracts, a sovereign could offer to exchange them for new ones. With the right incentives, most of the bondholders were likely to choose new, performing bonds over the prospect of default and years spent fighting to overcome sovereign immunity and scouring the world for attachable government assets. Within a decade of the first Brady bond deal, techniques such as exit consents and minimum participation thresholds paved the way for a string of relatively speedy debt exchanges that delivered substantial debt relief (Bi, Chamon, and Zettelmeyer, 2009; Panizza et al., 2009).[5]

As bond exchanges gathered momentum, more and more market participants argued that the official sector's war on unanimity in New York was misguided. Bond restructuring took less time than haggling with banks in creditor committees and dealing with their regulatory accounting constraints. CACs were a solution in search of a problem.

Yet to some in the official sector, CACs were the key to ending the era of big bailouts that started with Mexico in 1994 (Taylor, 2007). Here too, symbolic arguments made more sense than functional ones. The idea that New York–law contract changes could reduce the need for IMF lending ignored the fact that Mexico's vulnerability stemmed not from its foreign-law bonds, but from dollar-indexed domestic-law *tesobonos*, which might have been restructured unilaterally. The next round of bailouts responded to the crisis in Asia, with roots in cross-border interbank and corporate borrowing, not sovereign bonds. Russia, Brazil, and Turkey secured large IMF packages when the cost of rolling over their local currency—Treasury bills, which were governed by local law, became prohibitive (Roubini and Setser, 2004). Only in Argentina in 2001 did foreign bonds lie at the heart of the crisis, and even there, resolving the crisis would take much more than an orderly bond restructuring. For example, Argentina lost more reserves from deposit flight than bond repayment in 2000 and 2001 (Rosenberg et al., 2005; Setser and Gelpern, 2006).

Classic arguments over sovereignty loomed large over the debate about bailouts and bail-ins. For most U.S. officials, the idea that a treaty could trump financial contracts under New York law or that an international body could trump U.S. courts was simply unacceptable (Quarles, 2010). On the other hand, many market participants had an almost totemic attachment to the idea that "foreign law" and contracts properly drafted under the laws of a major financial jurisdiction would protect them from opportunistic sovereign debtors, even though only a handful of them had ever tried to vindicate their rights in court (Porzecanski, 2010).

Symbolism aside, the essential design change needed to bring the debate to an end was simple. The line in the contract that said that each bondholder had to consent to amend the bond's financial terms had to be struck. A new line specifying the supermajority needed to amend the terms would take its place.

Of course more could be done, and was done. Dislodging "sticky" boilerplate opened up the space to reconsider other terms in the contract, both those closely connected to the new majority amendment terms and others only tangentially relevant to them. An important but rarely mentioned set of changes in English-law sovereign bonds brought them closer to the standard emerging in New York. For example, the effective threshold required to bind all bondholders went up, as more contracts counted votes as a percentage of aggregate principal outstanding in place of the London market custom of counting bonds represented in a quorate meeting. In New York and London, the list of terms requiring supermajority consent for amendment grew longer to limit the scope for exit consents, which came to look coercive in the eyes of market participants after a string of bond exchanges. On the other hand, many issuers added terms that made it harder for individual creditors to accelerate and enforce their bonds (Weidemaier and Gulati, 2014; Bradley and Gulati, 2012). Concerns about conflicts of interest, such as sovereign debtors and entities controlled by them voting the bonds,[6] led to the introduction of disenfranchisement clauses, which deemed bonds owned or controlled by the debtor not to be "outstanding" for voting purposes.

Other terms were mooted but did not spread. For example, a drafting group made up of law practitioners who prepared model clauses under the auspices of the G10 shortly before Mexico switched to CACs in 2003 recommended that issuers consider using trustees to represent bondholders as a group and block lawsuits by individual holdouts (G10, 2002). Other suggestions included appointment of a negotiating representative in crisis, information disclosure, and moving toward a form of aggregated voting across multiple series.

ICMA issued recommendations for CACs in 2004 that were broadly in line with the G10 recommendations (ICMA, 2004). ICMA's model also advised sovereigns to precommit in their contracts to engage with creditor committees in the event of a restructuring. Some emerging- and mature-market issuers in the London market adopted such "engagement" clauses; almost none did in New York.

In sum, starting in 2003, virtually all new foreign-law bonds issued by emerging-market sovereigns in New York and London contained some form of supermajority amendment terms to facilitate the bond restructuring process. Changes in other parts of the contract responded to restructuring experience and concerns about new risks from CACs. Sovereigns experimented on the margins with designing CACs and safeguards. Nevertheless, long maturities and residual skepticism among a few issuers (notably China) meant that transition from unanimity to supermajority voting would take time. As of 2014, the IMF estimated that approximately one-fourth of all outstanding New York–law emerging-market bonds and approximately one-fifth of all foreign-law emerging-market bonds still required unanimous bondholder approval to amend financial terms (IMF, 2014a)

EVOLUTION TO REVOLUTION: 2003–2013

Despite a splash of publicity at the outset, the shift that began in 2003 had no material impact on the new issuance market. Foreign-law bonds with CACs traded like bonds without them.[7] Variations on CACs no longer made the news; they returned to the law firm conference rooms from whence they came.

Sovereign bond restructurings since 1997 suggested that CACs could be helpful, especially in small countries with a concentrated creditor base. Ukraine used CACs indirectly to amend three bonds and raise participation in its 2000 debt exchange. Uruguay used CACs to restructure a small Japanese-law bond but otherwise relied on the familiar combination of exchange offer and relatively mild exit consents in its 2003 debt operation (Buchheit and Pam, 2004). Moldova, Belize, Seychelles, St. Kitt's and Nevis, and Côte d'Ivoire all used CACs to amend their bonds (Duggar, 2013). But a couple of countries that had CACs in their English-law bonds, notably Pakistan back in 1999, chose not to use them at all. They were useful but hardly indispensable.

Aggregated CACs, first introduced by Uruguay in 2003, might have been a different matter. Uruguay's new bonds were issued as part of a comprehensive restructuring, replacing virtually the entire stock of its foreign debt. They allowed a full restructuring of all bonds with a vote of three-fourths of all the bonds taken together and two-thirds of each bond series. The lower per-series threshold would require holdouts to control more than one-third of a series to ensure that their bonds dropped out of a restructuring, compared to one-fourth in series-by-series CACs. Uruguay had initially mooted aggregation with a stock-wide vote only, but revived series-by-series voting as a parallel requirement when creditors complained. The new mechanism came to be known as "two-limb aggregation." It was the most significant precursor of the 2014 CACs; however, for a long time, it remained a minor footnote in emerging-market debt, introduced in a comprehensive restructuring and never tested either in the primary issuance market or as a tool in an actual restructuring.

Meanwhile, the risk of litigation in sovereign bond restructuring was no longer hypothetical. While still low, the incidence of lawsuits has increased dramatically since the 1980s (Schumacher, Trebesch, and Enderlein, 2012; IMF, 2013). To be sure, there is nothing wrong with lawsuits per se—contracts are supposed to be enforceable in court (Fisch and Gentile, 2005). The trouble with suing sovereign governments is that courts have limited power to fashion effective remedies against them, since most of their assets are inside their borders or immune from seizure. For a long time, this meant that lawsuits could irritate and embarrass governments into settling with holdouts but could do little to disrupt restructurings or harm bystanders.

Argentina's $86 billion default in 2001, followed by two rounds of restructuring in 2005 and 2010, changed all that.

The foreign bonds at the heart of Argentina's crisis were issued under New York law in the 1990s; they had no CACs. Even so, the government's first exchange offer in 2005 attracted just over three-fourths of its bond-holders, a lower participation rate than any other bond exchange that could not or chose not to use CACs. Commentators and market participants blamed the low take-up on Argentina's confrontational negotiating style and stingier than expected financial terms, not on any deficiency in the restructuring architecture (Porzecanski, 2005). A second exchange in 2010 brought participation to 93 percent. All the while, the government had been fighting thousands of lawsuits, mostly in Argentina. For the first decade after Argentina's crisis, creditors who sued under foreign law in Europe, Asia, and the United States had little to show for their efforts. However, in 2011, one group of holdout creditors appeared to hit paydirt: a U.S. federal court in New York enjoined payments on Argentina's restructured bonds issued in 2005 and 2010 until the holdouts were paid in full.

The remedy was based on another standard term in the bond contract, the pari passu clause, which had promised to treat creditors "in equal step" with one another and had served as rich fodder for arcane academic debates about the meaning of equality outside bankruptcy. The injunction upended the balance at the foundation of sovereign debt restructuring. Litigation turned from an irritant into a full-blown boycott, threatening bondholders, payment intermediaries, clearinghouses, and pretty much anyone else who could serve as a link between Argentina and the global financial markets (Weidemaier and Gelpern, 2013). At this writing, Argentina still refuses to pay the holdouts and has been unable to pay its restructured bonds or raise new debt since 2014. While the benefit of holdout strategy remains unrealized, the damage has metastasized. Those who argue that the injunctions are unimportant say that Argentina is "unique," in the sense that its restructuring tactics uniquely justify the nuclear remedy of enjoining a country from making any payments on its new, restructured bonds unless it paid its old, unrestructured bonds in full, including all past-due interest. Such reasoning is small comfort to other emerging-market issuers, who have started disclosing U.S. federal court rulings as a risk factor in new offering documents.

Between 2003 and 2013, investors in the emerging markets also shifted focus to bonds denominated in local currency and governed by local law. After a string of crises with roots in currency mismatches between the assets and liabilities of emerging-market economies, governments changed their approaches to saving and borrowing. They began accumulating large stocks of foreign currency reserves, reduced their need to issue foreign currency debt, and sought to borrow more at home. Borrowing in local currency would reduce mismatches and deepen local financial markets (Eichengreen and Hausmann, 1999; Inter-American Development Bank, 2006). At the same time, investors sought local-market exposure to profit from the expected appreciation of many emerging-market currencies. Some governments initially offered local currency debt governed by foreign law; however, investors were apparently unwilling to pay much for this feature, and it disappeared quickly (Tovar, 2005). Investors proved quite happy to accept local law for their local currency exposure. This was mildly puzzling, since investors who entered the local markets could hardly expect robust legal protections in a crisis. Russia restructured local-law debt in 1998; Argentina did it in 2002. Neither showed much concern for investor protections. Despite or because of this experience with domestic restructurings, no one broached the idea of introducing CACs in domestic-law emerging-market bonds.

When the Greek debt crisis began spreading across the euro area in 2010, sovereign debt restructuring architecture went from being a cyclical preoccupation in a $600 billion market for emerging-market debt to being the focus of attention in a €10 trillion market, overnight. One of the earliest responses to the debt crisis by European policy makers was to announce in the fall of 2010 that all new euro-area sovereign bonds should use CACs. The obligation to use clauses took effect in 2013, and the euro area's drafting committee choose to make two-limb aggregated CACs the standard in all euro-area government bonds, foreign and domestic (Gelpern and Gulati, 2013). Compared with market practice in both New York and London, euro-area CACs had lower voting thresholds for each of the two "limbs," notably two-thirds of the principal outstanding for all of the affected series, combined with 50 percent of the principal outstanding for each of the affected series, when voting by written resolution (Economic and Financial Committee Sub-committee on EU

Sovereign Debt Markets, 2012). Euro-area CACs also had more flexible disenfranchisement provisions, which would allow state-owned entities with "autonomy of decision" (including central banks and public pension funds) to vote government bonds.

Despite the energy poured into euro-area contract changes, the Greek debt restructuring of 2012 was carried out with little help from contracts. Like other euro-area issuers, Greece had issued most of its debt under its own law. When the time came to restructure, it enacted a law that allowed all of its local bonds to vote together in a single up-or-down vote and bind the dissenters. This statutory mechanism was cleverly marketed as a CAC, broadly reflecting the view that bondholder democracy was the basis of any legitimate sovereign restructuring. In all other respects, Greek "retro-CACs" had little in common with any other CACs: they were inserted in Greek contracts unilaterally by statute after the start of the crisis, not negotiated at the time of borrowing. They also included quorum and voting thresholds calculated to secure acceptance of the government's offer. The Greek model was functionally closer to class-wide voting in corporate bankruptcy than the prevailing bond-by-bond CACs.

The Greek restructuring also served as a graphic demonstration of the limits of series-by-series CACs. While foreign bonds were less than ten percent of the government's debt stock, they became a magnet for holdouts. Restructuring votes failed in nine out of seventeen foreign-law issues that Greece attempted to restructure. Slightly half of the total outstanding principal under foreign-law Greek bonds stayed outside the restructuring and, importantly, continued to be serviced on schedule. Most of the holdout bonds were governed by English law (Zettelmeyer, Trebesch, and Gulati 2013).

The success of statutory retro-CACs and failure of traditional series-by-series CACs in Greece together paved the way for CACs to come.

NEW MODEL NEEDED: 2013–2014

When the U.S. Treasury staff convened a group of issuers, investors, academics, and legal practitioners in the fall of 2013, the atmospherics were completely different from 2002. There were no G7 or G20 calls for a brand-new restructuring architecture. There was no talk of contract reform ending the era of big bailouts. Instead, the focus was on realistic and achievable changes to address two clearly defined problems: injunctions against Argentina and the failure of bond-by-bond CACs to secure broad participation in Greece's restructuring. In another contrast to 2002, the IMF joined the Treasury in promoting contract change. The IMF staff took SDRM off the table at the start, declaring that there was no support for revisiting treaties in its governing board. All energy went into contract design.

The wave of reforms at the turn of the century and the gradual adaptation and learning that went on since then were essential prerequisites to the 2014 changes. Nevertheless, the new low-key process led to a far bigger change in sovereign bond documentation than what had emerged from the public battles of the 1990s and early 2000s.

New clauses went beyond anything that had been in the market in either London or New York. They allowed the issuer to dispense with series-by-series voting altogether, either as a stand-alone restructuring tool or as part of two-limb aggregation. The attraction of polling each series had weakened in the eyes of investors over time. Greece's single vote of all bonds delivered an outcome that mapped to investor's expectations in a case where deep restructuring was obviously necessary—and it had become clearer that series-by-series voting could be gamed. Creditors who did not have blocking positions in individual series were at a disadvantage relative to creditors who did. An outcome that treated different bond issues fairly depended on how issuers decided to handle would-be holdouts with blocking positions. The presence of potential blocking positions made negotiation more difficult by creating varied and sometimes nontransparent creditor interests. As a result, the protection offered by series-by-series voting began to look illusory. For all but dedicated holdouts, it made good sense to embed investor protections elsewhere in the contract.

But aggregated voting across multiple issues on its own is also subject to the risk of abuse. On the one hand, all bonds—as unsecured creditors of the same rank—have an equal claim relative to the par value of the bond on the debtor's resources. On the other hand, bondholders come to the restructuring table with different financial interests and contractual claims, reflecting the terms of their bonds. Ensuring equitable treatment among them while protecting minorities entails further contract changes and creates challenging design problems.

In sum, 2013–2014 was the opposite of 2002–2003. Political symbolism was muted, while the design challenge was formidable. Successful reform required two things: broad agreement on the need for change and agreement on a template for the new design.

Consensus for change came from the obvious place: litigation against Argentina changed the game (Brooks and Lombardi, 2015; Stiglitz and Guzman, 2014). Until then, holding out had been perceived as a risky strategy unsuitable for all but the most determined activist investors. Participation rates were high (Das, Papaioannou, and Trebesch, 2012; Duggar, 2013), and the smattering of nonparticipants had been paid or bought out. The country and the creditors that went into the new instrument could move on. This did not happen in Argentina. Creditors who had agreed to accept new bonds with, in the case of the discount bonds, an initial face value of one-third of the old for the sake of moving on suddenly found their payments blocked. The old balance between risk and reward in sovereign restructuring was no more. While every distressed government might tell itself that it was not Argentina and did not merit the same punitive treatment, no country relished the prospect of making this argument in court. On the other hand, the appellate court rulings upholding the unprecedented injunctions against Argentina were explicit: sovereigns and their creditors were free to change their contracts if they wanted to avoid Argentina's fate.[8]

Thus, even though few governments and fewer creditors had much sympathy for Argentina, there was little doubt that the uncertainty about future payments reduced the market value of Argentina's restructured bonds. In the summer of 2014, Argentina's benchmark discount bonds traded at yields of 10 percent (a modest discount to their par value, as they had a relatively high coupon), while the bonds of Ecuador—a worse fundamental credit even back when oil was selling for more than $100 a barrel—traded at yields of around 7 percent. Clearing away the legal uncertainty would lead the bonds Argentina issued in its restructuring to trade up in value immediately. It was not difficult to show harm.

The impact of the injunction and its spillover effects compounded concerns based on growing evidence of strategic behavior by bondholders looking to build blocking positions in individual bonds (IMF, 2014b). Series-by-series voting set a transparent target for creditors who wanted to block amendment of their bonds (Makoff and Kahn, 2015). The Greek restructuring validated expectations that a bond that drops out of a restructuring would be paid in full, or at worst, restructured on advantageous terms. This dictated a simple investment strategy: buy a large stake at a deep discount in a bond maturing in the near term and threaten to sue unless paid in full. Investors looking to copy the success of the Greek English-law holdouts were rumored to have built up sizable positions in near-dated Cypriot bonds governed by English law. And even after setting aside Franklin Templeton's outsized position across a broad number of Ukraine's bonds, small groups of investors were reported to hold blocking positions in certain near-dated Ukrainian bonds (Ash, 2015).[9] The headaches from series-by-series voting seemed to snowball, even in England, where conventional wisdom held that the courts were unlikely to agree with the U.S. federal courts' interpretation of the pari passu clause.

Strategic free-riding using series-by-series CACs might be rational from the point of view of individual bondholders seeking to maximize returns; however, it does not necessarily serve the broader interest of all creditors. The funds paid to the holders of maturing Greek bonds governed by English law could have been used to make payments to all participants in the bond restructuring at no cost in aggregate to Greece. Moreover, the funds used to pay maturing Greek bonds governed by English bonds were borrowed from the euro area, adding to the burden of Greece's official debt.

On the other hand, the experience with a binding stock-wide vote in Greece was broadly positive. The statutory retro-CAC swept in all €178 billion (more than $230 billion at the exchange rate of the time) of Greece's domestic-law debt. This avoided any interruption of payments and avoided a technical default. CDS were triggered by the use of statute to bind creditors into a deal, not by formal default. This allowed Greek banks to continue to get financing from the European Central Bank (ECB), whose Greek debt holdings were excluded from restructuring altogether. The outcome—all holders getting the same package of new bonds—was analogous to the results of bankruptcy and made a certain amount of sense given Greece's deep distress and high debt levels. The resulting stock of Eurobonds has a reasonable payment structure and remained outside subsequent discussions of how to alter Greece's debt stock. After the bond restructuring, the official sector's unrestructured (in all but the most technical of senses[10]) debt was obviously the main problem.

Despite the audacious character of retro-CACs, the fact that they had been coordinated with creditors ahead of time and supported by the Institute of International Finance (IIF) made them surprisingly uncontroversial. Investors focused instead on the exclusion of ECB and national central bank bonds from the restructuring. While no doubt inequitable, this outcome reflected the leverage the ECB had over the negotiations as the only possible provider of liquidity support to the Greek banking system and thus the ultimate guarantor of Greece's continued participation in the euro.

In sum, Argentina and Greece had convinced market participants and issuers that series-by-series voting could create substantial uncertainty about a country's path through debt trouble and made it harder, not easier, for investors to price bonds as a country slipped toward default. This created an opportunity to consider changes that might result in a more predictable sovereign debt restructuring process. Discussion among practitioners, issuers, and investors indicated openness to go beyond fixing the interpretation of the pari passu clause. Judges revealed a dangerous misunderstanding of series-by-series voting in their repeated observations that the advent of CACs since 2003 had made holdouts a thing of the past. The realization that series-by-series CACS alone did not end holdouts supported a quick and deep consensus on the need for robust aggregation, which could support full participation in a restructuring and let the country and the market move on.

On the other hand, the experience of contract reform in 2003 reassured issuers and market participants that well-designed process improvements such as CACs would be accepted in the market and carry no price penalty (Gelpern and Gulati, 2015). We focus on the design of aggregation clauses next.

DESIGN

VOTING OPTIONS

The threshold choice for designing the new CACs is between single-limb and two-limb aggregation. Two-limb aggregation had two advantages. First, there were existing models acceptable to the market, notably the euro area's two-limb aggregated CACs with low approval thresholds, which would make it hard for potential holdouts to get blocking positions. Second, the presence of the second vote (really a second way of counting the same vote) provided a simple check against a discriminatory offer. As a result, there was no need to restrict the terms of the offer itself. Safeguards against discrimination were embedded in the voting procedure. By definition, any restructuring that got a supermajority of the all-series vote and simultaneously cleared a slightly lower threshold in the single-series vote would be deemed fair.

However, there were limits on what could be achieved through a two-limb structure, both from an issuer and a bondholder perspective. Existing two-limb structures did not foreclose the "blocking stake" strategy. This mattered less in the euro area, where all but Greece continued to issue under local law and arguably retained the tacit option of using retro-CACs if all else failed. In foreign-law bonds, raising the threshold for a blocking position in a series to 33⅓ or even 50 percent was not decisive. On the other hand, bondholders and lawyers voiced concerns—notably in London—about dropping the threshold on bond-by-bond voting below 50 percent, for fear of discrimination. For bondholders, virtually all plausible series-by-series voting scenarios led to game-theoretic options that could be exploited by an aggressive issuer or a determined holdout.

Allowing a single vote across series using an aggregation clause functionally similar to Greek retro-CACs offers an obvious alternative to two-limb aggregation. It eliminates the series-by-series tally and creates a choice between a restructuring binding on all polled creditors or a restructuring that fails for all. The result is a clean decision for all involved. This has advantages for the issuer but also for many creditors. The decision facing creditors in a bond-by-bond vote is more complex than is sometimes realized. In a market that trades, there is an advantage to holding the same instrument as others. The prospect of being "left behind" in a successful restructuring (that is, being left with an unrestructured bond) is unwelcome to a typical, nonactivist bondholder. A bondholder who wishes to reject the overall restructuring must do so by voting *no*. But by voting *no*, it is possible the bondholder will cause only his or her series to drop out of the restructuring and be left as an "unwilling holdout." A creditor consequently may prefer to remain in the old instrument if other creditors also vote against the deal and also may prefer to be bound into the deal if the deal does achieve critical mass rather than being an "involuntary" holdout stranded in an old and likely illiquid instrument. In series-by-series restructuring there is no way for a bondholder to vote against the restructuring as a whole but nonetheless agree to be bound if the overall restructuring ultimately achieves sufficient votes for approval.[11]

The argument for a single aggregated vote across all series is especially compelling if the issuer is seeking a comprehensive restructuring to restore its solvency after a payment default. Bondholders typically have the right to accelerate, which means that the maturity structure collapses after a default, as the full principal on all bonds is due. Legally, all the bonds become the same; each holder's stake is represented by the par value of its bond. In such circumstances, a vote of all bonds based on the par value of their bonds is easy to justify and execute. The main risk of such aggregation is that a supermajority of creditors could join the issuer and gang up to force discriminatory losses on a minority of their fellow investors. We return to this problem later in this section.

Aggregated voting is not needed for all cases. If the issuer's problem is caused by a single bond maturing in the near future, amending that bond's payment terms should be sufficient to address it. The single-bond scenario thus poses another design question: whether aggregation procedures should replace existing series-by-series voting or serve as one of several restructuring options option.

Limiting the number of voting procedures gives investors more certainty ex ante about the range of possible outcomes in distress. Such certainty comes at the cost of foreclosing flexibility to tailor restructurings to the issuer's circumstances. There are clearly cases when an individual bond might need to be restructured without a comprehensive restructuring, and there are also clearly cases where a comprehensive restructuring is needed. Informal consultations with investors revealed no interest on their part in foreclosing the targeted amendment option for one or several series. As a result, single-limb aggregation became an option, not a requirement.

The ICMA model ultimately included three voting procedures: series-by-series amendment, two-limb aggregation, and single-limb aggregation. The last option, which offers the strongest shield against opportunistic free riders, is only available under a set of restrictive conditions that serve as safeguards for investors. We discuss the safeguards later in this section.

Finally, investors should know ahead of time how their votes would be counted. When the sovereign borrower has a menu of options for restructuring, it commits to disclose its choice before taking the poll. Any votes cast are only valid for that procedure. If, for example, an aggregated vote fails to obtain the needed supermajority of all bondholders, but there are enough votes to amend the terms of several individual bond issues, the issuer cannot simply recount the votes to restructure the few issues. In theory, the issuer could conduct a second vote, but those voting to restructure their bonds individually would know that the aggregated vote had failed, and thus not all bondholders would be joining in the restructuring.

OFFER TERMS

As we noted earlier, there is no need to restrict the terms of the offer ahead of time in a series-by-series or two-limb aggregated vote. The series-by-series voting threshold substitutes process fairness for substantive oversight. An offer than is unfair to the holders of a one series would be rejected by the holders of that series. Single-limb aggregation removes this protection along with the risk that it could be used strategically by investors looking to secure a better payoff than other creditors.

Single-limb aggregation thus poses an additional challenge for designing substantive safeguards. The notion of voting by class of creditors comes from corporate bankruptcy. Bankruptcy classification and voting are supervised by the judge, who has the authority to protect minority creditors from an unfair or abusive offer. Relying entirely on contract, though, means that the court's role is more limited and is focused on assuring that the terms of the contract are followed. Only in extreme cases, where minorities are effectively expropriated, have courts intervened to invalidate the vote.[12]

The ICMA model resolves this problem by limiting single-limb aggregation to cases in which the sovereign makes a uniformly applicable offer to all its creditors. The meaning of "uniformly applicable" was actively debated in working groups and informal consultations. ICMA chose to define a uniformly applicable offer quite narrowly, as an identical offer made to the different bondholders per unit of par claim.

An "identical offer" can be an offer of identical terms (a prix fixe menu) or an offer to choose from the same à la carte menu. In either case, the same offer must be available to all creditors. There is not a prix fixe menu for one set of bonds and an à la carte menu for another. Menu terms can differ (for example, options of "par" and "discount" bonds, common in restructurings), so long as everyone gets to choose from the same menu. If one of the restructuring options on the menu is obviously better than the others, all the bondholders will choose that option. To avoid arguments over equivalence among menu items, the issuer was required to offer identical exit instruments to all.

The "same offer/same instruments" condition is more restrictive than other possible alternatives. For example, "same" is more limiting than "equal" or "equivalent." Conflicting arguments over equal treatment in the pari passu litigation involving Argentina demonstrate that equality can be in the eye of the beholder. Binding creditors who vote *no* into the instrument received by creditors who vote *yes* limits controversy over the equivalence of terms.[13]

In restructuring negotiations, the equivalence of different instruments with different cash flows depends on the interest rate used to discount the cash flows. Defining the requirement tightly limits the issuer's flexibility, but it also reduces the scope for disagreement over discount rates used to calculate the net present value (NPV) of cash flows to determine whether they are "equal." It is harder to claim discrimination if every investor is bound to receive an identical instrument.

The option to use single-limb aggregation to achieve identical NPV reduction (equivalent losses) across different instruments was ruled out in working group and market negotiations precisely to avoid endless arguments over appropriate discount rates. Foreclosing NPV-neutral exchanges using single-limb aggregation was a difficult choice. Some stakeholders, including issuers, sought to include NPV-neutral exchanges in single-limb aggregation to encourage participation among holders of near-dated bonds. However, putting NPV-neutral exchanges up to a single vote also raises hard issues. The simplicity of "same offer/same instruments" would be gone, replaced with arguments over what constituted equal NPV. What curve would be used? Who would decide the right discount rate for comparing future cash flows, especially in a world where the "exit" yield that equalizes different cash flows has to be decided ex ante but is only knowable ex post? Would different curves would be used for bonds denominated in different currencies? Using a dollar curve for euro-denominated bonds seems unfair, but using different curves would imply that bonds with equal par values and similar maturities denominated in different currencies would get different offers. Ultimately, the benefits of clarity and the desire to follow the prevailing sovereign restructuring and corporate bankruptcy practice, where voting is based on par value, won out.[14]

This outcome does not rule out NPV-neutral exchanges, which protect the maturity structure and generally favor investors at the front end of the curve. Such exchanges remain appropriate under some circumstances; they are typically used to avoid a payment default. However, because they would not meet the "same terms/same instrument" test, they would have to proceed using series-by-series or two-limb aggregated votes. Investors would know that if the NPV-neutral exchange failed, it could be followed by default and a comprehensive restructuring using single-limb aggregation. The single-limb backstop could help encourage participation in the exchange from holders of near-dated bonds. However, the restructuring could not bind near-dated series unless they voted for it.

Working group discussions also revealed that creditors needed assurance that they would not be penalized for voting *no*. The same offer means that investors who voted against the restructuring proposal/ exchange would receive the same instruments, on the same terms, as investors who voted for the deal. Rewards for voting, and for voting early, need not be prohibited so long as they were available to all bondholders pooled in a single-limb aggregated vote.[15]

Lesser complexities arise within the same terms/same instrument parameters, for example, with respect to interest. In sovereign restructuring practice, interest that has been accrued but not paid before the default is often paid out in the exchange, providing a bit of cash to some investors and equalizing the treatment of different bonds. (Otherwise a bond that received a coupon payment just prior to default is better positioned than bonds that were about to receive a coupon payment.) The treatment of past-due interest—interest that accrues after a default—is more contentious. Creditors, especially creditors with high coupon bonds, always want some recognition for past-due interest; however, restructuring practice varies in this area, while the amounts at stake can be substantial. The ICMA clauses define "same offer" as the same offer on par values, the same offer on all interest that had been accrued prior to the default, and the same offer on all past-due interest. Thus the offer to individual bonds could differ a bit, so long as the offer made on all par, all accrued but unpaid interest, and all past-due interest was the same. For example, offering no payment of past-due interest would meet the criteria of providing the same offer to all similarly situated creditors. The exact treatment of past-due interest would thus be a subject of negotiation or in the absence of formal negotiations, a critical decision that the issuer and its advisers would need to make before approaching their creditors with a comprehensive restructuring offer.

One interesting question is how to value zero-coupon bonds for the purposes of a restructuring. Zero-coupon bonds are one example of a broader category of bonds issued at discount to par. The answer is relatively simple: calculating the accrued principal value of the zero-coupon bond and using the adjusted par value as the basis for voting (see Box 6.1).

Other more complex features of a bond—embedded options—could be addressed in a similar way, when relevant. The logic of a uniformly applicable offer is that it makes the "same offer for the same features," so a bond with an embedded warrant might receive a different offer than a plain vanilla bond. But all warrants would need to get the same offer per equal warrant, and the par value of all plain vanilla bonds would need to receive the same offer. The flexibility in the pooling procedures in the ICMA model clauses also would help to manage a complex debt stock.

Yet the need for these features should not be overstated. Most emerging-market bonds governed by foreign law are fairly straightforward instruments—bullet maturity, coupon, fairly standard rather than bespoke legal provisions.

Box 6.1: Voting with zero-coupon bonds

ICMA model clauses indicate that a uniform offer must provide the same consideration or menu of consideration to each series of bonds and that the quantity of consideration is based on the par amount of the bondholder's claim. For most bonds, determining par claim is straightforward: the face principal amount of the bond. However, there are some bond structures in which the face principal amount is not the same as a par claim. The most common is a zero-coupon bond. A zero-coupon bond is issued for a price below par, and the bondholder earns the difference between this issue price and par over the life of the bond. A zero-coupon bond is a special case of the more general class of bonds with an "original issue discount." To recognize the full at-maturity principal claim of these bonds in a restructuring would be dilutive to other bond series, since it is equivalent to recognizing the future coupons of a par-issue coupon bond. Bankruptcy law makes special provision for bonds with original issue discount, generally disallowing any claim for "unamortized discount." Likewise, the euro area–model CACs include a method for calculating, for vote-counting purposes, an adjusted principal amount for zero-coupon bonds. This method consists of discounting the face amount of the bond from its scheduled maturity date to the record date of the restructuring, using as a discount rate the yield to maturity of the instrument at its issuance date. The ICMA clauses did not specify how the par claim for zeros should be calculated, but it is clear that there are good models for any emerging market that wants to issue a zero and include it in the aggregation pool.

VOTING THRESHOLDS

Choosing a voting threshold sufficient to assure fair treatment for all creditors is a distinct design challenge with single-limb aggregated CACs.

Market practice for series-by-series voting is not uniform. New York–law bonds typically allow holders of 75 percent of outstanding principal to bind all holders in a series. However, variation in effective thresholds within and across New York and London markets is enormous (Bradley and Gulati, 2012). Quorum requirements and alternative thresholds for postponed meetings make it hard to discern the effective threshold in any given case. English-law bonds typically allow amendment by a supermajority of two-thirds or three-fourths at a quorate meeting. If the quorum is 50 percent of the bond's par value, a supermajority of that quorum could amend the bonds. Postponed meetings may result in a quorum as low as 25 percent; however, in practice, low participation has not been a problem in sovereign restructurings.

There is a case that the voting threshold in single-limb aggregated voting should be high. The vote is binding on all and thus should have broad support from investors. For this reason, the ICMA clauses adopt the highest threshold consistent with existing market practice, a minimum requirement of 75 percent of the eligible stock.

Only affirmative votes in favor of the restructuring count toward the total; abstention is an effective "no" vote. This approach to tallying the votes rests on the assumption that there is little risk of passive creditors inadvertently blocking a restructuring they would want to support. The alternative to a comprehensive restructuring of all bonds is usually a comprehensive default and a prolonged period of nonpayment. Under the circumstances, creditors should be motivated to participate.

DISENFRANCHISEMENT

Institutions controlled by the issuer often can hold bonds that are a part of the restructuring. State-owned banks and state-owned pension funds, for example, may own their own countries international-law bonds. A country may also buy back its bonds at a discount and retain their votes. Emerging-market series-by-series and two-limb aggregated CACs and the G10 model clauses issued in 2002 all included provisions disenfranchising bonds held by institutions controlled by the sovereign. Control was normally defined as majority ownership or control of the board of directors. Bonds held by a privately owned bank regulated by the issuer would not lose their vote, but bonds owned by a state-owned bank would. These provisions were carried over into the 2014 ICMA model clauses.

As we noted earlier, euro-area aggregated CACs contain disenfranchisement provisions that are more permissive for the issuer. They allow voting by entities that might be owned or controlled by the sovereign but have "autonomy of decision." National central banks, state-owned banks, and public pension funds are the most likely bondholders in this category. This formulation of disenfranchisement is unique to the euro area. Working group members considered it inappropriate to extend this treatment to foreign-law debt of all mature and emerging-market issuers.

POOLING OR SUBAGGREGATION

Two-limb aggregation CACs allow the debtor to pool series for purposes of taking an aggregated vote. This feature gives issuers the capacity to classify bondholders for voting purposes. Aggregation procedures then apply within a pool rather than across the entire debt stock.

The subaggregation option can be important in a complex debt restructuring involving a variety of bond issues with different features and economic interests. Similar bonds—for example, all bonds denominated in the same currency or all zero-coupon bonds—could be placed in the same voting pool. Particularly complex bonds could also be placed in their own pool and restructured through a bond-by-bond vote.

With two-limb aggregation, pooling presents little risk of abuse. For example, in the euro CACs, each subaggregated series still gets to vote its own interests and must muster at least 50 percent of the outstanding debt to approve a proposal. On the other hand, single-limb aggregation does not have the safeguard of the series vote. The remaining safeguards are in the 75 percent approval threshold, and same offer/same instrument criterion. In theory, it is plausible for the debtor and its advisers to gerrymander a complex series of pools to discriminate among them. The "same offer/same instrument" constraint would apply within each pool but not across pools.

One safeguard considered but rejected was a requirement that all bonds in the same pool must have contiguous maturities. This would limit obvious attempts to gerrymander the voting pool. But it also generates additional complexity—notably when it comes to determining the maturity of instruments with embedded put and call options. There are also concerns about requiring the pooling of radically dissimilar bonds purely on contiguity grounds.

The ICMA model clauses did not in the end include any limitations on subaggregation and pooling. In part this is because the issuer normally would not want to splinter the voting pools too much, as a large number of pools reduces the basic benefit of aggregation. An issuer's interest in a successful restructuring also creates incentives to use pooling and subaggregation in a way that its investors recognized made sense, so as to maximize the odds of a successful vote.

The most potent protection against gerrymandering lies in the sovereign's need to get all bondholders to accept the deal. If a series is placed in a pool that is perceived by other bondholders as getting preferential treatment, others who consider themselves similarly situated would vote against the deal. Large discrepancies in treatment across different pools would only be accepted if the holders of the bonds in each pool believed their individual offer was fair and all similarly situated creditors would receive similar treatment.

INFORMATION DISCLOSURE

Disclosure of restructuring procedures and terms offered to all creditors (not just bondholders) is essential to protect the legitimacy of a vote of all creditors. This is especially important when multiple voting procedures could be used across diverse instruments. In addition, a fair vote requires equal access to information relevant to the restructuring decision. Investors should know not only the offer than they are receiving but also how the restructuring of their claims fits into the issuers' broader financial reorganization. ICMA's model consequently provides a covenant to assure full disclosure of the issuer's restructuring plans and financial condition.

The model information covenant requires the following conditions:

1. Full disclosure of any offers being made to other bonds and traded securities. Not all bonds have aggregation clauses. Those participating in the aggregated vote should know the terms being offered to bonds (and similar instruments) that are contractually not part of the aggregated vote. Similarly, if the issuer makes use of the pooling option, the bondholders know which bond series is in which pool and what package of new instruments and other considerations is being offered to holders of the instruments in each pool.

2. Disclosure of the issuer's intentions vis à vis other creditors than vis à vis other bondholders. This is a lower standard than the standard for

bonds, as it is the disclosure of the issuer's intended treatment of other groups of creditors rather than disclosure of the details of an actual offer. The standard for disclosure, though, should be higher for similarly situated creditors than for different categories of credits. Local-law instruments differ from foreign-law instruments. Official credits (Paris Club credits) typically differ from commercial bank loans and marketable debt securities. Official credits historically have been restructured through their own process, with terms negotiated between the issuer and its Paris Club creditors. The issuer can disclose its goals for the negotiations with bilateral creditors, but the Paris Club traditionally operates through consensus not an exchange of offers. Bondholders who want certainty on the terms of the Paris Club restructuring need to defer the restructuring of their claims until the conclusion of the Paris Club process.

3. The issuer is required to disclose its IMF program documentation and any new financing it is receiving, including any new official financing.

This falls short of a fully disclosed plan of adjustment in a bankruptcy proceeding, which makes clear the treatment of all relevant stakeholders and creditors. But the price of completeness is often delay. Building on existing practice, it seemed reasonable to require the issuer to disclose its full plan of adjustment for all bonded debt and to allow a vote on the bonded restructuring to proceed even in the absence of full clarity on the treatment of all other groups of creditors

The required disclosure builds on but goes beyond prior models, including Uruguay's 2003 clause and the G10/ICMA (G10, 2002; ICMA 2004) documentation standard. The net effect is a substantial increase in the disclosure required from an issuer at the time of its restructuring.

CALCULATION AGENT

Without a bankruptcy court to certify claims, a mechanism needs to be set up by contract to compute the par value of complex instruments and to fix the exchange rate used for calculating the value of bonds denominated in different currencies. If a country issues zero-coupon bonds, or other bonds sold at a significant discount (original issue discount), the par value of the bond for purposes of the vote may be defined to be something other than its face value. For example, as discussed in Box 6.1, the euro CACs had an elegant definition of the current par value of a zero-coupon bond—its accreted value, based on the interest rate on issuance.

SCOPE OF AGGREGATION ACROSS JURISDICTIONS

The ICMA aggregation clauses are limited to bonds governed by foreign law. Bonds governed by English law, New York law, Swiss law, and Japanese law could be combined in a single vote, provided all the instruments had the needed contractual provisions. Bonds governed by the issuers' own law would not be included in the aggregation pool.

This differs from the euro CACs, which were included in domestic- and foreign-law instruments. Both domestic- and foreign-law bonds can be part of the same aggregation pool under the euro-area model.

There are several reasons for this difference.

Documentation used in emerging-market (and for that matter G10) domestic-law bonds reflects each country's own history and legal tradition. Harmonizing the language used in local-law issuance would be a much deeper change than harmonizing the documentation used in New York–law and English-law bond issues, which generally follows the same basic legal templates.

Investors in foreign-law bonds also do not want to be aggregated in a single pool with the holders of domestic debt. While foreign participation in local markets has grown, in most countries, local investors—including regulated banks, insurance companies, and pension funds—hold the bulk of local market debt. The incentives facing these investors typically differ from the incentives of many investors in foreign-law bonds. For countries with more domestic-law than foreign-law debt, one-limb aggregation across both domestic- and foreign-law bonds raises the prospect that international investors could be bound into a proposal that draws support almost exclusively from local residents. Limiting the voting pool to bonds governed by a foreign law provided a simple and pragmatic solution to these concerns.

Finally, and most, importantly, countries already have scope for addressing collective action problems in their local market: local-law bonds. Greece illustrated that voting mechanisms can be introduced via statute as necessary.

ENGAGEMENT

ICMA's 2004 model CACs included recommended provisions for engagement with creditor committees in the event of a restructuring (ICMA, 2004). ICMA kept the recommendations in 2014, although they were not discussed in the working group and underwent minimal revision. This did not reflect hostility to creditor committees among any of the participants but rather two other factors. First, unlike aggregated CACs and pari passu terms, committees and engagement are already permitted in all existing sovereign bond contracts. Bondholders are free to call meetings and deputize representatives, typically by a vote of 25 percent of outstanding principal. Precommitting to particular engagement procedures did not appear to have the urgency of other reforms. Second, engagement terms recommended in 2004 failed to catch on in New York and were far from universal in London. This observation suggests that more research and design work is in order before extending official endorsement to any particular form of engagement.

There is every reason to expect that the widespread introduction of aggregation clauses will lead to more engagement with creditors during the restructuring process. An issuer has a much stronger incentive to negotiate with a committee of creditors than in the past. One difficulty with committees—after the end of the bank advisory committees of the 1990s—was that agreement with the committee did not necessarily bring in creditors who were outside. With aggregation, issuers can get 100 percent participation with the support of 75 percent of their creditors, making agreement with 75 percent more valuable than in the past. And in a complex restructuring with multiple pools of creditors and different offers to different pools, one way of avoiding disagreement on the composition of creditor pools is through close engagement with relevant creditor groups.

CONCLUSIONS

The issuance and adoption of ICMA-model aggregated CACs since 2014 testifies to the importance of design and process in reforming sovereign debt restructuring. In a stark contrast to the contract reforms of the late 1990s and early 2000s, this generation of reforms has won support from issuers, civil society groups, the sovereign debt bar, market participants, and international organizations. Agreement among diverse stakeholders on the design of a new model for the documentation for sovereign bonds issued by emerging markets and governed by foreign law paved the way for a relatively rapid and uncontroversial—though still incomplete—shift in documentation standards in both New York and England.

This reflects process learning and the buy-in achieved through the Treasury-initiated consultation process. It also reflects the maturity of the market. The debate was not driven by symbolism or fear that preparing for default and restructuring would encourage default and restructuring. Rather, making inevitable restructurings less chaotic and more predictable is now recognized to be a part of a healthy market. Advance preparation allows a faster path out of default and makes it easier for investors to price the likely outcome of the restructuring.

A low-key debate should not mask the scale of the change. Events since 2012 have demonstrated the value of well-designed contract provisions to guide restructuring. The new provisions went significantly beyond any existing contractual model and represent a far bigger substantive change in sovereign bond documentation than what had emerged from the public battles of the 1990s and early 2000s. While it will take some time for the existing stock of bonds with old CACs—or in some cases, no CACs—to turn over, the new aggregation provisions provide the contractual basis for replicating one key feature of bankruptcy—aggregated voting creditor classes.

At the same time, contract reform cannot fully replicate a full-blown bankruptcy regime based in statute or treaty. Clauses allowing for aggregated voting will help solve problems of coordination among different bond series but do not attempt to provide a framework for coordination across the full set of claims—local-law bonds, traditional Paris Club creditors, short-term bank lenders backed by a sovereign guarantee—on a distressed sovereign borrower.

More ambitious reform will require more substance and process learning, and in all likelihood, more trauma.

NOTES

1. The opinions in this essay are ours alone. The views expressed in the article do not reflect nor are they intended to represent the views of the Department of the Treasury or the government of the United States. The authors would like to thank Mark Sobel, Him Das, Francine Barber, and Domenico Lombardi for comments.

Kazakhstan was not shy. It placed a thirty-year bond at a yield of around 5 percent. Bids totaled $11 billion for $2.5 billion (face) of bonds on offer.

2. The financial crisis and regulatory reform experience since 2008 may have put the stakes in perspective for all involved.

3. The authors all participated in the informal working group on contract reform hosted by the U.S. Treasury Department.

4. English-law contracts evolved in reaction to innovations in New York, mostly with respect to voting mechanics and safeguards against manipulation (Gelpern and Gulati, 2009).

5. With exit consents, debtors asked bondholders participating in a debt exchange to vote in favor of amending nonfinancial but nevertheless important terms in the old bonds on their way out of them. If a majority voted to amend, nonparticipating bonds became illiquid and in some cases unenforceable (Buchheit and Gulati, 2002). While done within the "four corners" of the contract—and arguably central to the success of exchanges—exit consents worried creditors, who saw considerable potential for abuse. The restructuring process was riding too hard on using amendment provisions for a purpose other than they had been intended. To some, this suggested that creditors should take initiative in creating a fairer process for amending financial terms, but this was not the consensus view of creditors at the time.

6. CIBC Band & Trust Co. v. Banco Cent. do Brasil (886 F.Supp. 1105 [1995]).

7. Scores of academic pricing studies were so inconsistent that they looked incoherent. Some argued that CACs came with a price penalty. Others that they carried a benefit—for the same countries. Still others suggested no impact at all, though their explanations varied. All the studies pointing in different directions agreed on one thing: to the extent CACs had an impact on bond prices, it was very small. See Becker, Thaicharoen, and Richards, 2003; Eichengreen and Mody, 2004; Bradley and Gulati, 2012. A simple plot of a yield curve never suggested that CACs carried a price penalty. For example, bonds with the new aggregation clauses trade in line with bonds that lack the new aggregation clauses of the same maturity. However, there is evidence that some legal provisions start to have an impact on market pricing as bonds slide closer to default.

8. See NML Capital, Ltd. v. Republic of Argentina, 699 F.3d 246 (2d Cir. 2012); and NML Capital, Ltd. v. Republic of Argentina, 727 F.3d 230 (2d Cir. 2013).

9. The U.S. mutual fund Franklin Templeton had been a large buyer of Ukraine's debt and as a result of its large position likely held over a third of many other bond issues. However, there is no indication that it bought the bonds with the intent of gaining leverage over the restructuring.

10. Member states did agree to change the payments profile of the debt Greece owed to the European Financial Stability Fund in 2012.

11. The nonactivist bondholder faces two questions in a complex series-by-series restructuring but has only one vote with which to respond: First, is the overall restructuring acceptable? Second, is the restructuring unfair to a particular series? A single aggregated vote with constraints on the offer to assure fairness reduces the question posed to the bondholder to "Is the overall restructuring acceptable?"

12. Assenagon Asset Management SA v. Irish Bank Resolution Corporation Ltd [2012] EWHC 2090 (Ch); see also Jane Croft, "Bondholders may challenge 'unfair' restructuring measures," April 28, 2013. Accessed April 29.www.ft.com/cms/s/0/a0866b3e-ae74-11e2-8316-00144feabdc0.html#axzz3izZIxTv3.

13. Mexico's first New York–law bond required the offer to be the same to all bonds but did not further clarify that the offer needed to be "on the same terms," though the context supported the "same terms" interpretation. Mexico has since clarified the clause to conform to ICMA's New York–law template. A few outstanding bond issues that copied Mexico still miss the four words, though subsequent issues are following the ICMA template. From Working Group, IMF Board, and ICMA discussions, it is clear that this was not supposed to be a departure.

14. IMF, 2014a.

15. Azevedo and Alvarez v Imcopa Importacao, Exportaacao e Industria de Oleos Ltda and other companies, All ER (D) 33 (Aug 2012); see also Joseph Cotterill, "The consent of the (bondholder) governed." April 22, 2013. Accessed April 23. http://ftalphaville.ft.com/2013/04/22/1469152/the-consent-of-the-bondholder-governed.

REFERENCES

Ahmed, Faisal Z., Laura Alfaro, and Noel Maurer. 2010. "Lawsuits and Empire: On the Enforcement of Sovereign Debt in Latin America." *Law and Contemporary Problems* 73 (no. 4): 39–46.

Ash, Tim. 2014. Standard Bank. Weekly market commentary.

Becker, Torbjorn, Yunyong Thaicharoen, and Anthony Richards. 2003. "Bond Restructuring and Moral Hazard: Are Collective Action Clauses Costly?" *Journal of International Economics* 61 (no. 1): 127–161.

Bi, Ran, Marcos Chamon, and Jeromin Zettelmeyer. 2011. "The Problem That Wasn't: Coordination Failures in Sovereign Debt Restructurings." IMF Working Paper 11/265, Washington, D.C.

Bradley, Michael, and Mitu Gulati. 2012. "Collective Action Clauses for the Euro-zone: An Empirical Analysis." Working Paper. http://papers.ssrn.com/sol3/papers.cfm?abstract_id=1948534 (accessed January 13, 2013).

Brooks, Skylar, and Domenico Lombardi. 2015. "Sovereign Debt Restructuring: Issues Paper." CIGI Papers No. 64, Waterloo, Ont.

Brooks, Skylar, Martin Guzman, Domenico Lombardi, and Joseph E. Stiglitz. January 2015. "Identifying and Resolving Inter-creditor and Debtor-Creditor Equity Issues in Sovereign Debt Restructuring." CIGI Policy Brief No. 53, Waterloo, Ont. www.cigionline.org/publications/identifying-andresolving-inter-creditor-and-debtor-creditor-equityissues-sovereign-de.

Buchheit, Lee C. 1995. "How to Negotiate Eurocurrency Loan Agreements." Euromoney, London.

——. 1998. "Majority Action Clauses May Help Resolve Debt Crises." *International Financial Law Review* 17.

Buchheit, Lee C., and Mitu Gulati. 2002. "Sovereign Bonds and the Collective Will." *Emory Law Journal* 51 (no. 4): 1317–1363.

Buchheit, Lee C., and Jeremiah S. Pam. 2004. "The Pari Passu Clause in Soveriegn Debt Instruments." *Emory Law Journal* 53 (special edition): 870–922.

Buchheit, Lee C., Mitu Gulati, and Ignacio Tirado. 2013. "The Problem of Holdout Creditors in Eurozone Sovereign Debt Restructuring." Duke Law Working Paper. *IMF Staff Papers* 35: 644.

Chamon, Marcus, Julian Schumacher, and Christoph Trebesch. 2015. "Foreign Law Bonds: Can They Reduce Sovereign Borrowing Costs?" University of Munich (Economics) Working Paper.

Claessens, Stijn, Daniella Klingbiel, and Sergio L. Schmuckler. 2007. "Government Bonds in Domestic and Foreign Currency." *Review of International Economics* 15 (no. 2): 370–403.

Clare, Andrew, and Nicolas Schmidlin. 2014. "The Impact of Foreign Governing Law on European Government Bond Yields." City University London (Cass) Working Paper.

Clifford Chance. 2014. "New ICMA Collective Action and Pari Passu Clauses." www .cliffordchance.com/briefings/2014/10/new_icma_sovereigncollectiveactionandpar .html.

Choi, Stephen, and Mitu Gulati. 2006. "Contract as Statute." *Michigan Law Review* 104: 1129–1173.

Choi, Stephen, Mitu Gulati, and Eric A. Posner. 2011. "Pricing Terms in Sovereign Debt Contracts." *Capital Markets Law Journal* 6 (no. 2): 163–187.

Cline, William. 1995. *International Debt Reexamined*. Peterson Institute: Washington, D.C.

Das, Udaibir S., Michael G. Papaioannou, and Christopher Trebesch. August 2012. "Sovereign Debt Restructurings 1950–2010: Literature Survey, Data, and Stylized Facts." IMF Working Paper/12/203, Washington, D.C.

Diaz de Leon Carrillo, Alejandro. 2016. "Mexico's Adoption of New Standards in International Sovereign Debt Contracts—CACs, Pari Passu and a Trust Indenture." *Capital Markets Law Journal* (forthcoming).

Du, Wenxin, and Jesse Schreger. 2015. "Local Currency Sovereign Risk." Harvard University (Economics) Working Paper.

Duffie, Darrell, Lasse Hejje Pedersen, and Kenneth J. Singleton. 2003. "Modelling Sovereign Yield Spreads: A Case Study of Russian Debt." *Journal of Finance* 58 (no. 1): 119–159.

Duggar, Elana. 2013. "Argentina Is Unique—Implications for Sovereign Debt Restructurings." A Cato Institute Forum, held December 11.

Economic and Financial Committee of the European Union. 2013. "Common Understanding on Implementing the EU Commitment Regarding the Use of Collective Action Clauses (CACs)." http://europa.eu/efc/sub_committee/pdf/common _understanding_cacs_en.pdf (accessed January 15, 2013).

Economic and Financial Committee of the European Union, Sub-committee on Sovereign Debt Markets. 2014. "Implementation of the EU Commitment on Collective Action Clauses in Documentation of International Debt Issuance, Brussels, November 12" (ECFIN/CEFCPE(2004)REP/50483 final). http://europa.eu/efc /sub_committee/pdf/cacs_en.pdf.

———. 2012. "Euro Area Model CAC 2012." http://europa.eu/efc/sub_committee/cac /cac_2012/index_en.htm (accessed April 23, 2013).

Economist, The. 2013, April 20. "An Illusory Haven: What Lessons Should Investors Learn from the Argentine and Greek Restructurings?" www.economist.com/news /finance-andeconomics/21576391-what-lessons-should-investorslearn-argentine -and-greek-restructurings.

Eichengreen, Barry. 2003. "Restructuring Sovereign Debt." *Journal of Economic Perspectives* 17 (no. 4): 75–98.

Eichengreen, Barry, and Ricardo Hausmann. 1999. "Exchange Rates and Financial Fragility." Proceedings–Economic Policy Symposium–Jackson Hole, Federal Reserve Bank of Kansas City, 329–368.

Eichengreen, Barry, and Ashoka Mody. 2004. "Do Collective Action Clauses Raise Borrowing Costs?" *Economic Journal* 114 (no. 495): 247–264.

Eichengreen, Barry, and Richard Portes. 1995. "Crisis? What Crisis? Orderly Workouts for Sovereign Debtors."

Fisch, Jill E. and Gentile, Caroline M. 2004. "Vultures or Vanguards? The Role of Litigation in Sovereign Debt Restructuring." *Emory Law Journal* (53): 1047.

Franco-German Declaration. 2010. http://ebookbrowse.com/franco-german-declaration -deauville-18-10-2010-pdf-d221247911 (accessed January 15, 2013).

Gadanecz, Blaise, Ken Miyajima, and Chang Shu. 2014. "Exchange Rate Risk and Local Currency Sovereign Bond Yields in Emerging Markets." BIS Working Paper 474.

Gelpern, Anna. 2014. "A Sensible Step to Mitigate Sovereign Bond Dysfunction." http://blogs.piie.com/realtime/?p=4485#.VBlnUiofqW8.email.

———. 2016. "Domestic Debt and Alien Comforts." *Capital Markets Law Journal* (forthcoming).

Gelpern, Anna, and Mitu Gulati. 2006. "Public Symbol in Private Contract: A Case Study." *Washington University Law Quarterly* 84: 1627–1715.

———. 2009. "Innovation After the Revolution: Foreign Sovereign Bond Contracts Since 2003." *Capital Markets Law Journal* 4 (no. 1): 85–103.

———. 2013. "The Wonder-Clause." 2013. *Journal of Comparative Law* 41: 367–385. Also *Georgetown Law Faculty Publications and Other Works*. Paper 1281. http:// scholarship.law.georgetown.edu/facpub/1281.

———. 2015. "Contract Terms and Sovereign Debt Pricing: The View from a Government Debt Manager's Perspective." Duke Law School Working Paper.

Gros, Daniel, and Thomas Mayer. 2010. "How to Deal with Sovereign Default in Europe: Create the European Monetary Fund Now!" Center for European Policy Studies 202. www.ceps.eu/ceps/download/2912 (accessed January 13, 2013).

G10. 1997. "The Resolution of Sovereign Liquidity Crises." Bank of International Settlements. August.

———. 2002. *Report of the G-10 Working Group on Contractual Clauses*. September. www.bis.org/publ/gten08.pdf (accessed January 13, 2013).

G22. 1998. Report of the Working Group on International Financial Crises. October. http://www.imf.org/external/np/g22/ifcrep.pdf.

Gugiatti, Mark, and Anthony Richards. 2003. "The Use of Collective Action Clauses in New York Law Bonds of Sovereign Borrowers." Working Paper Series. http:// papers.ssrn.com/sol3/papers.cfm?abstract_id=443840 (accessed January 15, 2013).

Gulati, Mitu, and Frank Smets. 2013. "The Evolution of Eurozone Sovereign Debt Contracts." Unpublished Manuscript.

Häseler, Sönke. 2009. "Collective Action Clauses in International Sovereign Bond Contracts—Whence the Opposition?" *Journal of Economic Surveys* 23 (no. 5): 882–923.

Inter-American Development Bank. 2006. *Living with Debt: How to Limit the Risks of Sovereign Finance, 2007 Report*. Washington, D.C.

International Capital Market Association. 2004. "Standard Collective Action Clauses (CACs) for the Terms and Conditions of Sovereign Notes." October 28.

International Capital Market Association. 2011. Response to Consultation Dated 23 July 2011 on Collective Action Clauses to be Included in Euro Area Sovereign Securities. www.icmagroup.org/assets/documents/Maket-Practice/Regulatory-Policy

/Sovereign-Debt-Information/ICMA%20CAC%20response%202%20September%202011.pdf (accessed January 10, 2013).

———. June 2014a. ICMA Sovereign Bond Consultation Paper Supplement.

———. August 2014b. Standard Aggregated Collective Action Clauses ("CACS") for the Terms and Conditions of Sovereign Notes.

International Monetary Fund. 2003a. "Proposed Features of a Sovereign Debt Restructuring Mechanism." Washington, D.C. www.imf.org/external/np/pdr/sdrm /2003/021203.pdf (accessed January 13, 2013).

———. 2003b. "The Restructuring of Sovereign Debt—Assessing the Benefits, Risks, and Feasibility of Aggregating Claims." Washington, D.C. www.imf.org/external /np/pdr/sdrm/2003/090303.pdf.

———. April 2013. "Sovereign Debt Restructuring—Recent Developments and Implications for the Fund's Legal and Policy Framework." Washington, D.C. www.imf .org/external/ np/pp/eng/2013/042613.pdf.

———. September 2014a. *Strengthening the Contractual Framework to Address Collective Action Problems in Sovereign Debt Restructuring. Staff Report.* Washington, D.C.

———. June 2014b. *The Fund's Lending Framework and Sovereign Debt—Preliminary Considerations. IMF Staff Report.* Washington, D.C.

JP Morgan. 2014. 6 November. Conference call. Transcript available on request.

Krueger, Anne. April 2002. "A New Approach to Sovereign Debt Restructuring." International Monetary Fund, Washington, D.C.

Makoff, Gregory, and Robert Kahn. February 2015. "Sovereign Bond Contract Reform: Implementing the New ICMA Pari Passu and Collective Action Clauses." CIGI Papers No. 56, Waterloo, Ont. www.cigionline.org/publications/sovereign -bond-contract-reform-implementing-newicma-pari-passu-and-collective -action-c.

Miyajima, Ken, Madhusudan Mohanty, and Tracy Chan. 2012. "Emerging Market Local Currency Bonds." BIS Working Paper 391.

Mody, Ashoka. 2004. "What Is an Emerging Market?" IMF Working Paper 177, Washington, D.C.

Mauro, Paolo, Nathan Sussman, and Yishay Yafeh. 2006. "Bloodshed or Reforms? The Determinants of Sovereign Bond Spreads in 1870–1913 and Today." CEPR Discussion Paper 5528.

Nordwig, Jens. 2015. "Legal Risk Premia During the Euro Crisis: The Role of Credit and Redenomination Risk." University of Southern Denmark Working Paper.

Ocampo, José Antonio. 2014a. "Guest Post: Implications of the US Supreme Court Ruling on Argentina." *Beyond BRICS* (blog), *Financial Times*, June 23. http://blogs.ft.com/beyond-brics/2014/06/23/guestpost-implications-of-the-us -supreme-court-ruling-onargentina.

Panizza, Ugo, et al. 2009. "The Economics and Law of Sovereign Debt and Default." *Journal of Economic Literature* 47: 1.

Porzecanski, Arturo. 2006. "Dealing with Sovereign Debt: Trends and Implications." In: Chris Jochnick and Fraser A. Preston (eds.), *Sovereign Debt at the Crossroads: Challenges and Proposals for Resolving the Third World Debt Crisis.* Oxford University Press: Oxford.

Porzecanski, Arturo. 2010. "When Bad Things Happen to Good Sovereign Debt Contracts: The Case of Ecuador." *Law and Contemporary Problems*, Fall.

Quarles, Randal. 2010. "Herding Cats: Collective-Action Clauses in Sovereign Debt— The Genesis of the Project to Change Market Practice in 2001 Through 2003." *Law and Contemporary Problems* 73 (no. 4): 29–38.

Rosenberg, Christoph, Brad Setser, Ionnis Halikas, Brett House, Jens Nystedt, and Christian Keller. 2005. "Debt-Related Vulnerabilities and Financial Crises: An Application of the Balance Sheet Approach to Emerging Economies." IMF Occasional Paper 240, Washington, D.C.

Roubini, Noriel, and Brad Setser. 2004. *Bailouts or Bail-Ins? Responding to Financial Crises in Emerging Economies*. Washington, D.C.: Institute for International Economics.

Schadler, Susan. August 2012. "Sovereign Debtors in Distress: Are Our Institutions Up to the Challenge?" CIGI Papers No. 6, Waterloo, Ont. www.cigionline.org /publications/sovereigndebtors-distress-are-our-institutions-up-challenge.

Schumacher, Julian, Christoph Trebesch, and Henrik Enderlein. 2012. Sovereign Defaults in Court: The Rise of Creditor Litigation 1976–2010 (December 16, 2012). http:// papers.ssrn.com/ sol3/papers.cfm?abstract_id=2189997. Unpublished manuscript.

Setser, Brad. 2010. "The Political Economy of SDRM." In *Overcoming Developing Country Debt Crises*, ed. Barry Herman, José Antonio Ocampo, and Shari Spiegel, et al. New York: Oxford University Press.

Setser, Brad, and Anna Gelpern. 2006. "Pathways Through Financial Crisis: Argentina." *Global Governance: A Review of Multilateralism and International Organizations* 12, no. 4 (October): 465–487.

Stiglitz, Joseph, and Martin Guzman. 2014. "Argentina's Griesafault." *Project Syndicate*, August 7. www.projectsyndicate.org/commentary/joseph-e—stiglitz-andmartin -guzman-argue-that-the-country-s-default-willultimately-harm-america.

Sturzenegger, Federico, and Jeromin Zettelmeyer. 2007. *Debt Defaults and Lessons from a Decade of Crises*. Cambridge, Mass.: MIT Press.

Taylor, John B. 2002. "Sovereign Debt Restructuring: A U.S. Perspective." In: *Remarks at the Conference Sovereign Debt Workouts: Hopes and Hazards?* Washington, D.C.: Institute for International Economics.

——. 2007. *Global Financial Warriors: The Untold Story of International Finance in the Post–9/11 World*. New York: Norton.

Tirado, Ignacio. 2012, December 8. "Sovereign Insolvency in the Euro Zone Public and Private Law Remedies." http://ssrn.com/abstract=2186730.

Tovar, Camilo E. 2005. "International Government Debt Denominated in Local Currency: Recent Developments in Latin America." *BIS Quarterly Review* (December). http://ssrn.com/abstract=1645868.

United Nations. 2015. "Basic Principles on Sovereign Debt Restructuring Processes"(A/69/L.84). September 11. http://unctad.org/en/pages/newsdetails.aspx ?OriginalVersionID=1074.

Weidemaier, Mark C., and Anna Gelpern. 2013. "Injunctions in Sovereign Debt Litigation." Georgetown Law Faculty Publications and Other Works. Paper 1319. http://scholarship.law.georgetown.edu/facpub/1319.

Weidemaier, Mark C., and Mitu Gulati. 2014. "A People's History of Collective Action Clauses," *Virginia Journal of International Law* (no. 54): 1–95.

Weidemaier, Mark, Robert Scott, and Mitu Gulati. 2012. "Origin Myths, Contracts, and the Hunt for Pari Passu." *Law & Society Inquiry* 37. http://ssrn.com/abstract= 1633439 (accessed January 10, 2013).

Zettelmeyer, Jeromin, Christoph Trebesch, and Mitu Gulati. 2013. "The Greek Debt Restructuring: An Autopsy." *Economic Policy* 28 (no. 75): 513–563.

CHAPTER 7

Contractual and Voluntary Approaches to Sovereign Debt Restructuring

THERE IS STILL MORE TO DO

Richard Gitlin and Brett House

The international community took important steps during 2014 and 2015 to improve the global infrastructure through which it deals with cases of sovereign debt distress—steps on which further progress should be built. The development of better model language for bond contracts, as promulgated by the International Capital Markets Association (ICMA, 2014) and largely endorsed by the International Monetary Fund (IMF, 2014b), should make these bonds simpler to restructure when countries experience payment difficulties. Similarly, the reform of some IMF lending practices (IMF, 2014a, 2015) will likely make the Fund more effective at helping indebted countries avoid unnecessary restructurings. Together, these changes ought to make future episodes of sovereign debt distress less costly for both debtors and creditors. Concurrent with these developments, the United Nations General Assembly (UNGA) Resolution 68/304 "Towards the Establishment of a Multilateral Legal Framework for Sovereign Debt Restructuring Processes" (UN, 2014) passed by a split vote on September 9, 2014. The resolution expressed the will of some member states to move toward the creation of a multilateral statutory framework for sovereign debt restructuring. It echoed calls by the G77 in the 1970s and in other recent UN resolutions (UN, 2010, 2011, 2012) for an orderly approach to sovereign debt restructuring. Coming more than a decade after the rejection of the IMF's Sovereign Debt Restructuring Mechanism (SDRM; Krueger, 2001) in 2003, this UNGA resolution signals continued interest in treaty-based approaches to enhancing our sovereign debt tool kit. On September 10, 2015, the UNGA passed a second resolution endorsing "Basic Principles on Sovereign Debt Restructuring Processes" (UN, 2015). While heralded as a breakthrough achievement by its supporters, these basic principles fall well short of creating a multi-lateral legal framework, and their modesty signals that this process is not likely to advance further in rapid succession.

Taken together, these innovations underscore that there is no need to choose between strictly contractual or voluntary approaches versus statutory or treaty-based agreements to improve the machinery of sovereign debt restructuring. The arguments by firm partisans for one side or another present a false and what is now an arid and counterproductive choice: both sets of approaches have their strengths and weaknesses—pros, cons, and exclusive features that have already been aired extensively. Neither path provides a perfect combination of optimal results, efficiency, and political feasibility; zero sum–style advocacy for one approach to the exclusion of the other is likely to delay rather than accelerate reform. As the September 2015 vote on UNGA Resolution 69/319 demonstrates, a global consensus on even something as limited as a set of basic principles on sovereign debt restructuring remains elusive. But in an era of record debt levels in many countries (Bank for International Settlements [BIS], 2014a, 2014b; Dobbs et al., 2015) and heightened consequences attached to any policy mistake, it is important to identify where the next incremental steps can be feasibly taken to sustain the reform momentum generated in recent years. Identifying these steps is the purpose of the present chapter.

In charting a route toward further reform, it is notable that the votes on the 2014 and 2015 UNGA resolutions highlighted some of the same fault lines that undermined the IMF's SDRM proposal. Several of the countries that withheld support for the SDRM in 2003 either opposed the 2014 and 2015 UNGA resolutions or abstained from the votes on them. Among others, Japan, the United Kingdom, and the United States—the three countries under whose legal frameworks most external sovereign debt is issued and in whose major financial centers most sovereign debt is traded—voted against both resolutions. In particular, the United States opposed the assertion in the UN Basic Principles of a sovereign's putative right to undertake a discretionary restructuring of its debt (Charbonneau, 2015) and pressed for further discussions on these matters to be hosted at the IMF rather than the UN. If there is any doubt that this represents at least a temporary impasse for statutory and treaty-based approaches to sovereign debt restructuring, consider how difficult it was to get the 2010 package of IMF reforms ratified in the U.S. Congress even with the explicit backing of the White House and U.S. Treasury. At least for the moment, a great deal more can be done through contractual and voluntary channels to make sovereign debt workouts smoother and more effective than can be achieved through narrowly statutory routes.

Additional efforts should be pursued with vigor to improve the voluntary and contractual means of assisting sovereigns in debt distress. This chapter lays out a pragmatic plan for the pursuit of this agenda. It first takes stock of the achievements of recent years. It then lays out a set of complementary initiatives that would support and extend the latest advances. If the proposed work program outlined below were implemented, substantial progress would be made without the difficulties that treaty negotiations inspired by the UN resolutions would likely encounter.

RECENT DEVELOPMENTS SET THE STAGE FOR MORE PROGRESS

The IMF staff usefully—and bravely—reopened the discussion of sovereign debt restructuring at the Fund's executive board meeting in April 2013 after eight years of quiet and, in so doing, substantially shifted the terms of this debate. The difficulties encountered by Greece in its 2012 debt treatments, the continued pursuit of Argentina by creditors in the U.S. courts, and the prospect of more sovereign financial distress in the coming years together created a natural opportunity for the Fund to reengage on metalevel sovereign debt restructuring issues. After decades in which the presumption had been that sovereign debt restructuring should be intentionally costly to provide governments an incentive for proactive adjustment and a disincentive for gratuitous default, the IMF staff argued that the real problem is not that restructurings happen "too much, too soon" but rather that they tend to be "too little, too late" (IMF, 2013). That is, they provide too little debt relief to return a country to sustainability and they come too late to prevent substantial damage to the debtor country, its creditors, and, often, global financial markets.

In its consideration of the 2013 IMF staff paper, the Fund's board endorsed both the staff diagnosis and a proposed work program built on this assessment. The IMF's sensible plan has four parts: (1) reform of IMF analyses, processes, and lending practices; (2) improvement of the contractual infrastructure for debt restructuring; (3) creation of a clearer framework for official sector involvement in treating distressed sovereign debt; and (4) review and possible expansion of the IMF's policies on lending into arrears. The first two agenda items are direct responses to problems encountered in dealing with the debt crises in Greece and Argentina, but they also address broader systemic challenges and go far beyond attempts to refight yesterday's wars. The last two items confront issues that have received years of lip service but little action. The IMF's work program is both appropriately ambitious and eminently feasible.

The IMF board's endorsement of this four-point plan opened up the way for two subsequent staff papers on sovereign debt distress (IMF, 2014a, 2014b). IMF board discussions in response to the first of these papers added the option of debt rescheduling or "reprofiling" to IMF-supported programs, even if—and in some cases, especially when—exit sustainability is questionable. Explicit board endorsement of the option of reprofiling under IMF programs adds official support to an approach to alleviating debt distress that has already been implemented in cases such as Uruguay and the Dominican Republic in the early 2000s. By providing a middle path between the binarisms of a fully financed public bailout and the expectation that a restructuring is a prerequisite for official liquidity support, the IMF should be able to provide extra breathing room to distressed debtor countries to sort out their affairs and, perhaps, avoid debt write-downs that are typically costlier for both creditors and debtors than lighter reschedulings. By allowing this option when the solvency of a debtor country is uncertain, the board's decision also reduces the implicit pressure on the Fund staff to certify that a lending program would produce sustainability in cases in which this is contested.

The first paper (IMF, 2014a) also foreshadowed the eventual elimination of what has become known interchangeably as the "systemic waiver," "systemic exception," or "systemic exemption" regarding the Fund's rules on exceptional access to IMF resources. The 2010 waiver created an exception to limits on Fund lending in circumstances in which "there is a high risk of systemic spillovers" (IMF, 2010). Schadler (2014) details some of the problems with this fudge. First, it represents terrible process in policy making: rather than coming at the end of a deliberation on how limits to the Fund's discretion should be modified while still curtailing the threat of moral hazard, the waiver was inserted by the IMF board in the midst of the specific lending decision on Greece. Second, it is inherently unfair: the waiver allows massive lending to small countries that are inside monetary unions without permitting commensurate support to similar countries outside currency zones. This narrowly violates the Fund's long-standing cornerstone principle of equality of treatment, although the main beneficiary of such exceptional lending is arguably the IMF's entire membership. Finally, it is the wrong remedy: as the eurozone crisis has shown, contagion is not curtailed by large public bailouts but rather through appropriate policies and predictable action. Getting rid of this waiver would be a useful bit of postcrisis tidying up.

Although IMF board discussions on ending the systemic waiver occurred in 2015, they did not conclude until January 2016 when elimination of the waiver became a condition of US ratification of the 2010 IMF quota reform. Schadler's (2014) contention that the IMF's preferred-creditor status should be challenged to force the abolition of the systemic waiver proved unnecessary. In any event, this would have solved one problem by creating another: financing provided by the IMF in the midst of a crisis, when all other sources of liquidity are closed, clearly merits a senior carve-out from any subsequent restructuring. Instead of ending the Fund's senior-creditor status, the fact that the Fund's exceptional access criteria proved too binding for the IMF to deal with a relatively small country such as Greece has arguably helped to add further pressure on the United States to ratify the agreed 2010 IMF quota increase (Congress of the United States of America, 2015) while also providing an impetus for the rest of the world to move ahead regardless of U.S. Congressional support through developments such as the BRICS countries' new Contingent Reserve Agreement (House, 2015b). Under the doubling of the IMF's quota shares, far fewer countries' borrowing needs will look "exceptional," thereby rendering any need for a systemic waiver moot. Removal of the waiver should prompt also a serious review of the form and transparency of the Fund's debt-sustainability analysis (DSA) framework to ensure that clearly unsustainable debt burdens trigger a move to restructuring rather than exceptionally large lending packages.

The second IMF paper (IMF, 2014b) puts the Fund stamp of approval on the improved model language for sovereign bond contracts published by ICMA in August 2014 (ICMA, 2014) following a series of informal multistakeholder consultations. When adopted by issuers, the new language features three optional configurations that, inter alia, introduce cross-series aggregation as a standard feature of sovereign bonds' collective action clauses (CACs) and narrow the implications of sovereign bonds' pari passu provisions to exclude the ratable payment interpretation provided by U.S. District Court Judge Thomas Griesa.[1] Griesa's reading of pari passu and his accompanying injunctive remedy precludes Argentina from servicing the bonds from its 2005 and 2010 debt exchanges without also making proportionate payments to bondholders that refused to accept the terms of these restructurings—all of which tips the balance of power in a debt workout disproportionately toward creditors (see Chodos, 2016). The newly agreed CAC model language and related circumscriptions on bonds' pari passu provisions should remedy this by making it harder for minority creditors to hold up restructurings. Nevertheless, an indebted sovereign will still face a nontrivial challenge in assembling the majorities needed among its creditors to trigger even these new clauses and a subsequent debt restructuring.

The new IMF- and ICMA-endorsed language will move new sovereign bond contracts closer to an expression of a Goldilocks-like trade-off between debtor and creditor interests. The language has been quietly and quickly adopted by a succession of borrowers, led by Kazakhstan, Mexico, Vietnam, and Ethiopia, without any apparent effect on demand for this paper (House, 2015b). This mirrors the smooth inclusion of CACs in bonds issued under New York law from 2003 onward:[2] creditors have welcomed the greater certainty engendered by the new clauses. Of course, sovereign issuers do not adopt model contract language verbatim or uniformly, and even the Fund (IMF, 2014b) declined to endorse the ICMA paper's advocacy of creditor engagement and representative committee clauses, as also supported by DeSieno (2016). Some interpretative uncertainty will be attached to this language until it is tested in the courts: clever lawyers and particular cases could still undo the apparent gains it offers. But what is most striking about the ICMA-endorsed collective action, aggregation, acceleration, and pari passu provisions is that, once widely incorporated in sovereign debt contracts, they would create a de facto facsimile of many of the key de jure features of the final 2003 version of the failed SDRM proposal (see IMF, 2003; Rieffel, 2003: 268–269).

Over time, these initiatives will likely, together, reduce some of the costs of sovereign debt restructuring (see figure 7.1). The option to reprofile or reschedule debt obligations even when solvency is unclear,[3] and the recently agreed expansion of the IMF's LIA policy (IMF 2015), together give a distressed sovereign breathing room to deal with its problems in the midst of a crisis: they reduce the in medias res costs of debt treatments by either obviating the need for a heavy restructuring or by allowing one to be organized in an orderly, pre-default manner

A. Outstanding policy gaps before, during, and after restructuring

Ex ante
- No standing venue for debt reform, creditor-debtor discussions
- No systematic engagement with non–Paris Club Official creditors
- Inhibitions to tapping IMF lending still too strong
- Insufficient encouragement for lender/debtor discipline

In medias res
- No automatic standstill mechanism for countries in debt distress
- IMF crisis lending overly constrained in presence of debt-service arrears

Ex post
- Non-participating creditors have disproportionate leverage
- Payments systems vulnerable to attachment

B. Existing and potential responses

Legend
Underway
Pending

Restructuring timeline

Ex ante	*In medias res*	*Ex post*
• **Sovereign Debt Forum (SDF)**	• IMF reprofiling	• CACs: **accelerate rollovers**
• **Wider OSI engagement**	• IMF LIA policy expansion	• Aggregation
• **IMF FCL/PLL reform**	• **Sovereign contingent debt**	• Pari Passu reform
• **Consensus debtor/creditor principles**		• **Immunize payment systems**
		• **Protect investment/trade dispute settlement systems**

Figure 7.1   Costs of sovereign debt restructuring, policy gaps, and proposed responses.

with IMF support. Better CACs, narrowed pari passu provisions, and aggregation across creditors should together reduce the ex post cost of restructuring by making the terms of a debt treatment harder to undermine once they have been agreed upon. But these provisions will become powerful only once enough new bonds bearing them replace existing outstanding debt. This will likely take over a decade, since 40 percent of emerging market debt issued under New York law has residual maturities of 10 years or more (IMF, 2014b). Debtor countries could accelerate the rollover of this outstanding debt through swaps, but the IMF reports that sovereigns have not indicated much interest in doing so (2014b). Some encouragement and facilitating support from the IMF and others could be useful to move forward on exchanges of new paper for these existing bonds.

Nevertheless, as common-sense and helpful as these developments clearly are, and as useful as the 2014 and 2015 UN resolutions may be in sustaining pressure for additional reform, none of these innovations directly address the core problem of "too little, too late" that the IMF identified in 2013. They do not reduce the ex ante costs of restructuring: they do little to encourage sovereigns to deal with their debt problems proactively; they provide only an indirect and partial discipline on lender and borrower behavior; and they do not reduce the inhibitions country authorities face in seeking early, preventative assistance from the IMF.

There is urgency for more action to improve the world's responses to sovereign debt distress. Incremental, voluntary, and contractual approaches offer the most tractable way to achieve these gains—without undermining the possibility of future statutory or treaty-based initiatives. High levels of public indebtedness in many countries mean their public authorities currently have little margin to compensate for policy mistakes, further slowdowns in real-sector growth, or greater weakness in commodity prices: global debt vulnerabilities have increased substantially since the beginning of the 2008 financial crisis. Sovereign debt stocks have ballooned in developed economies (BIS, 2014a, 2014b), deleveraging still has a long way to go in many sectors (Bologna, Miglietta, and Cacavaio, 2014), and household balance sheets remain stretched (Dobbs et al., 2015). Emerging- and frontier-market foreign-currency bond issuance by corporate borrowers has expanded (Uy and Zhou, 2016) and is a time bomb set to explode as yields normalize. According to IMF data, many low-income countries that had the bulk of their debt written off at the turn of the millennium are already back in danger: some forty poor countries are in medium to severe debt distress (Kaiser, 2015). Puerto Rico's debt crisis highlights problems lurking in many countries at the subnational level. Vulnerabilities can quickly cascade between sectors, and both private and subnational public debt problems can rapidly become sources of sovereign debt distress, as the experiences of many emerging markets (Rosenberg et al., 2005) and the recent crises in Ireland and Spain demonstrate.

The IMF's intention to engage non–Paris Club official creditors more clearly in sovereign debt treatments will, when implemented, be a good next step to bring down the upfront barriers to restructuring, but more can and needs to be done, not just to reduce the ex ante costs of restructuring, but also to cut further the in medias res and ex post costs. The remainder of this chapter provides some practical suggestions on how these goals could be realized in the years ahead.

EX ANTE: MAKE IT EASIER TO PREVENT
AND TREAT DEBT DISTRESS

When it comes to sovereign debt problems, an ounce of prevention is worth multiple ounces of cure. Access to such preventative medicine needs to be made cheaper, easier, and more routine to reduce the likelihood that debt treatments, when they happen, come too late to prevent significant damage to a debtor country's economy and avoidable costs to its creditors. The creation of a noninstitutional sovereign debt forum (SDF), as proposed by Gitlin and House (2014a), would provide a standing, independent venue in which creditors and debtors could meet on an ongoing basis to address incipient sovereign debt distress in a preemptive fashion. Continuous and inclusive discussion within an SDF would help blunt the trigger problem and stigma that inhibit governments from seeking international assistance at the earliest stage of payment difficulties. An SDF would also ensure that there is a perpetual research and reform process on sovereign debt issues so that improvement of the system is not allowed to go dormant, as it did during 2003–2010. It could also provide for the involvement of new sovereign creditors and private lenders in debt treatments in a more equitable, inclusive, and upfront manner, in line with the engagement, transparency, and creditor committee clauses that ICMA (2014) has proposed and DeSieno (2016) advocates. The histories of noninstitutionalized, but nevertheless precedent-bound bodies such as the Paris and London Clubs, the Extractive Industries Transparency Initiative, and even the successive negotiating rounds for the General Agreement on Tariffs and Trade bear testament to the potential effectiveness of a "soft law" SDF built on understandings rather than treaties. Proposals by Kaiser (2010, 2016) and Ocampo (2014, 2016) could later add arbitration processes to the SDF's simple design if sufficient support for such measures were ever to emerge.

Preemptive and preventative financing from the IMF also needs to be made more attractive to debtor countries. The channels through which the IMF provides such support, the Flexible Credit Line (FCL) and the Precautionary Liquidity Line (PLL), have rarely been used. Since the FCL's introduction in March 2009, only three countries— Colombia, Poland, and Mexico—have sought (even then, only after *much* encouragement) arrangements under the FCL, despite market conditions that should have implied substantial interest from many countries in accessing a well-designed, preemptive liquidity window. Only two countries—former Yugoslav Republic of Macedonia and Morocco— have used the PLL, despite its looser qualification criteria compared with the FCL. Although the FCL and PLL are indeed more *flexible* than the Contingent Credit Line (CCL), their unloved and unused predecessor, countries still do not see enough net value in the FCL and PLL compared with the perceived costs attached to a request for qualification to generate demand for these crisis-prevention and crisis-mitigation financing products.

It should be no slight to the IMF to suggest that it is time to go back to the FCL/PLL drawing board: getting the terms of credit facilities such as the FCL and PLL properly balanced is tough work. The last comprehensive review of the IMF's lending facilities took place in 2011; the next is due in 2016. The Fund made some tweaks to the FCL and PLL in 2014, but they do not appear to have been sufficient to make either credit line meaningfully more attractive to IMF member countries. More should be done to make the FCL/PLL more appealing: the facilities' qualification criteria and processes need to be loosened, the predictability by which approved resources can be drawn upon needs to be improved, the duration of support under both facilities needs to be made more flexible, the scale of potential borrowing needs to be made larger, and the facilities' borrowing terms need to be made less punitive.

At the same time, preventative guidelines for borrowers and creditors—such as the Institute of International Finance's "Principles for Stable Capital Flows and Fair Debt Restructuring" (IIF, 2012), the UN Conference on Trade and Development's "Principles on Responsible Sovereign Lending and Borrowing" (UNCTAD, 2012), and the UN's new "Basic Principles" (UN, 2015)—need additional work to make them into more effective codes of conduct. At present, the IIF principles are relatively long on expectations of debtors, but are more parsimonious in their demands of creditors. Both borrowers and lenders could benefit from a clearer charter for prospective behavior. In contrast, UNCTAD's "Principles" and the UN's "Basic Principles" are more symmetric in their design, but have received limited buy-in from private-capital market participants and the governments of financial centers. There needs to be a unified set of guiding principles, something akin to the UN's "Principles for Responsible Investment", adapted for both sovereign borrowers and their creditors: principles that are balanced in their treatment of both competing interests, widely endorsed, and routinely used as a reference point to guide financing decisions.

IN MEDIAS RES: GIVE DISTRESSED COUNTRIES
MORE BREATHING ROOM

The revived proposal for two forms of state-contingent debt most recently articulated by the Banks of Canada and England (Brooke et al., 2013) should be acted upon by well-regarded sovereign debt issuers. The idea of state–contingent sovereign debt has been around for some time (Borensztein and Mauro, 2004; Barkbu, Eichengreen, and Mody, 2012; Mody, 2013), but its potential has not been fully exploited. Mexico issued oil-indexed bonds in the 1970s; in the 1990s, Mexico, Nigeria, Uruguay, and Venezuela issued Brady bonds, whose returns were tied to commodity prices; and Costa Rica, Bulgaria, and Bosnia-Herzegovina issued gross domestic product (GDP)-linked bonds under Brady restructurings in the 1990s. More recently, Argentina in 2005 and Greece in 2012 issued GDP-linked warrants as sweeteners in their respective debt exchanges.

The first form of contingent sovereign debt proposed by Brooke and colleagues (2013), sovereign "cocos" (that is, "contingent convertibles"), consists of bonds that automatically extend their maturity upon realization of a prespecified trigger linked to a liquidity crisis. The term is borrowed from corporate cocos, bonds that convert into equity when a firm's stock reaches a prespecified strike price; clearly, the analogy is partial, since there is no notion of equity in a sovereign context. Brooke and colleagues (2013) propose tying activation of a sovereign bond's coco provisions to initiation of an IMF-supported program, but other triggers more removed from the sovereign's discretion would be both feasible and more insulated from moral hazard, such as ratings downgrades, increased collateral requirements on a sovereign's debt from clearing systems, or violation of a prespecified floor on official foreign-exchange reserves. The second contingent form proposed by Brooke and colleagues (2013), GDP-linked bonds, carries principal and interest provisions that vary with a country's GDP to preserve the sovereign's solvency in bad times and to compensate creditors in good times for the increased risk they bear. Debt service on these bonds could also be tied to global or regional growth, key commodity prices, global interest rate indices, or other major aggregates that materially affect the financial health of the sovereign, but are both independent of the government's discretionary actions and verifiable by third parties.

The main virtue of sovereign cocos and other performance-linked debt lies in their automatic provision of breathing room to a country that gets into trouble owing to forces ostensibly outside its control. Countries with highly volatile economies and those in which monetary policy is bound into a currency union stand to benefit the most from the issuance of such debt, but all potential issuers would see the need to make wrenching, growth-hindering fiscal adjustments in the midst of a crisis dampened. The international system as a whole would also be better off: there would be less political pressure on the IMF to lend into circumstances that do not merit its support, the possibility of an automatic standstill would increase pressure on creditors to discipline their lending, and private lenders would be "bailed-in" to crisis resolution efforts with their exposure and engagement maintained. Granted, state-contingent automatic standstills do not provide a means to address intercreditor equity issues or enable debtor-in-possession financing in the manner a statutory framework could. Additionally, just like the new CAC language, it would take years for state-contingent debt to replace a substantial share of a country's debt stock. Still, even limited issuance of these instruments would be an improvement on the status quo.

A strong group of industrialized countries and emerging market sovereigns could usefully come together under an agreed program of issuance to make sovereign cocos and other state-contingent debt a more common feature of the foreign-law sovereign debt landscape. Worries that state-contingent debt cannot be priced by the market are misplaced. The market assigns prices to the Argentine and Greek warrants; modeling their price behavior is straightforward. There is little involved in pricing a coco that does not already feature in pricing standard fixed-income instruments. While it is true that some asset managers would not immediately be able to invest in state-contingent debt under their existing investment mandates, it is also likely that these mandates would be modified as this debt becomes more ubiquitous and liquid (House, 2015a).

The approved extension (IMF, 2015) of the IMF's policy on lending into arrears (LIA) to cover past-due debt to bilateral official creditors is a natural complement to wider issuance of state-contingent sovereign debt: both could reduce in medias res debt restructuring costs. The LIA policy, which was born of efforts in the late 1990s and early 2000s to ensure private-creditor participation in debt workouts, allows the Fund to lend to member countries in arrears to their private creditors so long as the country is making "good faith" efforts to conclude a collaborative agreement to treat these debts. Permitting the Fund to lend to countries in default on private bonds and loans goes some way to balance creditor and debtor leverage in the negotiating process. The extension of this policy to arrears on bilateral official debt provides more breathing room to illiquid sovereigns, reduces incidences of avoidable restructuring, and is consistent with the spirit of comparable treatment. Further extension of the LIA policy should be contemplated.

EX POST: MAKE AGREED RESTRUCTURINGS STICK

The new ICMA- and IMF-endorsed model CAC and pari passu language is a huge advance in lowering the ex post costs of sovereign debt restructuring, but as has already been noted, it will be several years before a critical mass of existing debt has been rolled over and replaced with bonds bearing this new language. Intentional, concerted action should be considered to realize more quickly the benefits of this new approach to writing sovereign bond contracts. Collectives of emerging-market borrowers, such as the BRICS countries, G-24, ASEAN, or others could work together to reduce the cost of large-scale debt exchanges and preempt any concerns that such exchanges in any way indicate a debtor country is concerned about its liquidity or solvency. Further assistance could come from long-term institutional investors and the IIF, who have generally welcomed the increased certainty that the new contractual provisions will bring; capital markets authorities in London and New York, where most foreign-law bonds are issued; and the IMF. Any upfront costs would likely be more than compensated for by long-run savings for all of these actors. The United Kingdom and the United States could also investigate the possibility of retrofitting through legislation the new CAC and pari passu language into existing bonds issued under their legal frameworks, much as Greece added an ex post facto aggregative CAC into its domestic-law bonds to facilitate its 2012 debt exchange.

For at least as long as debt that does not bear the 2014 CAC and pari passu language remains outstanding, the *NML Capital Limited v. Argentina* cases in the New York courts show that payment and clearing systems also need to be insulated from attachment by holdout creditors. Belgium (Government of Belgium, 2004) passed legislation in 2004 that shields the Euroclear payment system from attachment threats; Luxembourg provides similar protections for Clearstream. In the early part of this decade, the United Kingdom (Government of the United Kingdom, 2011) passed legislation that offered protection from attachment under English law to the forty-odd heavily indebted poor countries that saw most of their external debt written off under global debt relief programs that began in 1996. Action should be undertaken to add such immunities to payment systems under New York law and to broaden these immunities in English, European, and other jurisdictions.

Trade and investment treaties and their dispute settlement mechanisms need similar protections. Some creditors have argued that trade and investment treaties give foreign-law bondholders the same rights as foreign direct investors, and these creditors have worked to insert claims on sovereign debt into these treaties' international arbitration processes (St. John and Woods, 2014). Some treaties and sovereign bond contracts explicitly prohibit such actions (e.g., the North American Free Trade Agreement), but many do not, which leaves an avenue for holdout creditors to reopen settled debt restructurings. Though this has received much less attention than NML's hunt of Argentina in the New York courts, some Italian creditors have also pursued Argentina under the Argentina-Italy bilateral investment treaty through the International Centre for Settlement of Investment Disputes. Governments should move to eliminate the incipient threat of copycats by adding annexes to their key bilateral and plurilateral trade and investment treaties to rule out this kind of litigation.

CONCLUSION: A FEASIBLE AGENDA FOR ACTION

More can and should be done to enhance the prevailing contractual and voluntary approach to sovereign debt restructuring. Building on the improvements to contractual provisions widely endorsed in recent years and the IMF's move to support reprofiling in cases in which debt sustainability is uncertain, the proposals outlined above could help ensure that future debt treatments are not "too little, too late" for distressed sovereigns. None of these efforts would require difficult treaty negotiations or the significant erosion of any actor's leverage in existing processes. This work program should be at the core of the international agenda in the years ahead, in fulfillment of the G20's commitments to improve sovereign debt restructuring (G20, 2014).

Even if every element of this plan is implemented, efforts to improve the mechanics of sovereign debt restructuring will not be finished. Few contracts, laws, or institutions tend to remain perpetually effective even once reformed: most are eventually undermined or superseded by clever litigation, unintentional consequences, or unexpected circumstances.

In anticipation of such developments, this work program would provide a sound precursor and foundation for a range of more ambitious proposals, including those outlined by Ocampo (2016), Herman (2016), Kaiser (2016), and Raffer (2016).

Sovereign debt restructuring will likely remain a perfectible project for many years to come. The reform program outlined in this chapter would ensure the momentum currently generated on this project continues to build toward better results.

NOTES

The opinions expressed in this chapter represent the personal views of the authors and should not be attributed to the institutions with which they are affiliated. The authors are grateful to Timothy DeSieno, Martin Guzman, and Franz Henne for their insightful reviews and helpful comments. Any remaining errors or omissions remain the responsibility of the authors. The Jeanne Sauvé Foundation provided critical support for the preparation of this chapter and its assistance is gratefully acknowledged.

1. Gelpern (2014) provides a concise summary of the new model CACs, the more delimited pari passu clause, and their implications.

2. By late 2005, 75 percent of all new emerging-market foreign-law sovereign bond issues included CACs; by 2010, more than 90 percent of all new issues included them (Helleiner, 2009; IMF, 2013).

3. The IMF's 2013 move to publish its debt sustainability templates and include debt sustainability analyses in its Article IV consultations makes assessments of solvency much more transparent; it also positions these DSAs more effectively as a basis for a consensus among creditors on how to address a sovereign's financing problems. See: www.imf.org/external/pubs/ft/dsa.

REFERENCES

Bank for International Settlements. 2014a. *BIS Quarterly Review*. March. Basel. www.bis.org/publ/qtrpdf/r_qt1403.pdf.

———. 2014b. *BIS Quarterly Review.* December. Basel. bis.org/publ/qtrpdf/r_qt1412.pdf.

Barkbu, Bergljot, Barry Eichengreen, and Ashoka Mody. 2012. "Financial Crises and the Multilateral Response: What the Historical Record Shows." *Journal of International Economics* 88 (no. 2): 422–435.

Bologna, Pierluigi, Arianna Miglietta, and Marianna Cacavaio. 2014, October 14. "EU Bank Deleveraging." Brussels: VoxEU. www.voxeu.org/article/eu-bank-deleveraging.

Borensztein, Eduardo, and Paolo Mauro. 2004. "The Case for GDP-indexed Bonds." *Economic Policy* 19 (no. 38): 166–216.

Brooke, Martin, Rhys Mendes, Alex Pienkowski, and Eric Santor. 2013. "Sovereign Default and State-Contingent Debt." Bank of Canada Discussion Paper 2013-3, Ottawa, Ont. www.bankofcanada.ca/2013/11/discussion-paper-2013-3.

Charbonneau, Louis. 2015. "UN Nations Approve Principles for Sovereign Debt Restructuring." Reuters, September 10. www.reuters.com/article/2015/09/10/us-un -sovereign-debt-idUSKCN0RA2KS20150910.

Chodos, Sergio. 2016. "From the Pari Passu Discussion to the 'Illegality' of Making Payments." In *Too Little, Too Late: The Quest to Resolve Sovereign Debt Crises*, ed. Martin Guzman, José Antonio Ocampo, and Joseph E. Stiglitz, chapter 4. New York: Columbia University Press.

Congress of the United States of America. 2015. "H.R.2029 - Consolidated Appropriations Act, 2016." *Public Law No: 114-113*, December 18. www.congress.gov /bill/114th-congress/house-bill/2029/related-bills.

DeSieno, Timothy. 2016. "Creditor Committees in Sovereign Debt Restructurings: Understanding the Benefits and Addressing Concerns." In *Too Little, Too Late: The Quest to Resolve Sovereign Debt Crises*, ed. Martin Guzman, José Antonio Ocampo, and Joseph E. Stiglitz, chapter 9. New York: Columbia University Press.

Dobbs, Richard, Susan Lund, Jonathan Woetzel, and Mina Mutafchieva. 2015. "Debt and (Not Much) Deleveraging." February. Washington, D.C.: McKinsey Global Institute. www.mckinsey.com/insights/economic_studies/debt_and_not _much_deleveraging.

G20. 2014. Leaders' Communiqué, November 16. www.g20.utoronto.ca/2014/2014 -1116-communique.html.

Gelpern, Anna. 2014. "A Sensible Step to Mitigate Sovereign Bond Dysfunction." *Real Time Economic Issues Watch* (blog entry). August 29. http://blogs.piie.com /realtime/?p=4485.

Government of Belgium. 2004. "Law of November 19, 2004 Amending the Law of April 28, 1999 to Transpose the Directive 98/26/EC of May 19, 1998 on Settlement Finality in Payment Systems and Settlement of Securities Transactions." *Official Gazette of Belgium*, December 28.

Government of the United Kingdom. 2011. "Government Acts to Halt Profiteering on Third World Debt Within the UK." Press release, May 16. www.gov.uk/government /news/government-acts-to-halt-profiteering-on-third-world-debt-within-the-uk.

Gitlin, Richard, and Brett House. 2014a. "A Blueprint for a Sovereign Debt Forum." CIGI Papers No. 27, Waterloo, Ont. www.cigionline.org/publications/blueprint -sovereign-debt-forum.

——. 2014b. "Further Reform of Sovereign Debt Restructuring: An Agenda for 2015." CIGI Policy Brief No. 54, Waterloo, Ont. www.cigionline.org/sites/default/files /pb_no54_0.pdf.

Helleiner, Eric. 2009. "Filling a Hole in Global Financial Governance? The Politics of Regulating Sovereign Debt Restructuring." In *The Politics of Global Regulation*, ed. Ngaire Woods and Walter Mattli, 89–120. Princeton, N.J.: Princeton University Press.

Herman, Barry. "Toward a Multilateral Framework for Recovery from Sovereign Insolvency." In *Too Little, Too Late: The Quest to Resolve Sovereign Debt Crises*, ed. Martin Guzman, José Antonio Ocampo, and Joseph E. Stiglitz, chapter 11. New York: Columbia University Press.

House, Brett. 2015a. "The World Should Listen to Greece's Big Idea About Debt." *Quartz*, February 9. http://qz.com/340448/the-world-should-listen-to-greeces-big -idea-about-debt.

———. 2015b. "It's the US That Has the Most to Lose If Congress Keeps Blocking IMF Reform." *Quartz*, February 11. http://qz.com/342144/its-the-us-that-has-the -most-to-lose-if-congress-keeps-blocking-imf-reform.

———. 2015c. "Here's Why Hedge Funds Will Never Be Able to Hold Debtor Countries Hostage Again." *Quartz*, February 19. http://qz.com/346677/heres-why-hedge -funds-will-never-be-able-to-hold-debtor-countries-hostage-again.

Institute of International Finance. 2012. *Principles for Stable Capital Flows and Fair Debt Restructuring*. Report and addendum. Washington, D.C.: IIF Joint Committee on Strengthening the Framework for Sovereign Debt Crisis Prevention and Resolution. www.iif.com/topics/principles-stable-capital-flows-and-fair-debt-restructuring.

International Capital Markets Association. 2014. "Standard Collective Action and Pari Passu Clauses for the Terms and Conditions of Sovereign Notes." August www.icmagroup.org/Regulatory-Policy-and-Market-Practice/Primary-Markets /collective-action.

International Monetary Fund. April 2003. *Report of the Managing Director to the International Monetary and Financial Committee on a Statutory Sovereign Debt Restructuring Mechanism*. Washington, D.C. www.imf.org/external/np/omd/2003/040803 .htm.

———. 2010. "Greece: Staff Report on Request for Standby Arrangement." IMF Board Paper, May. Washington, D.C. www.imf.org/external/pubs/cat/longres .aspx?sk=23839.0.

———. 2013. "Sovereign Debt Restructuring: Recent Developments and Implications for the Fund's Legal and Policy Framework." IMF Board Paper, April. Washington, D.C. www.imf.org/external/np/pp/eng/2013/042613.pdf.

———. 2014a. "The Fund's Lending Framework and Sovereign Debt—Preliminary Considerations." IMF Board Paper. June. Washington, D.C. www.imf.org/external /np/pp/eng/2014/052214.pdf.

———. 2014b. "Strengthening the Contractual Framework to Address Collective Action Problems in Sovereign Debt Restructuring." IMF Board Paper. October. Washington, D.C. www.imf.org/external/pp/longres.aspx?id=4911.

———. 2015. "Reforming the Fund's Policy on Nontoleration of Arrears to Official Creditors." IMF Board Paper. December. Washington, D.C. www.imf.org/external /pp/longres.aspx?id=4911.

Kaiser, Jürgen. 2010. "Taking Stock of Proposals for More Ordered Workouts." In *Overcoming Developing Country Debt Crises*, ed. Barry Herman, José Antonio Ocampo, and Shari Spiegel, chap. 15. Oxford: Oxford University Press.

———. 2015. "Make a Reform Process Visible and Sustainable." Presentation at the Frameworks for Sovereign Debt Restructuring Conference, held November 17 at Columbia University, N.Y.

———. "Making a Legal Framework for Sovereign Debt Restructuring Operational." In *Too Little, Too Late: The Quest to Resolve Sovereign Debt Crises*, ed. Martin Guzman José Antonio Ocampo, and Joseph E. Stiglitz, chapter 12. New York: Columbia University Press.

Krueger, Anne. 2001. "International Financial Architecture for 2002: A New Approach to Sovereign Debt Restructuring." Address to the National Economists' Club annual members' dinner hosted by the American Enterprise Institute, Washington, D.C. www.imf.org/external/np/speeches/2001/112601.htm.

Mody, Ashoka. 2013. "Sovereign Debt and Its Restructuring Framework in the Euro Area." Bruegel Working Paper No. 2013/05, Brussels. www.bruegel.org/publications /publication-detail/publication/788-sovereign-debt-and-its-restructuring -framework-in-the-euro-area.

Ocampo, José Antonio. 2014. "The UN Takes the First Step to Debt Restructuring." *Beyondbrics* (guest post), *Financial Times*, September 10. http://blogs .ft.com/beyond-brics/2014/09/10/guest-post-the-un-takes-the-first-step-to-debt -restructuring.

———. 2016. "A Brief History of Sovereign Debt Resolution and a Proposal for a Multilateral Instrument." In *Too Little, Too Late: The Quest to Resolve Sovereign Debt Crises*, ed. Martin Guzman, José Antonio Ocampo, and Joseph E. Stiglitz, chapter 10. New York: Columbia University Press.

Raffer, Kunibert. 2016. "Debts, Human Rights, and the Rule of Law: Advocating a Fair and Efficient Sovereign Insolvency Model." In *Too Little, Too Late: The Quest to Resolve Sovereign Debt Crises*, ed. Martin Guzman, José Antonio Ocampo, and Joseph E. Stiglitz, chapter 15. New York: Columbia University Press.

Rieffel, Lex. 2003. *Restructuring Sovereign Debt: The Case for Ad Hoc Machinery.* Washington, D.C.: Brookings Institution.

Rosenberg, Christoph, Ioannis Halikias, Brett House, Christian Keller, Jens Nystedt, Alexander Pitt, and Brad Setser. 2005. "Debt-Related Vulnerabilities and Financial Crises. An Application of the Balance Sheet Approach to Emerging Market Countries." IMF Occasional Paper No. 240, Washington, D.C.

Schadler, Susan. 2014. "The IMF's Preferred Creditor Status: Does It Still Make Sense After the Euro Crisis?" CIGI Policy Brief No. 37, March. Waterloo, Ont. www.cigionline.org/publications/imfs-preferred-creditor-status-does-it-still-make -sense-after-euro-crisis.

St. John, Taylor, and Ngaire Woods. 2014. "Ukraine Versus the Vultures." *Project Syndicate*, March 17. www.project-syndicate.org/commentary/ngaire-woods-and -taylor-st—john-warn-that-the-country-s-investment-treaties-could-undermine -debt-restructuring-efforts.

United Nations. 2010. "External debt sustainability and development." UNGA Resolution 65/144. New York. www.un.org/en/ga/search/view_doc.asp?symbol=A/RES/65/144.

———. 2011. "External debt sustainability and development." UNGA Resolution 66/189. New York. www.un.org/en/ga/search/view_doc.asp?symbol=A/RES/66/189.

———. 2012. "External debt sustainability and development." UNGA Resolution 67/198. New York. www.un.org/en/ga/search/view_doc.asp?symbol=A/RES/67/198.

——. 2014. "Towards the Establishment of a Multilateral Legal Framework for Sovereign Debt Restructuring Processes." UNGA Resolution 68/304. New York. www .un.org/ga/search/view_doc.asp?symbol=A/RES/68/304&Lang=E.

——. 2015. "Basic Principles on Sovereign Debt Restructuring Processes." UNGA Resolution 69/319. New York. www.un.org/ga/search/view_doc.asp?symbol=A /RES/69/319&Lang=E

United Nations Conference on Trade and Development. 2012. "Principles on Promoting Responsible Sovereign Lending and Borrowing." January. Geneva. http:// unctadxiii.org/en/SessionDocument/gdsddf2012misc1_en.pdf.

Uy, Marilou, and Shichao Zhou. 2016. "Sovereign Debt of Developing Countries: Overview of Trends and Policy Perspectives." In *Too Little, Too Late: The Quest to Resolve Sovereign Debt Crises*, ed. Martin Guzman, José Antonio Ocampo, and Joseph E. Stiglitz, chapter 2. New York: Columbia University Press.

CHAPTER 8

Sovereign Debt Restructuring

A COASEAN PERSPECTIVE

James A. Haley

In the words of the great American social philosopher Yogi Berra, "It's déjà vu all over again" with respect to sovereign debt restructuring: in late 2014, Mexico successfully issued New York law bonds incorporating revised collective action clauses (CACs).[1] The new clauses, which strengthen existing provisions to assuage creditor coordination problems and promote the timely, orderly restructuring of sovereign debt, were developed by the International Capital Market Association (ICMA) in collaboration with the U.S. Treasury, the International Monetary Fund (IMF), and the Institute for International Finance.

A little more than a decade ago, Mexico likewise demonstrated leadership in introducing first-generation CACs in its New York–law bonds. At the time, CACs were viewed as the cornerstone of the "voluntary" approach to sovereign debt restructuring in the debate between backers of a market-led approach to address creditor coordination problems and advocates of a formal statutory approach incorporating elements of domestic bankruptcy frameworks.[2] Mexico's introduction of CACs in February 2003, together with the recognition that statutory approaches lacked the political support needed to be implemented, effectively ended the debate and relegated the statutory approach to the proverbial back burner.[3]

Significant progress was made in terms of sovereign debt restructuring in the years between the initial Mexican bond issue with CACs and today. Soon after Mexico's pathbreaking 2003 issue, three-quarters of all new sovereign bond issues included CACs; by 2010, more than 90 percent of all new issues included these clauses. Moreover, through much of the past decade, sovereign debt restructurings were completed with relative speed and were notable for the absence of litigation.[4] Indeed, the experience was such that by late 2011 supporters of the contractual approach could claim vindication. If not the "best of all possible worlds" of Voltaire's Dr. Pangloss, the process for restructurings seemed at least to be working; then came Greece and Argentina.

By early 2012, the sovereign debt restructuring landscape had changed. With more than 90 percent of its debt stock governed by domestic law, Greece retroactively inserted an aggregated collective action mechanism across its bonds with voting thresholds very favorable to the debtor, much to the chagrin of its bondholders. Meanwhile, holdout creditors of Argentina who chose not to participate in earlier restructurings secured a favorable judgment upholding a pari passu clause in the 1994 Fiscal Agency Agreement that forbids Argentina to pay other debts unless it also pays the holdout creditor on a pro rata basis, which in the court order providing injunctive relief is interpreted as "ratable" payments.[5]

These "new challenges" have resurrected "old debates" about the merits of contractual versus statutory approaches to sovereign debt restructuring.[6] And Anna Gelpern, a longtime, self-proclaimed skeptic of bankruptcy for sovereigns, surveying recent debt restructuring experiences, has concluded: "The existing system for reducing sovereign debt is deeply dysfunctional and produces bad law."[7] The arbitrary nature of retroactive insertion of CACs in Greek debt and the use of pari passu against investors that accepted restructured bonds have tarnished the Panglossian perspective on sovereign debt restructurings that prevailed just a few years ago and have reenergized efforts to facilitate more predictable outcomes for creditors and debtors and fairer treatment across creditors. The ICMA model clauses on which Mexico's late-2014 bond is based are a response to these concerns of predictability and fairness.

As a preview of what follows, I make three (admittedly unoriginal) points.

First, the new clauses are a useful and potentially important instrument for dealing with the problem of holdout creditors. Indeed, given that they address key weaknesses and obvious problems in existing bonding "technology," the ICMA clauses are undoubtedly a "big deal."[8]

Second, the new clauses are not a panacea. This assessment reflects the fact that it will take some time for these clauses to be embedded in the stock of outstanding bonds. The benefits from them, meanwhile, can be expected to dissipate over time as contractual practices evolve. Moreover, whatever their merits, the new clauses do not address the issues of unenforceability and discharge of sovereign debts.

Third, the debate between voluntary/contractual and statutory approaches is a false dichotomy. Contractual approaches will necessarily be incomplete and the design of "institutions," whether bankruptcy provisions embodied in formal treaty or the responses of existing international financial institutions, will influence the outcome of sovereign debt restructurings.

The first of these points is factual and, I think, noncontroversial. The latter two are more conjectural in nature and subject to possible debate.

IMPACT OF NEW CLAUSES

The ICMA model clauses adopted by Mexico and other issuers in late 2014 are intended to make it harder for holdout creditors to disrupt future sovereign debt restructurings by addressing the aggregation problem under the series-by-series voting process that has been incorporated in CACs since 2003. In series-by-series voting, a small minority of creditors controlling a single bond issue can impede a restructuring acceptable to the broad majority of investors holding other series. The problem is that creditors will be reluctant to reduce their claims on distressed sovereigns if other creditors are not also participating in the restructuring. As a result, if a small minority of investors in a single bond issue refuses to accept modified terms, they could potentially block the entire restructuring. Rather than risk failure, sovereign debtors may pay the minority creditors in full. But paying off the minority creates an incentive for holdout investors to "free ride" on the majority of creditors that are prepared to reduce their claims.[9]

To make it harder for holdout creditors to disrupt future bond restructurings, the ICMA model clauses allow issuers to organize a vote across bond series in two ways, in addition to the existing series-by-series mechanism.[10] The first method is a "two-limb" voting process in which the threshold for single series approval is reduced from 75 to 50 percent, subject to approval by two-thirds of the entire pool of bondholders. The second modification to voting proposed by the ICMA model clauses is "single-limb" voting by all bondholders, across all series, with a 75 percent threshold for amending terms. Given the potential for abuse by minority creditors, the single-limb rule requires the issuer to offer the same menu of participation options to all creditors—the "uniform consideration" clause.[11]

The power of the proposed changes comes from the reduction in the ability of minority investors to block restructurings. The change from series-by-series voting to the single-limb mechanism is striking, particularly in cases in which the sovereign has a large number of outstanding bond issues, some with relatively small nominal amounts outstanding. Under such conditions, blocking the restructuring of a single series in a series-by-series vote requires a relatively modest investment. In contrast, the single-limb approach requires a much larger investment, equivalent to 25.1 percent of the entire outstanding debt stock. For a large issuer with a large stock of debt, this could represent an insurmountable obstacle. At the same time, a 75 percent threshold is sufficiently high that successful restructurings will continue to be difficult to achieve, requiring the cooperation of the broad majority of creditors. In this regard, it is interesting to note the incentive that the single-limb mechanism provides for the debtor to work with supportive creditors in designing a voting strategy that maximizes the likelihood of success to the benefit of most creditors.

The ICMA clauses also refine the troublesome language of pari passu clauses that, in the hands of holdout creditors and following a favorable judicial ruling in New York, has led Argentina into selective default and thrust the issue of sovereign debt restructuring once more onto the international policy agenda. By neutralizing the notion of ratable payments, the new clause should reduce the risk of copycat litigation. There is residual uncertainty regarding contractual interpretation, however, and only time will tell whether the new clause will achieve its objective.

MARKET EVOLUTION AND BONDING TECHNOLOGY

Notwithstanding the potential benefits from ICMA model clauses, the environment for sovereign debt restructuring will likely remain challenging.[12] In the first instance, the benefits from aggregation mechanisms will take time to accrue owing to the stock/flow issue: the IMF estimates that roughly 30 percent of the US$900 billion in outstanding bonds globally will mature in more than 10 years.[13] The potential for holdouts will clearly remain for some time to come. In the interim, there is a risk that the partial introduction of mechanisms to facilitate restructuring could increase the risk of free riding, as ease of restructuring bond issues with ICMA clauses increases the potential returns from disrupting restructurings.[14]

More generally, there are residual challenges to a purely contractual framework for debt restructuring coming from a number of sources.

The first is interpretation uncertainty. The new ICMA model clauses will be subject to judicial interpretation; as demonstrated with respect to pari passu in the case of Argentina, such rulings may not adhere to prevailing opinion. Over time, the meaning and interpretation of new clauses will be clarified, defined, and incorporated in jurisprudence, reducing the degree of uncertainty. But there will be uncertainty that will affect behavior of debtors and creditors alike.

In addition, regardless of their merits, the new clauses do not address the basic issues of unenforceability and debt discharge that plague sovereign debt restructurings.[15] In contrast to domestic commercial bankruptcies, sovereigns suffering from excessive debt cannot secure a judicial discharge of debts that binds all creditors and prevents disruptive litigation and asset stripping. And apart from nuisance attempts to seize assets, there is very little that creditors can do to force payment from sovereigns that do not pay their debts. As a result, it is reasonable to assume that sovereign debt contracts will have a self-enforcing element. While better contract design can assist a sovereign seeking a cooperative solution that preserves asset values for creditors and restores the economy to growth, there will be residual uncertainty concerning "ability" and "willingness" to honor existing contracts.[16]

One implication of this uncertainty is that, short of some internationally binding agreement that enforces the use of standard, nonvarying terms, contractual approaches will be subject to innovation and evolution as market conditions and the needs of sovereign borrowers change. There may well be circumstances in which sovereign borrowers and potential investors develop innovations that immunize an issue against a particular formulation of an aggregation clause.[17] Moreover, the introduction of "near-debt" instruments, which share some equity features, may be helpful in reducing the vulnerability of a sovereign's balance sheet in response to adverse shocks within a certain range, but could complicate restructuring in the event of a much larger shock. Finally, the potential for governments to legislate institutional barriers to efficient recontracting cannot be discounted.

A FALSE DEBATE?

The upshot of this dynamic view of market evolution and contract design is that the benefits of a particular contract innovation are likely to erode over time.[18] Although better contracts should deliver better outcomes in terms of lower deadweight losses to creditors and sovereign borrowers, the size of those benefits will be subject to uncertainty.

In theory, we should be indifferent with respect to approaches if they result in the same outcome in equilibrium—defined such that neither the creditors nor the borrower seeks to modify the payment schedule (mutually agreed to in the case of voluntary outcomes or imposed in the case of statutory bankruptcy frameworks). This might be the case, say, if the obligations under debt contracts are articulated clearly and resulting rights over the sovereign's tax revenues so defined are effectively enforced.

In this regard, advocates of voluntary approaches implicitly invoke the so-called property rights school to support their case. In his pioneering paper, *The Problem of Social Costs*, Ronald Coase argued that, in the absence of transactions costs, bargaining between private parties will ensure the efficient allocation of resources, irrespective of the initial distribution of ownership rights.[19] In practice, however, as Arrow (1979) demonstrated, this proposition is equivalent to saying that the outcome is Pareto-optimal.[20]

This result depends critically on strict assumptions with respect to the information sets of the different players. Specifically, that every player knows every other player's payoff as a function of the strategies played—the offers and counteroffers that the other side will make in response to their offers. The failure of the underlying postulates of the bargaining approach can result in a situation in which the two sides get stuck in a Pareto-dominated point. The problem is that rather than converge on a stable equilibrium, successive iterations of offers and counteroffers are based on misperceptions of what the other side is prepared to accept. This could account for protracted sovereign debt restructurings in which economic losses grow and asset values shrink, ultimately resulting in restructurings that in the words of the IMF, are "too little, too late."[21]

More fundamentally, in contrast to the basic assumption of the property rights school, resource transfers from the debtor to the creditor are not well defined in the case of sovereign debt: there may well be ex ante agreement on payments between creditor and debtor, but there is weak enforcement ex post; indeed, in many jurisdictions, unenforceability is enshrined in law to promote the comity of nations.[22] Meanwhile, the "unintelligibility" of the legal rules governing sovereign restructuring, as one legal scholar characterizes the status quo, creates uncertainty that amounts to a transactions cost, violating the postulates of the Coase theorem.[23]

This discussion underscores a false dichotomy between "contractual" and "statutory" approaches and rightly emphasizes the issues of enforceability and limitation of contract design—practical problems that the property rights school assumes away by recourse to zero transactions costs and full information. There is reason to believe that Coase would approve of this focus on enforceability and contract design. Nearly thirty years after its publication, he feared his seminal paper had been misinterpreted.

He wrote, "Its influence on economic analysis has been less beneficial than I had hoped." His aim, he said, was not simply to describe what life would be in a world without transaction costs, but rather, "to make clear the role which transaction costs do, and should, play in the fashioning of the institutions which make up the economic system." What has become known since as the "Coasean World,"—where rational actors transact freely without need for institutions, firms, or even law—"is really the world of modern economic theory, one which I was hoping to persuade economists to leave."[24]

A Coasean perspective on sovereign debt restructuring recognizes that institutions, whether bankruptcy provisions embodied in formal treaty or promulgated through a "soft law" approach in the policies of existing international financial institutions, will influence the outcome of debt restructurings.[25] These policies jointly affect the pace and progress of the process. For example, strict access limits on the size of IMF support packages with clearly defined conditions for exceptional access could influence negotiations between sovereign borrowers and their creditors by anchoring expectations of IMF assistance in the event of severe balance of payment difficulties.[26] But absent some means to contain the fallout from limiting financing, attempts to impose strengthened access limits and constrain discretion may not be credible and would not, therefore, affect behavior. Similarly, an internationally recognized stay on litigation (or "standstill") sanctioned by the IMF or some other international body could allow for the orderly restructuring of claims and provide the sovereign time to introduce policies that "grow the pie" to the benefit of domestic citizens and foreign creditors alike. And IMF lending into arrears, which provides access to financing to avoid a draconian compression of imports, can be thought of as the analogue of debtor-in-possession financing for sovereigns.[27] IMF lending has potential external effects, however, in that its preferred creditor status can subordinate private claims and complicate debt restructurings, particularly if there is a nonnegligible probability that further restructuring may be required in the future.

In this world, the contractual approach and efforts to integrate key elements of domestic bankruptcy in the framework for sovereign debt restructuring are not mutually exclusive; in fact, they complement each other. This is observed at the domestic level, where bargaining occurs and voluntary debt restructurings are completed "in the shadow of the courthouse," because creditors and borrowers know the consequences of failure. The threat of an involuntary solution "through the courthouse" creates an incentive to do the deal privately, while well-developed legal rules reduce the uncertainty attached to potential outcomes and guide voluntary settlements.[28] The sovereign debt analogue, perhaps, is the risk that failure to reach agreement on a debt restructuring in the context of an IMF-supported program could lead to an economic collapse detrimental to all parties.

This Coasean perspective is also aligned with the agency costs approach to understanding the problems of sovereign debt and the role of the IMF.[29] In this approach, the IMF can act as a bonding mechanism to assist countries' access international capital markets by virtue of its superior monitoring ability derived from its ongoing policy dialogue and confidential discussions with national authorities. Committing to IMF-supported programs allows sovereign borrowers to benefit from higher levels of borrowing and on more favorable terms than would be possible without the IMF. The outstanding question, though, is whether there are additional public policy interventions that, in conjunction with traditional IMF support, could facilitate better outcomes should it be necessary to recontract a debt.[30]

So, where do we stand with respect to the contractual approach to sovereign debt restructuring?

We should, clearly, welcome the potential benefits from ICMA model clauses. The introduction of such clauses should mitigate some of the problems arising from the new challenges posed by the Greek restructuring and the litigation against Argentina. But it is both too early and too risky to declare that these clauses represent the best of all possible worlds. In the presence of weak enforcement and absent debt discharge, contractual approaches will necessarily be incomplete. Because sovereign debt contracts are incomplete, they will need to be restructured in the face, say, of severe negative shocks to output. Clear rules of the game—whether in formal statutory frameworks or in the policies adopted by the institutions of international cooperation—would provide guidance to this process and facilitate timely, orderly restructurings. In this respect, we need to understand the institutional environment in which these clauses are used and, where appropriate, make necessary changes to institutional practice, even if the political will does not exist to take more fundamental steps.

NOTES

Helpful comments from Martin Guzman, Paul Jenkins, Trevor Lessard, and Nicholas Marion are gratefully acknowledged. The usual caveat applies.

1. The Mexican bond was not the first to incorporate the revised clauses. A few days earlier Vietnam had made a private placement incorporating the ICMA clauses; Kazakhstan had also issued bonds that include most elements of the new terms prior to Mexico.

2. The apotheosis of the statutory approach was the proposal for a Sovereign Debt Restructuring Mechanism developed by IMF staff under the direction of then first deputy managing director Anne Krueger.

3. See the discussion in Ocampo (2016).

4. See IMF (2013).

5. The court's interpretation is such that, if Argentina pays 100 percent of the amounts owing on restructured bonds, it must pay 100 percent of the amounts owing on the un-restructured bonds held by the holdouts.

6. Haley (2014).

7. Gelpern (2013b).

8. Gelpern (2014).

9. In the March 2012 Greek restructuring, foreign (U.K.) law bonds were not restructured and were paid in full.

10. An excellent discussion of these issues is found in Makoff and Kahn (2015).

11. In effect, this feature replicates provisions in U.S. bankruptcy law under which all bonds are accelerated to par in the event of bankruptcy, putting all bondholders on an equal footing in the negotiation process.

12. Proposals for the further evolution of the contractual approach include an automatic standstill provision and creditor engagement clauses, requiring sovereign issuers to convene and negotiate with representative creditor committees as a condition of "good faith" negotiations. For a discussion of the potential benefits and drawbacks of creditor committees, see DeSieno (2016).

13. IMF (2014).

14. See Makoff and Kahn (2014). Pitchford and Wright (2010) have suggested, for example, that collective action clauses and other measures to facilitate timely, orderly restructurings increase the returns to holding out intended to extract greater returns from the sovereign.

15. Gelpern (2013a).

16. It is curious that appeals are made to the "sanctity of contracts" in this context. Contracts between private parties are amended under domestic bankruptcy laws, leaving the debtor in possession of the firm's assets when there is a public policy interest to do so and legal tests are met; it is unclear why a contract between a private creditor and sovereign government (representing social interests) should be inviolate.

17. The risk of such innovations is exacerbated by the problem of excessive debt accumulation arising from the absence of a clear priority of claim in sovereign debt. Bolton and Jeanne (2007), meanwhile, argue that sovereign lenders can increase the likelihood of repayment in the presence of weak contract enforcement by making their claims more difficult to restructure. While such contracts increase the debt capacity of the sovereign borrower in good times, they result in higher deadweight losses in bad states of the world in which a recontracting is required. More recently, Halonen-Akatwijuka and Hart (2013) have contended that parties may deliberately write incomplete contracts (or contracts that are less complete than is feasible). The intuition behind their result is that the specification of remedies in the event of a particular event may increase influence expectations with respect to events not subject to state-contingent clauses and lead to higher deadweight losses.

18. As an example, a legal ruling in London in July 2012 could potentially limit the use of exit consents—an innovative legal strategy that had facilitated many restructurings over the previous decade. Under exit consents, bondholders agreeing to a restructuring through a debt exchange simultaneously "consent" to amendments in the nonfinancial terms of the old bonds from which they are "exiting." These changes reduce the underlying value of the old bonds. Since changes to nonfinancial terms typically require a lower voting threshold, the use of exit consents had thus been an effective means to reduce the incentive to holdout. London courts struck down the use of exit consents on the grounds that they violated English law and the terms of the trust deed of the bonds under litigation. The judgment supported the claims of holdout investors that the clauses in question amounted to an abuse of power by the majority and were "oppressive and unfair" to the minority.

19. Coase (1960).

20. Arrow (1979). Pareto optimality implies that neither party can be made better off without putting the other in an inferior position. The proof is the "folk theorem" of cooperative games: both sides will continue to bargain and strike side agreements until there is no possible outcome that is preferred by either.

21. IMF (2013).

22. See, e.g., the U.S. Foreign Immunities Act.

23. See Gelpern (2013b). I am indebted to an anonymous reviewer for this point.

24. Extract from the University of Chicago Law School, "The Problem of Social Cost," Coase in memoriam, www.law.uchicago.edu/lawecon/coaseinmemoriam /problemofsocialcost.

25. For a discussion of the "soft law" approach, see Guzman and Stiglitz (2016).

26. See the discussion in Brooks and Lombardi (2016).

27. Under most domestic bankruptcy regimes, a court-sanctioned stay on proceedings and DIP financing reduces the costs of damaging creditor runs. Existing creditors benefit from the breathing space provided to the debtor to reorganize and propose an orderly restructuring to the benefit of all creditors; similarly, while new lending under DIP financing enjoys priority, it helps preserve the asset values of all creditors by, e.g., keeping the firm in operation, preserving the capital of the firm as a "going concern," and allowing for the introduction of measures to return the operation to profitability. Protection from litigation benefits creditors by preventing

the rush to the courthouse and the dissipation of asset values through a disruptive liquidation of assets under fire sale prices.

28. A sovereign debt forum—a venue for the sharing of information and a repository of sovereign debt restructuring "best practices"—could reduce uncertainty and facilitate timely debt restructurings by reducing information asymmetries and building trust. See Gitlin and House (2016).

29. Tirole (2002).

30. One possibility, in addition to calls for more work on mechanisms to facilitate restructuring, might be to provide guarantees on restructured debts to reduce the potential costs associated with serial restructuring. Uncertainty associated with the threat of future restructurings could be dissipated by breaking claims into two components. The first component would be a non-state-contingent element based on very robust assumptions (to avoid a "balanced on a knife-edge" scenario), which would benefit from the guarantee. The second component would entail a state-contingent element providing upside returns to creditors in the event of stronger-than-expected growth owing to favorable shocks, with the IMF performing monitoring and third-party verification in accordance with its role in addressing agency problems.

REFERENCES

Arrow, Kenneth J. 1979. "The Property Rights Doctrine and Demand Revelation Under Incomplete Information." In *Economics and Human Welfare*, ed. M. Boskin. New York, Academic Press: 23–39.

Bolton, Patrick, and Olivier Jeanne. August 2007. "Structuring and Restructuring Sovereign Debt: The Role of Bankruptcy Regime." International Monetary Fund Working Paper WP/07/192, Washington, D.C.

Brooks, Skylar, and Domenico Lombardi. 2016. "Private Creditor Power and the Politics of Sovereign Debt Governance." In *Too Little, Too Late: The Quest to Resolve Sovereign Debt Crises*, ed. Martin Guzman, José Antonio Ocampo, and Joseph E. Stiglitz, chapter 3. New York: Columbia University Press.

Coase, Ronald. 1960. "The Problem of Social Costs." *Journal of Law and Economics* 3 (October): 1–44.

De Sieno, Timothy. 2016. "Creditor Committees in Sovereign Debt Restructurings: Understanding the Benefits and Addressing Concerns." In *Too Little, Too Late: The Quest to Resolve Sovereign Debt Crises*, ed. Martin Guzman, José Antonio Ocampo, and Joseph E. Stiglitz, chapter 9. New York: Columbia University Press.

Gelpern, Anna. 2013a. "Contract Hope and Sovereign Redemption." *Capital Markets Law Journal* 8 (no. 2): 132–148.

——. 2013b. "A Skeptic's Case for Sovereign Bankruptcy." *Houston Law Review* 50: 1095–1127.

——. 2014. "ICMA CACs v. 2.0: Mexico Moves in New York." *Credit Slips*, November 10.

Guzman, Martin, and Joseph E. Stiglitz. 2016. "Creating a Framework for Sovereign Debt Restructuring That Works." In *Too Little, Too Late: The Quest to Resolve*

Sovereign Debt Crises, ed. Martin Guzman, José Antonio Ocampo, and Joseph E. Stiglitz, chapter 1. New York: Columbia University Press.

Haley, James A. May 2014. "Sovereign Debt Restructuring: Old Debates, New Challenges." CIGI Papers No. 32, Waterloo, Ont.

Haley, James A., Halonen-Akatwijuka, Maija, and Oliver D. Hart. April 2013. "More Is Less: Why Parties May Deliberately Write Incomplete Contracts." NBER Working Paper 19001, Cambridge, Mass.

International Monetary Fund. 2013, April 26. "Sovereign Debt Restructuring—Recent Developments and Implications for the Fund's Legal and Policy Framework." Washington, D.C.: https://www.imf.org/external/np/pp/eng/2013/042613.pdf.

——. October 2014. "Strengthening the Contractual Framework to Address Collective Action Problems in Sovereign Debt Restructuring." Washington, D.C.: https://www.imf.org/external/np/pp/eng/2014/090214.pdf.

Makoff, Gregory, and Robert Kahn. *Sovereign Bond Contract Reform: Implementing the ICMA Pari Passu and Collective Action Clauses*, CIGI paper no. 56, February 6, 2015: https://www.cigionline.org/publications/sovereign-bond-contract-reform -implementing-new-icma-pari-passu-and-collective-action-c.

Ocampo, José Antonio. 2016. "A Brief History of Sovereign Debt Resolution and a Proposal for a Multilateral Instrument." In *Too Little, Too Late: The Quest to Resolve Sovereign Debt Crises*, ed. Martin Guzman, José Antonio Ocampo, and Joseph E. Stiglitz, chapter 10. New York: Columbia University Press.

Pitchford, Rohan, and Mark L. J. Wright. December 2010. "Holdout in Sovereign Debt Restructuring: A Theory of Negotiation in a Weak Contract Environment." NBER Working Paper 16632, Cambridge, Mass.

Tirole, Jean. 2002. *Financial Crises, Liquidity Provision and the International Monetary System*. Princeton, N.J.: Princeton University Press.

CHAPTER 9

Creditor Committees in Sovereign Debt Restructurings

UNDERSTANDING THE BENEFITS AND ADDRESSING CONCERNS

Timothy B. DeSieno

It is not difficult to argue that creditor committees are the single most useful tool for addressing current concerns about sovereign debt restructuring. Sovereign creditors are frequently concerned that restructurings inadequately address their commercial and process concerns, in some recent cases leading to restructurings that impose concessions that unfairly impinge their interests. Sovereign issuers are frequently concerned that their ability to achieve important creditor concessions is impaired when their debt is in the form of widely held bonds, and real creditors may be hard to identify and to locate for purposes of understanding concerns and preferences. Both constituencies are concerned by what is currently labeled "the holdout problem," which describes the ability of some bondholders not to agree to a proposed restructuring and instead to seek to collect on their unrestructured claims, potentially disrupting others' agreed objectives.

Many stakeholders and experts are debating how to address these concerns. Proposals range from International Monetary Fund (IMF)–required debt reprofiling, to enhanced collective action clauses, to revised pari passu clauses, to an independent forum of experts, to a system of mandatory mediation. Each of these ideas has merits and drawbacks, and there would seem to be sense in examining all possibly useful tools.

I contend, however, that most key players in the field are paying too little attention to creditor committees, even though such committees are the tool that has enabled most consistent and effective progress on these concerns throughout the history of restructuring *bond* debt. Many leading organizations have long advocated the central importance of creditor committees in debt restructuring exercises.[1] There is no reason for any deviation from that viewpoint just because the debt in question happens to have been issued by a sovereign instead of a private entity. The brief outline below may aid in assessing known benefits and means for addressing perceived drawbacks of creditor committees.

KNOWN BENEFITS

COMMITTEES STREAMLINE A RESTRUCTURING PROCESS FOR ISSUERS

The formation of a representative committee provides an issuer a credible, user-friendly, single forum in which to make proposals and to advance its interests.[2] If a committee includes representatives of the key stakeholders, and if it is well-advised, the committee can work to build intercreditor consensus, removing the complexity of that task from the issuer. In addition, consensus is usually speedier via a committee, as most creditors will usually feel they can trust "a group of their own" more readily than they can trust the issuer. This dynamic enables an efficient process that imposes less administrative burden on the issuer. The recent cases of Greece and Belize, while perhaps subject to criticism for other reasons, have demonstrated how committees can form and serve this useful purpose in modern sovereign bond restructurings.[3]

COMMITTEES REDRESS INFORMATION IMBALANCES

A primary reason for creditors to organize in connection with a restructuring exercise is to counteract the natural information imbalance that exists between issuers, who are closely familiar with the details of their own affairs, and creditors, who are not close to the day-to-day governance of an issuer. In order to ensure an issuer shares a universe of broadly useful information, it helps if a representative group of creditors can assemble and agree on what is needed. With that agreement, the issuer can be confident that information requests are targeted and are not overly time-consuming, ad hoc, or designed to gather unnecessary or even strategically harmful information. The mission of the committee is to amass sufficient detail to negotiate a reasonable deal, based on expectations that are as matched as possible with those of the issuer. The best pathway to matching expectations is to match information bases sensibly. Experience with committees demonstrates their efficiency in this work. Again, the recent cases of Greece and Belize, in addition to the ongoing work in the case of Grenada, demonstrate that committees play a constructive role in the informational aspects of modern sovereign debt restructurings.[4]

COMMITTEES ENABLE CONFIDENTIALITY

As in any debt restructuring exercise, confidentiality is key to a successful sovereign debt restructuring. No stakeholder wants confidential information leaked to the public that could harm the issuer or that could harmfully affect the progress of restructuring discussions. All stakeholders will understandably be concerned about the risk that discussions with multiple bondholders could lead to information leaks, even in the absence of bad intentions. A committee helps address this risk, first by limiting the number of creditors with whom the issuer shares information. Second, committee members would ordinarily sign a confidentiality agreement that prohibits dissemination of confidential information except via agreed mechanics, using agreed materiality considerations, and at agreed times. These arrangements enable a more robust exchange of information, which in turn enables better matching of expectations, which in turn enables more efficient deal making.[5]

COMMITTEES ENHANCE SUPPORT FOR CONSENSUAL DEALS (MINIMIZING HOLDOUTS)

Perhaps the most fundamental benefit of a committee is the weight its views can lend to other creditors' favorable consideration of a proposed restructuring (or of an interim standstill or a temporary payment cessation; if such steps are demonstrably sensible, committees can support their implementation as well, and that support will be more persuasive to other creditors than any ex ante, rules-based equivalent). In amassing support for a proposed deal (or other interim step), and in diminishing the attraction of a creditor holdout strategy, the supportive views of a well-crafted and well-informed creditor committee are unmatchable. If creditors understand that a committee has been close to the design of the proposed terms, that the committee consists of creditors whose interests are the same as theirs (or at least clearly aligned with them), and that the committee supports the proposed terms as being reasonably fair and sustainable in the circumstances, then creditors take enhanced comfort that they too should support the proposal. On the other hand, creditors often suspect that a proposal designed without meaningful and organized input from a committee is more likely to favor those stakeholders who *did* design the terms, likely impairing the (absent) creditors disproportionately. Such suspicions, especially if reasonably grounded in the publicly available information, can materially enhance the attraction of a holdout strategy. In general, a creditor will select a holdout strategy only if it is confident that its rights otherwise would be impaired disproportionately, and if the holdout strategy includes a cost-effective means for recapturing some of the lost value. Creditors do not choose a holdout strategy lightly, and meaningful involvement and support from a demonstrably capable committee make holding out all the less interesting or attractive.

ADDRESSING PERCEIVED DRAWBACKS

DO COMMITTEES SLOW PROGRESS TOWARD A DEAL?

It is sometimes asserted that committees slow progress toward a restructuring proposal. First, there is a fear that a committee can be slow to form as creditors assess how best to advance their interests. In times of crisis, the delay can be damaging. Second, it can take time to engage a committee and to advance the diligence, confidentiality, and negotiating processes that are involved.

On the first point, practical experience is different: creditors are usually ready to organize quickly once it is clear there is work to be done. Often, such an organization forms within hours or days of relevant developments or announcements. On the other hand, if a committee is slow to form, there would be no need for an issuer to slow its own restructuring efforts. Either way, there is no need to lose time over committee formation.

On the second point, it is important to examine the costs and benefits of the alternatives to a committee. In the absence of a committee, does the issuer plan a series of informal consultations with creditors, and how much time will that effort take, especially if larger creditors require more than one consultation as the process unfolds? But also, how successful would a noncommittee process be? If a noncommittee process leads to market suspicion and material holdouts, especially if material creditor concessions are proposed, those results will counterbalance any perceived increase in speed gained by declining to engage a committee.

DO COMMITTEES INCREASE THE EXPENSE OF A DEAL?

It is sometimes asserted that committees increase the expense of a restructuring deal. Most usually, committees engage expert advisers, financial and legal, to aid them in their work. These advisers come with a cost, and the issuer is asked to bear that cost. Of course, it is difficult to argue with the idea that there is an expense entailed in dealing with a committee. But issuers readily accept this cost in the end, at least when the advisers' work helps lead to a deal that is widely supported by the creditor community, enabling the issuer to achieve its larger goals. The added expense always pales in comparison to the benefit of a successful deal, especially one that follows the best practices of creditor engagement the IMF, the World Bank, and INSOL International generally advocate. At the same time, it is important that committees' expenses be carefully controlled. In addition to a possible expense-management function of an overarching body that might play a useful role on this subject, committees themselves are powerful regulators of the expense of the restructuring exercise. Committees know that all stakeholders ultimately bear the cost of any expense, even if the issuer pays. Practical experience shows that committees limit their advisers' roles to their pure areas of expertise, and committees are increasingly in the habit of requiring budgets and cost efficiency of their advisers.

DO COMMITTEES OVERLY EXPAND CREDITORS' POWER?

Some are of the opinion that a creditor committee may overly strengthen the position of a sovereign's creditors, weakening an issuer's ability to achieve needed creditor concessions. One could surely posit scenarios in which a committee might enhance already existing power of a sovereign's creditors in ways that could potentially be dangerous. For example, any group of creditors that alone has the power to materially affect new lending to a sovereign might be overly empowered by a committee, which could institutionalize such power. In the era before Brady bonds, for example, when private sector lending to sovereigns was driven by globally powerful banks, we could imagine a sovereign becoming concerned. On the other hand, in today's world of sovereign bond issuances, widely disbursed bond holdings, and few, if any, incentives or mechanics for investors to cooperate to "blacklist" any country, we contend any parallel fears are overdone. With the exception of Argentina, to whom most investors are agreed further sovereign lending is unwise (in no small part due to Argentina's very decision to advance its proposed restructuring while declining to engage any creditor committees), investment views about any given country can vary quite widely among investors in both primary and secondary markets. Investors simply lack the concentrated power that global banking syndicates once enjoyed.

HOW CAN COMMITTEES BE SUPERVISED?

Some have also asked whether it would be possible to standardize and to supervise committee behavior so as to provide comfort to issuers that committees will be predictably constructive. Practical experience indicates that creditors in general are quite effective at regulating their own activities, including tempering hostile actions against a stressed issuer. Committees tend to behave responsibly toward the objective of maximizing value sustainably in light of the known economic dynamics and constraints.

On the other hand, a creditor committee is by definition an advocate for creditors, and issuers might gain comfort from knowing creditor committees have to abide by an agreed set of operating rules. It is exactly this idea that motivated our proposed amendment to the IMF's lending into arrears policy on the topic (which is attached hereto as Appendix A). The attached document regulates important items such as (1) committee formation and representativeness, (2) the terms on which an issuer is to reimburse a committee's expenses, (3) the means for ensuring the issuer's confidential information remains confidential, and (4) the core operations of the committee, such as refraining from litigation, maximizing speed and minimizing cost, and supporting agreed terms with other creditors. Between creditors' genuine responsibility and regulations such as these, committees would be empowered to serve their core functions of enabling restructuring deals and minimizing holdouts.

Still, it would seem to be sensible to examine the possibility of establishing a supervisory body that would observe issuer-committee restructuring efforts and assist in maintaining a constructive approach and resolving disputes (e.g., the "Standing Committee" mentioned in Appendix A). Any body tasked to do that work must be (1) demonstrably expert in debt restructuring and (2) just as importantly, fully impartial— it cannot be a body that has any current stake in sovereign debt, such as any of the existing multilaterals or the Paris Club or the London Club.

OTHER CONCERNS

In a 2009 paper, Lee Buchheit listed a collection of "Potential Drawbacks" to a creditor committee in a sovereign debt restructuring.[6] To the extent not already addressed above, each is discussed briefly below.

First is a concern that that once a sovereign engages a committee, it is difficult "to divorce" that committee. Aside from the healthy disciplining effect such a limit might have were it to be true, issuers in the past have indeed disengaged from creditor committees when the process was insufficient or unsatisfactory to the issuer. That outcome is not ideal, but declining to get married because divorce is difficult might not be the best reasoning.

Second is a concern that different constituencies might form committees, and it might be difficult to coordinate them all. Aside from the point that it would be even more difficult to coordinate the multiplicity of creditors without any semblance of organization, there is the well-known mechanism of establishing an umbrella committee, with subcommittees as needed, to offer the best streamlining possible.[7]

Third is a concern is that committee membership may shift over time. Aside from asking why the changing of one or more seats in a committee should be problematic so long as the committee remains representative, it is worth noting this concern is inconsistent with practical experience. Serving on a committee entails material trading limits for a creditor, since a committee member is generally exposed to inside information. A creditor chooses to get on a committee only after carefully considering the impact on its trading strategy, and no creditor changes this decision lightly.

Fourth is a concern that committee members will misuse confidential information. Aside from asking for examples of bondholder committee members behaving in that way in the current regulatory environment (none have been reported), it is worth noting there is nothing unique about sovereigns that makes this risk any higher than it is in any other context, say in connection with a corporate debtor, where nobody seems to oppose committees.

In sum, each of these concerns can be addressed by stakeholders who desire to do so, as part of a good faith effort to strike a reasonable and sustainable restructuring deal.

CONCLUSION

Practical experience working with creditor committees over the past several decades affirms their constructive approach and their utility to a good faith issuer that really wants to achieve consensus on a fair and sustainable debt restructuring. Certainly, the committee process can raise concerns, and effort to address those concerns is worthwhile. Standardization and even supervision would seem to be worth exploring. But it is those topics toward which the energy of debate should be directed, and not toward a continued discussion about whether committees should be used at all. Committees are too valuable to the restructuring process, and in time they will be found to exceed any of the other tools under discussion for addressing identified risks and achieving prompt, fair, and sustainable debt restructuring.

Outline of Proposed Amendment to IMF Policy on Support for Governments Restructuring Sovereign Bond Debt

1. **General.** No government shall be entitled (a) to restructure its sovereign bond debt and (b) to enjoy any new financial support from the IMF, from and after the date (the "Commencement Date") that the IMF first discovers that such government plans or intends to restructure its sovereign bond debt, unless such government shall have fully complied with either the "Committee Guidelines" or the "Publication Guidelines" below. To the extent the IMF's lending into arrears rules are implicated, a government's compliance with these Guidelines shall be deemed to constitute its "good faith effort."[8]

2. **Committee Guidelines.** Unless the government shall fully comply with the "Publication Guidelines" below:

   a. If a single bondholder committee (a "Committee") that includes holders not affiliated with the government of at least [25]% of the government's total external bond debt shall not have formed within [__] days of the publication of the Commencement Date, the government may proceed to restructure its sovereign bond debt in any legal manner.

   b. If a single Committee shall have formed within [__] days of the publication of the Commencement Date, the government shall engage and finance (as defined below) the Committee. If the Government believes it would be useful, (using form documents to be designed) the government may finance a meeting of bondholders—or a series of them in the case of multiple bond issues—convened for the purpose of authorizing the Committee to act, although in a nonbinding fashion, on behalf of all bondholders in the restructuring discussions. Unless a committee's role shall have been expressly rejected at a quorate bondholders' meeting, such a committee shall be deemed to be the Committee for purposes of these Guidelines.

c. For purposes of these Guidelines, "engage and finance" shall mean:

- execute a letter agreement (the "Committee Letter Agreement") with representatives of the Committee (using a form document to be designed) containing the government's commitment to work with the Committee toward a consensual deal and to reimburse the Committee's reasonable expenses for so long as the government shall be in discussions with the IMF, subject to earlier termination upon completion of the bond-related deal;

- provided the Committee engages legal advisers within [__] days of its formation, execute a letter agreement with one legal advisory team (using a form document to be designed) containing the government's commitment to pay the reasonable cost of the advisory team's services;

- either publish all documents in accordance with the "Publication Guidelines" below or execute a confidentiality agreement with representatives of the Committee (using a form document to be designed) committing to share confidential information with self-selected "restricted" Committee representatives for a limited period and committing to publish all shared material nonpublic information on an agreed schedule; and

- timely abide its undertakings in each of the foregoing agreements and negotiate in good faith with the Committee toward a consensual deal that (i) is based on the collection of information that the government has shared with its creditors, (ii) respects contractual rights, (iii) includes and is based on an agreed set of governmental policies and policy reforms, (iv) is designed to match the parties' views of the government's debt sustainability, (v) provides comparable treatment to all types and classes of debt claims, and (vi) is solicited and documented in full consultation with the Committee and its advisers.

3. **Committee Responsibilities.** For so long as the government is in compliance with the Committee Guidelines above, and for as long as the Committee Letter Agreement remains in effect, the Committee shall be obligated to undertake the following actions (which shall be specified in the Committee Letter Agreement):

   a. The Committee shall serve as the representative for bondholders in the restructuring discussion process, cooperating with the government and the other creditors in a good faith effort to achieve agreement.

   b. The Committee and its members shall refrain from litigation or other collection activity against the government, and consistent with market practice, the Committee shall support the government in opposition to the litigation or collection activity of other bondholders.

   c. The Committee shall cooperate with the government in the sharing of confidential information in a manner that assists the Committee in its deliberations, and the Committee shall strictly honor its confidentiality undertakings at all times.

   d. Consistent with market practice, the Committee shall assist the government in attempting to build market consensus in support of any proposals that the government and the Committee jointly support.

   e. Consistent with market practice, the Committee shall cooperate with the government in a reasonable way so as to maximize the speed of the restructuring process and to minimize its cost.

4. **Publication Guidelines.** Unless the government shall fully comply with the "Committee Guidelines" above:

   a. The government shall provide to the IMF written permission (using a form document to be designed) to publish on the IMF website (i) every document that the government provides to the IMF from and after the Commencement Date through the date of publication of the exchange offer or equivalent, except to the extent that a confidentiality-bound standing committee of investor representatives (the "Standing Committee"), in consultation with the IMF staff, determines that a document is not relevant or material to the consideration of any proposed restructuring terms and (ii) every document delivered to the IMF within the [__] days prior to the Commencement Date that the Standing Committee, in consultation with the IMF staff, determines is relevant or material to the consideration of any proposed restructuring term.

The IMF shall have so published each such document within [__] days of having received such document (or the written permission to publish, if later).

NOTES

1. See, e.g., International Monetary Fund Legal Department, Orderly & Effective Insolvency Procedures (Washington, D.C., 1999); World Bank, The World Bank Principles for Effective Insolvency and Creditor Rights Systems (Washington, D.C., December 21, 2005); and INSOL International, Statement of Principles for a Global Approach to Multi-Creditor Workouts (London, 2000).

2. A creditor committee is an informal group of holders of debt obligations who agree to work together to communicate with and negotiate with their common debtor. The committee is normally not imbued with any special power or ability to bind anybody. Instead, a committee's power and influence is informal and derives from the size of the aggregate amount of debt that its members hold; if they hold a lot, their views will not only be representative, but they may alone go a long way toward being sufficient creditor support for any given restructuring proposal that the debtor may propose.

3. In both cases, the issuers achieved meaningful debt relief in a process that involved engagement with a committee, for which the committees expressed their support.

4. The Grenada Note Holder committee has engaged in meaningful diligence, with the support of a committee advisory team and the cooperation of the Grenada authorities.

5. There is a great deal of convergence in the form and text of these confidentiality agreements, even if they have become somewhat more complex in the wake of certain U.S. court rulings in corporate Chapter 11 proceedings.

6. Lee C. Buchheit, "Use of Creditor Committees in Sovereign Debt Workouts," Business Law International 10 (2009): 205.

7. Umbrella committees consist of representatives from multiple creditor constituencies who all agree to work together as a single unit facing the issuer. The theory is the streamlining effect of such a unified organization can make for more efficient discussions. Usually, the various constituencies that make up such an umbrella committee will coordinate (and negotiate) among themselves as needed and then present a common front to the issue.

8. Accordingly, these guidelines will require augmentation so as to include other relevant aspects of the "good faith effort" already prescribed by the IMF.

PART IV

Proposals for a Multinational Framework for Sovereign Debt Restructuring

PRINCIPLES, ELEMENTS, AND INSTITUTIONALIZATION

CHAPTER 10

A Brief History of Sovereign Debt Resolution and a Proposal for a Multilateral Instrument

José Antonio Ocampo

The global financial architecture cannot rely exclusively on emergency lending to manage sovereign debt crises for two major reasons. First, emergency lending may result in unsustainable levels of external indebtedness. Second, it may generate moral hazard for creditors, as official emergency lending is very often used to effectively bail out the private sector. Furthermore, the absence of an effective debt workout mechanism forces debtors to adopt excessively contractionary adjustment policies during crises, which may have negative long-term effects in terms of access to and cost of financing. The international financial architecture must, therefore, have both emergency financing mechanisms to manage situations of illiquidity and debt workouts to manage unsustainable debt burdens. The dividing line between the two has been traditionally been seen as that between "liquidity" and "solvency," but this line is not easy to draw, as in many cases the lack of liquidity financing may lead to insolvency. In fact, one of the major arguments in favor of emergency financing is to prevent problems of illiquidity from turning into insolvency.

The only regular mechanism of this type in place is the Paris Club, which deals exclusively with official creditors. The system has otherwise relied on ad hoc arrangements and voluntary renegotiations. It also relies on informal and imperfect coordination of debtors and creditors, complementary bilateral and multilateral financing, and International Monetary Fund (IMF) guidance. However, the problem with this patchy "non-system" is that debt restructurings generally (or even always) come too late, after overindebtedness has had devastating effects on countries and thus on their capacity to service debts. This is also an inefficient outcome from the point of view of creditors, as it reduces the effective value of their assets. It is also horizontally inequitable, as it does not treat all debtors or all creditors uniformly.

A BRIEF HISTORY OF DEBT RESOLUTION AND
THE RISE OF THE CURRENT "NON-SYSTEM"

Debt defaults and renegotiations have a long history, which matches the sequence of boom-bust cycles of international finance. Before the Second World War, the typical mechanism was voluntary negotiations between creditors and sovereign states, followed (if they failed) by intergovernmental arbitration—but also, and on more than a few occasions, by military intervention.[1] Interestingly, when the latter did not happen, this regime tended to grant greater degrees of relief from private creditors than the current system, but only after lengthy lags in negotiations, which allowed arrears to accumulate to the point where they even exceeded the original principal (Suter and Stamm, 1992). Furthermore, the mix of default and debt renegotiations often produced a better result for debtor countries than the current system in both macroeconomic performance during default and the debt burden after renegotiations. This comes across clearly in a comparison of Latin America in the 1930s versus the 1980s: default was one of the mechanisms that supported recovery during the 1930s, whereas debt service was a major drag in the 1980s; in turn, the debt renegotiations after the 1930s default were more generous than those that took place under the Brady Plan in the early 1990s (Ocampo, 2014).

The destruction of international finance during the Great Depression led to the absence of significant private financing for several decades and, consequently, of demands for sovereign debt workouts. Because official financing became the dominant form of financing, renegotiations with official creditors took center stage. The mechanism created was the Paris Club, which emerged out of Argentina's traumatic renegotiations with creditors in 1956 but became a regular institution thereafter, although its agreements have never had a clear legal status. With the reconstruction of an international private financing mechanism in the 1960s, boom-bust cycles of financing came back and with them defaults and debt renegotiations. The boom in financing to developing countries was very strong in the 1970s, particularly in the second half of the decade, when it was associated with the recycling of petrodollars. This was followed by the first contemporary phase of debt renegotiations, which started in the late 1970s and peaked in the 1980s (Panizza, Sturzenegger, and Zettlemeyer, 2009; Cruces and Trebesch, 2013).

The "London Clubs" were set up in the late 1970s to renegotiate bank debts; these are not a formal arrangement but a generic name for a mechanism of voluntary debt renegotiations, similar to the procedure followed before the Second World War. However, negotiations with private creditors in the 1980s were mainly done under the leadership of the U.S. government and with support from the IMF, which followed at the time a policy of not lending to countries that were in arrears with private creditors. Although creditor committees played a central role in coordinating banks, the positive view taken by their leaders as a mechanism to facilitate the return of market access and growth (Rhodes, 2011) contrasts with the perception of them as a mechanism that tilted the negotiation in favor of creditors and, in any case, did not produce either growth or a rapid return to markets (Ocampo, 2014). Rather, an alternative perception of the way the Latin American debt crisis was managed in the 1980s is that it was successful in avoiding a banking crisis in the United States, but only by displacing its effects to debtor countries.

Indeed, the failure of the early waves of reschedulings (Devlin, 1989) finally led U.S. authorities to promote complementary mechanisms: additional financing through the 1985 Baker Plan and an ad hoc debt relief initiative, the Brady Plan, in 1989. The latter became one of the sources of the new wave of renegotiations in the first half of the 1990s. It provided limited relief, particularly when compared with the renegotiations of the 1930s defaults in the 1940s and 1950s, but it helped create a bond market for emerging-country debt that became the framework for renewed financing in the 1990s. It also led to a change in IMF policy in favor of the principle of "lending into arrears," which was also adopted in 1989, accepting the principle that the IMF could finance countries in arrears so long as they continued to negotiate with creditors "in good faith"; it was modified in 1998–1999 to include bonds and a less stringent interpretation of what negotiating in good faith means (IMF, 2002). However, neither the Brady Plan nor the related policy of lending into arrears served, as could have been possible, as a framework to develop a multilateral debt workout mechanism, a proposal that was at the center of recommendations by some institutions since the 1980s—notably the United Nations Conference on Trade and Development (UNCTAD).

A new wave of defaults and renegotiations would soon come as the result of a sequence of crises in the emerging economies unleashed in East Asia in 1997. Many took the form of voluntary reschedulings, specifically debt exchanges in which bumps in the debt service schedule were smoothed out, with maturities effectively extended. Since these reschedulings were voluntary, the terms of the new bonds had to be attractive enough to induce creditors to participate. So as Spiegel (2010) has shown, even in cases when some investors experienced short-term losses, returns to investors were quite good over the long term. A few, more traumatic renegotiations did provide larger relief, particularly those with Russia in 1998 and Argentina in 2005 and 2010. As discussed later in this chapter, the latter took center stage in recent debates as a result of successful demands by holdouts in U.S. courts in 2012–2013.

In the case of low-income countries, public sector financing continued to play the major role. The problems of their indebtedness led to years of serial rescheduling at the Paris Club, accompanied by new credit leading to debt overhangs. Under strong pressure from civil society (particularly the Jubilee 2000 Alliance), these countries became the focus of another ad hoc initiative: the Heavily Indebted Poor Countries Initiative (better known by the acronym HIPC), launched in 1996 and strengthened in 1999, and the subsequent Multilateral Debt Relief Initiative (MDRI) of 2005. The major differences between these initiatives and the Brady Plan were their focus on low-income countries and the inclusion of relief and later of write-offs of multilateral debts.

THE PROBLEMS OF THE CURRENT NON-SYSTEM AND THE CASE FOR A DEBT WORKOUT MECHANISM

The existing framework mixes, therefore, the Paris Club for official debts, voluntary renegotiations with private creditors, and occasional ad hoc debt relief initiatives (the Brady Plan and HIPC/MDRI). It has two fundamental deficiencies.

First, as the IMF (2013: 1, 7, 15) has recognized, "debt restructurings have often been too little and too late." This view is shared by many other analysts (see, e.g., Bucheit et al., 2013). In fact, on several occasions, renegotiations (including those within the Paris Club) have been a way of postponing rather than solving the problem. Furthermore, due to limited relief offered at each stage, renegotiations have frequently been sequential, effectively postponing their potential benefits. The debt overhang that persists for several years has devastating effects on countries but also has adverse effects on creditors, given the limited capacity of debtors to pay. In short, the current non-system does not guarantee a "fresh start" or a "clean slate," the conditions that are generally identified as the basic characteristics of a good bankruptcy procedure at the national level.

The second deficiency is that existing mechanisms do not guarantee equitable treatment, neither of different debtors nor of different creditors. Indeed, a repeated criticism of the member countries of the Paris Club members is that private creditors do not accept the restructuring conditions agreed by the members of the club, while still benefiting from the reduction of the burden on debtor countries (an issue that was particularly important in the HIPC Initiative). In turn, private creditors argue that they are forced to take larger haircuts in cases in which the Paris Club only agrees to reschedule payments (the typical situation in the case of middle-income countries), as the capacity to pay private debts is reduced by limited growth, the lack of official debt reductions, *and* the "preferred creditor status" of multilateral financial institutions.

The case for an orderly debt workout mechanism can thus be made on both efficiency and equity grounds (Stiglitz, 2010). From the point of view of efficiency in debt markets, it would guarantee appropriate incentives for creditors and debtors to negotiate good contracts, allowing both to properly assess the risks they are incurring and recoveries in case of default, and thus to estimate the adequate risk spreads of the particular loan or bond issue. Creditors should also feel sufficient confidence that their property rights are adequately protected in case of default. At the same time, the rules should avoid incentives for the borrower, if it runs into difficulties, to unduly postpone the decision to renegotiate or default, as that would also undermine the asset values of creditors.

In turn, equity considerations require that all debtors and creditors be treated equitably, which should include seniority principles for different obligations—in particular, seniority for financing that is made available during the period of restructuring. In turn, this requires the system to avoid free riders and, particularly, to eliminate the capacity of holdouts to initiate legal disputes that affect the interests of creditors who participate in well-structured collective action. Equity conditions also require that a debtor does not offer exceptional prerogatives to creditors who provide financing at high costs when it starts to face payment difficulties, as this would undermine the asset value of other creditors.

Obviously, well-structured contracts are an essential element of capital markets. However, it would be impossible to include all possible contingencies in contracts. It would also be costly or outright impossible for individual creditors to monitor all other debt contracts a debtor has incurred. Furthermore, different contracts would not necessarily be consistent with one another and they could also vary according to different legal traditions. For all these reasons, negotiations have to be considered a normal way of handling unforeseen events and, if such events happen, to aggregate claims under rules that are fair and respected by all parties. In short, a well-functioning debt workout regime can actually reduce risks and transaction costs, even in the case of unexpected events that may lead to default.

A major issue is whether a potential debt workout mechanism could generate moral hazard for either debtors or creditors. Given the view of many debtors that the negotiations with creditor committees are imbalanced and, particularly, that IMF support comes with strong conditionality, it is quite unlikely that the expectation of debt restructuring would generate incentives to overborrow. Indeed, as already noted, experience indicates that borrowing countries tend rather to postpone the use of restructuring mechanisms, largely to maintain good relations and avoid confrontation with private creditors. In the words of Bucheit and colleagues (2013: V), "incentives are stacked against timely recognition and restructuring of unsustainable debts."

There might be more significant moral hazard concerns in relation to lenders, particularly for those who consciously incur in risks because they perceive that they can sell their assets before an eventual default. But even these concerns are unlikely to be important relative to the really important fact: the "contagion of optimism" that characterizes booms, followed by the opposite "contagion of pessimism" that characterizes busts, with herding behavior generating the associated boom-bust cycles. In short, the way in which overborrowing is monitored during booms to prevent crises should, of course, be a major concern of macroeconomic policy and of international cooperation, and it is unlikely that a properly designed debt workout mechanism would worsen the moral hazard problem. Indeed, overborrowing has generally been present in a system that lacks such a mechanism.

However, creditors' moral hazard issues can become a major problem when a crisis erupts and there are expectations that official resources will be supplied. Under these circumstances, a delay in debt restructuring does represent a bailout of private creditors, with the flight of private capital forcing a larger amount of official financing. If the debt is in fact unsustainable, official financing will have "socialized" private obligations. This situation will also force creditors who have not jumped the ship to incur larger debt losses in the case of a restructuring, thus generating major intercreditor equity issues. This creates a strong argument for timely actions to manage unsustainable debt burdens. The management of the 2010–2012 Greek crisis can be considered one of the best examples in history of a situation in which delay in debt restructuring led to a major socialization of debts by eurozone governments and institutions, under conditions that, moreover, left the country with debt ratios that most analysts considered unsustainable.

INCOMPLETE REFORM EFFORTS IN RECENT DECADES

The lack of a multilateral framework for dealing with international debt crises involving private creditors has been a major concern of many analysts in recent decades. Thus, since the 1970s there have been multiple proposals to create international debt/bankruptcy courts or forums for mediation or eventual arbitration of problems of overindebtedness. These initiatives proliferated after the 1994 Mexican crisis and especially after the 1997 Asian crisis. The corresponding proposals came from both the political right, who consider the elimination of moral hazard associated with public guarantees to private credits is an essential prerequisite for the good functioning of financial markets, as well as from the left, who saw excess debt levels as a strong obstacle to development.

The major initiative at the time was the decision of the G10 central bank deputies to launch in February 1995 a G10 working party, whose May 1996 report proposed introducing new provisions in bond contracts—collective action clauses (CACs), though they were not named as such in the report—to facilitate consultations and cooperation in the event of a crisis (G10, 1996). The report was based, in turn, on proposals by Eichengreen and Portes (1995). In the late 1990s, this view was aided by the frustration of Paris Club members with the unwillingness of private creditors to cooperate with the club's relief efforts. Although this initiative continued to be in the background, thanks to European support, it never received the explicit endorsement of the U.S. Treasury (Gelpern and Gulati, 2010). The inability to agree on the generalization of CACs was paradoxical, given the fact that there was already a tradition of using such provisions in London bond issues, in which creditor coordination is handled by a trustee who is given the prerogative of negotiating or initiating legal proceedings. Most sovereign bonds, however, were issued under New York law and required unanimous consent for their financial terms to be changed; moreover, the fiscal agents that distributed payments from the debtor in New York bonds did not have the powers of the trustee under British law. It could be added that creditors felt well protected by New York law, under which bond contract conditions were very difficult to change, at least until they faced actual defaults.

In turn, the major attempt to negotiate a statutory approach to sovereign debt crises—a Sovereign Debt Restructuring Mechanism (SDRM)—was led by the IMF in 2001–2003, with initial encouragement from the U.S. Secretary of the Treasury Paul O'Neil. The objective, in the terms of Krueger (2001, 2002), then IMF deputy managing director, was to create a catalyst that would encourage debtors and creditors to come together to restructure unsustainable debts, thus facilitating an orderly, predictable, and rapid restructuring while protecting asset values and creditors' rights. A major issue behind this proposal was also the sense that in a financial landscape in which bond financing, rather than bank lending, was playing the prominent role, the growing heterogeneity of creditors had intensified the collective action problems associated with managing debt overhangs and increased the number of speculators who had bought bonds at distressed prices and who were interested in litigation rather than in participating in restructuring (i.e., they preferred to remain as holdouts).

The proposal varied through the period when it was considered, particularly in relation to the role of the IMF in the process. This reflected the debates that the initial proposals raised, particularly the opposition to the IMF having a very active role in debt negotiations or in the approval of the final agreements. According to the proposal, the mechanism would be triggered by the debtor country, leading to a renegotiation process with some core features: (1) qualified majority voting, with the possibility of aggregating debts within broad categories; (2) stay of credit enforcement (which was dropped by the time of the final proposal); (3) protecting collective creditor interests by adopting policies that protected asset values, which could include controls on capital outflows to prevent capital flight; and (4) establishing a process for private creditors to potentially agree to give seniority to new private lending during a crisis; short-term trade financing (involving banks) and interbank claims were understood to be exempt from restructuring, as their disruption would impose a severe economic burden and lessen the likely recovery of value by bondholders. Given the strong opposition to the inclusion of domestic debts in these restructuring processes, it was in the end accepted that the proposal would generally involve only external debts. It was presumed, nonetheless, that in cases in which governments had substantial domestic bonds outstanding, a parallel process under domestic law would restructure those bonds, and the external creditors would not approve the restructuring of their claims unless satisfied that the burden-sharing with holders of domestic bonds was fair in some sense.[2] The mechanism required, in turn, independent arrangements for verification of creditors' claims, resolution of disputes, and supervision of voting. In the final versions of the proposal, the mechanism would be put in place by an amendment of the IMF Articles of Agreement, which would create a new judicial organ with safeguards that guaranteed it would operate independently of the executive board and the board of governors of the IMF.

This proposal was rejected by both the United States, under clear pressure from its financial sector and the internal opposition within the Treasury from Under-Secretary for International Affairs John B. Taylor and various developing countries (notably Brazil and Mexico) who feared that it would end up limiting, or increasing their costs of, access to international capital markets at a time when it was quite limited. There was also a clear opposition from the private sector to the IMF being at the center, given the conflict of interest (since it is also a creditor), whereas civil society opposed IMF involvement due to the conflict of interest from being both a creditor and a decision maker, and because of the conditionality associated with its programs. This is why ad hoc voluntary renegotiations continued to be the norm. In the early twenty-first century, the most important examples have been the Argentine debt renegotiations of 2005 and 2010 and the Greek renegotiation of 2012.

THE RECENT DEBATE AND A PROPOSAL

One of the major problems with this voluntary approach had been that those parties that do not accept the terms of the agreements (the holdouts) were able to go to the courts to claim full payment. These demands have been successful in several cases in the past, a fact that obviously discourages participation in renegotiations. The alternative solution to this problem was the spread, since 2003, of CACs for international bonds issued in the United States; as previously noted, this mechanism was already used in other markets, especially in London. This mechanism defines in the debt contract the majorities necessary to restructure a sovereign bond issue. As we have seen, this alternative had been increasingly favored in conceptual terms since the 1994 Mexican crisis but only received its final impetus as a result of the search by the U.S. government and financial sector for alternatives to the SDRM (Gelpern and Gulati, 2010).

The use of CACs in New York contracts became widespread after the decision by one of the major debtors opposed to the SDRM—Mexico—to include those clauses in a bond issue in March 2003; they then found that the premium paid for CACs was, if anything, negligible. The corroboration of this fact in later issues by other countries dispelled the fear that CACs would raise the cost of borrowing and led to their generalization. This trend was combined with agreements on "codes of conduct." The one that stands out is the "Principles for Stable Capital Flows and Fair Debt Restructuring in Emergency Markets," adopted in 2005 by the Institute of International Finance (IIF, 2005). The code was slightly amended after the Greek restructuring.

The IMF (2013) has recently underscored several deficiencies of this market-orientated approach. The first is that incentives remain for both debtor countries and creditors to delay restructurings, which implies that they tend to come too little and too late. Furthermore, the unsuccessful Argentinean litigation in U.S. courts in 2013–2014 on the interpretation of the pari passu clause[3] has exacerbated the collective action problems by increasing the leverage of holdouts, as it has prohibited Argentina from making payments on its restructured debts if it does not pay in full its unrestructured debt. The incentives to participate in any restructuring would thus be significantly reduced. On the other hand, the need to aggregate different claims by including aggregation clauses in debt contracts is now broadly accepted and essential to guarantee intercreditor equity. Aggregation has been required in eurozone bonds since 2013, with 75 percent of bondholders across all relevant issues required to approve a proposed restructuring, plus 66.66 percent of the holders of each individual bond issue.

Based on the problems raised by Argentina's litigation, the International Capital Market Association (ICMA, 2014a, 2014b) and the IMF (2014) proposed the inclusion of aggregation clauses in debt contracts and a revision of the pari passu clause[4]. Mexico again led the way, including the new clauses in a November 2014 debt issue in New York—Kazakhstan had done so for a new issue in London in October—with no effects on the cost of the issue. Mexico also changed from having a fiscal agent to having a trustee represent the bondholders in negotiation with debtors (the London system). Following the 2003 experience, when Mexico led the way in introducing CACs in New York issues, these conditions are likely to spread. In any case, aggregation does not exclude the possibility of blocking majorities in individual issues[5] and fails to guarantee the coherence between bond and other debt contracts, particularly with syndicated bank lending. Also, according to the IMF (2013), the impact of credit default swaps has not been fully tested, certainly reduces the incentive to participate in debt renegotiations, and introduces a whole new set of actors into the process.

To these considerations we could add that, although the revised CACs will help manage future problems, they would not solve the legacy of existing debt for some time and will leave other problems unaddressed (see Guzman and Stiglitz 2016). The traditional division between external and internal debt is also being blurred by the increasing participation of international funds in the domestic debt markets of emerging economies. Furthermore, the traditional separation between official and private creditors, and those of the restructuring mechanisms each of these creditor groups uses, has been made more complex by the rise of official lenders who are not members of the Paris Club (notably China). The inequities that could be generated between the two realms of restructuring have already been noted. This may imply that in the future "aggregation" may refer not only to liabilities with private creditors but to *all* obligations, including multilateral lending, with proper seniority rules, favoring in particular creditors who provide funding during crises.

In a parallel way, the United Nations has been part of this debate, with its 2002 Monterrey Consensus on Financing for Development reflecting the call for financial crisis management mechanisms "that provide for fair burden-sharing between public and private sectors and between debtors, creditors and investors" (United Nations 2002: para. 51). This has led to numerous consultations in the context of the UN's Financing for Development process (Schneider, 2014). The UN Commission of Experts on Reforms of the International Monetary and Financial System, better known as the Stiglitz Commission (United Nations, 2009), made important proposals in this area, and UNCTAD has, in turn, launched some "Principles on Sovereign Lending and Borrowing."

The need to have a better framework for debt resolution remains, therefore, one of the major gaps of the international financial architecture. It has led to extensive debate, which referred in the past to emerging economies but now also to the European periphery,[6] and to numerous proposals on how to reform the system.[7] Following Schneider (2014), we can say there are three basic ways forward. The first one would be to improve the "contractual technology." This would require the need to generalize the use of aggregation clauses in bond contracts. This is the approach taken by the eurozone countries since 2013 and more recently by the ICMA and the IMF. The basic problem is how to manage creditors who may still obtain a blocking position for a particular bond issue. It would also require the generalization of the new pari passu clause and of the system of trustees to represent bondholders in negotiations, and perhaps some formal standstill provision. Even the best of all solutions in this area face, in any case, the problems previously mentioned: the long transition that has been associated with the fact that CACs only began to be used in New York in 2003, aggregation clauses that are only just now starting to spread, and the additional problems associated with: the management of debts with the private versus the official sectors, external versus domestic liabilities, and credit default swaps.

The second route is the negotiation of a statutory regime, which would create an international debt court or similar institution with clear rules on priority of claims and intercreditor equity that would be legally enforceable in the main financial markets. According to the foregoing analysis, this institution would ensure that the agreed international principles of a fresh start, equitable sharing of haircuts, and priority of claims against the debtor government were followed. It would thus correct the two main flaws in the ad hoc structure that has arisen over time: it would lead to restructurings that benefit both creditors and debtors (the essence of a good arrangement in this field), and it would give equitable treatment to different debtors and creditors according to principles that could be agreed internationally. The Stiglitz Commission has put on the table the most interesting proposals in this field (UN, 2009: chap. 5). The mechanism could also work on the basis of case-by-case arbitration panels convened by the relevant parties under internationally agreed arbitration rules (Kaiser, 2013) or an "oversight commission" made up by three countries that are members of a multilateral legal framework in this area, as proposed by Argentina during the ongoing UN negotiations (Republic of Argentina, 2015).

The best alternative in my view would be to mix the voluntary and statutory solutions by creating a mechanism similar to the World Trade Organization's (WTO) dispute settlement mechanism,[8] in which there is a sequence of voluntary negotiations, mediation, and eventual arbitration that take place with preestablished deadlines, thus generating strong incentives to reach agreement under the "shadow of the court"; the existence of the mechanism could also encourage its timely use, but this is not guaranteed. The process would start with the declaration of moratorium by the debtor country, which would unleash the negotiations. As in national bankruptcy regimes, the first step would be the attempt by the defaulting country to reach a voluntary agreement with its creditors. The process should also serve as a framework to coordinate the positions of creditors within and across different classes of lenders (eventually including official creditors, both Paris Club members and nonmembers). If this first stage fails within the agreed deadline, the institution in charge would move to mediating in the dispute as an "honest broker." Again, if the deadline for this second stage ends without an agreement, or if requested by both parties before the deadline, this broker would arbitrate the dispute, leading to a decision that is legally binding for all parties. As in national "debtor-in-possession financing," this broker would also have the authority to ask creditors to provide new financing to the country undergoing debt restructuring. These new debts, as well as all financing provided when the country is in default (e.g., IMF "lending into arrears," loans by multilateral development banks and official bilateral creditors, and private trade financing) would have seniority over defaulted debts.

The mechanism could be created as an independent body under the UN system. This would require negotiating a new international treaty, which would be a time-consuming effort both in terms of negotiations and ratifications, with the possibility that countries that host major financial centers (notably the United States and the United Kingdom) would not ratify it. So a better alternative would be that which was tried in 2001–2003: an amendment to the IMF Articles of Agreement, so long as it could function through a system of *independent* panels of experts and a body with final judicial decision-making capacity, similar to those used under the WTO's dispute settlement mechanism. This is implicit in Krueger's (2002) proposal that the debt resolution organ would operate independently of the IMF's executive board and the board of governors and with strong provisions to avoid interference from the IMF staff, directors, or member states.

A complementary but major task of multilateral development cooperation is to support countries that have undergone debt restructuring to have a smooth and hopefully speedy return to markets. Multilateral development banks (MDBs) can play a crucial role in this regard, through cofinancing or the issue of guarantees to new debt issues by countries. A sovereign debt restructuring facility within the IMF, combining IMF lending and debt restructuring, could also play that role (Buchheit et al., 2013) but is less desirable, as many more countries are willing to use MDBs rather than IMF facilities.

The workout mechanism designed should deal primarily with sovereign debts, but there are two other individual cases that should be taken into account. They are private sector debts that are "nationalized" during crises as part of bailouts, particularly of financial sectors, and cases in which private sector debts cannot be serviced because they would intensify balance of payments problems. In the first case, the external liabilities should be treated as corporate debts that should be renegotiated as such, as part of the cleaning of the balance sheet of the institution involved, and may therefore involve larger amounts of haircuts. This procedure would help reduce the pressure exercised by foreign creditors to take over private sector debts during crises, which has been a practice in many emerging and developing countries in the past and has added substantial amounts of previously private sector debt to the sovereign state's obligations. In the case of balance of payments crises, an agreement should be reached as to how domestic private debtors can convert their payments in local currency into foreign exchange.

Finally, three complementary mechanisms would be desirable—and some of them (particularly the first one) actually required for a mechanism of this sort to operate. The first is an international registry of debt, which would be best managed by the institution in charge of debt restructuring. The second is the creation of effective mechanisms for creditor coordination for individual renegotiations, a problem that has become more complex given the diversity of creditors. This should be part of the rules that establish the eventual mechanism. The third is a sovereign debt forum, which could be a multistakeholder process organized under the umbrella of the UN Financing for Development process, thus providing for the participation not only of governments and international institutions but also of the private sector and civil society.

NOTES

This chapter is part of a book on the international monetary system being prepared by the author for the World Institute for Development Economics Research of the United Nations University.

1. This is true even though the international legal framework was the "Convention Respecting the Limitation of the Employment of Force for the Recovery of Contract

Debts," adopted as part of a set of conventions on the laws of war at The Hague in 1907. This was a response to a practice that had been typical in the nineteenth century, but there was no reluctance to use force on subsequent occasions (e.g., Dominican Republic in 1916).

2. See Hagen (2005). This is the most authoritative account, as the author was at the center of the negotiations.

3. This clause has been generally interpreted as giving creditors equal ranking, but it has come to be interpreted by the New York District Court Judge Thomas P. Griesa as equal "ratable payments," which increases the negotiating power of holdouts, affects third parties, and may even undermine the doctrine of sovereign immunity.

4. Change of language was introduced to eliminate any interpretation requiring ratable payments (see previous note 3).

5. This is what happened with some London issues in the Greek renegotiations of 2012; at the time there were, in any case, no aggregation clauses.

6. See, e.g., the essays collected by Herman, Ocampo, and Spiegel (2010a) and Paulus (2014), respectively.

7. See an inventory of proposals in IMF (2013); the excellent survey by Panizza, Sturzenegger, and Zettlemeyer (2009) of the economic and legal issues involved; and Herman (2016), Kaiser (2016), Howse (2016), and Raffer (2016).

8. My own early ideas on the subject were included in Herman, Ocampo, and Spiegel (2010b). Of course, in contrast to the WTO mechanism, which involves controversies among countries, the mechanism would involve a negotiation between a debtor country and private creditors (but also, eventually, a mix of private and official creditors).

REFERENCES

Buchheit, Lee C., Anna Gelpern, Mitu Gulati, Uga Panizza, Beatrice Weder di Mauro, and Jeromin Zettlemeyer. 2013. *Revising Sovereign Bankruptcy, Report of the Committee on International Economic Policy and Reform*. Washington, D.C.: Brookings Institution.

Cruces, Juan, and Cristoph Trebesch. 2013. "Sovereign Defaults: The Price of Haircuts." *American Economic Review: Macroeconomics* 5 (no. 15): 85–117.

Devlin, Robert. 1989. *Debt and Crisis in Latin America: The Supply Side of the Story*. Princeton, N.J.: Princeton University Press.

Eichengreen, Barry, and Richard Portes. 1995. *Crisis? What Crisis? Orderly Workouts for Sovereign Debtors*. London: Centre for Economic Policy Research.

G10. May 1996. *The Resolution of Sovereign Liquidity Crises: A Report to the Ministers and Governors Prepared Under the Auspices of the Deputies*. Jean-Jacques Rey (chairman). www.bis.org/publ/gten03.pdf.

Gelpern, Anna, and Mitu Gulati. 2010. "How CACs Became Boilerplate: Governments in 'Market-Based' Change.'" In *Overcoming Developing Country Debt Crises*, ed. Barry Herman, José Antonio Ocampo, and Shari Spiegel, chap. 13. New York: Oxford University Press.

Guzman, Martin, and Joseph E. Stiglitz. 2016. "Creating a Framework for Sovereign Debt Restructuring That Works." In *Too Little, Too Late: The Quest to Resolve*

Sovereign Debt Crises, ed. Martin Guzman, José Antonio Ocampo, and Joseph E. Stiglitz, chapter 1. New York: Columbia University Press.

Hagen, Sean. 2005. "Designing a Legal Framework to Restructure Sovereign Debt." *Georgetown Journal of International Law* 36 (no. 2): 299–402.

Herman, Barry. "Toward a Multilateral Framework for Recovery from Sovereign Insolvency." In *Too Little, Too Late: The Quest to Resolve Sovereign Debt Crises*, ed. Martin Guzman, José Antonio Ocampo, and Joseph E. Stiglitz, chapter 11. New York: Columbia University Press.

Herman, Barry, José Antonio Ocampo, and Shari Spiegel, eds. 2010a. *Overcoming Developing Country Debt Crises*. New York: Oxford University Press.

——. 2010b. "Conclusions: Towards a Comprehensive Sovereign Bankruptcy Regime." In *Overcoming Developing Country Debt Crises*, ed. Barry Herman, José Antonio Ocampo, and Shari Spiegel, chap. 17. New York: Oxford University Press.

Howse, Robert. "Toward a Framework for Sovereign Debt Restructuring: What Can Public International Law Contribute?" In *Too Little, Too Late: The Quest to Resolve Sovereign Debt Crises*, ed. Martin Guzman, José Antonio Ocampo, and Joseph E. Stiglitz, chapter 14. New York: Columbia University Press.

Institute of International Finance. 2005, March 31. "Principles for Stable Capital Flows and Fair Debt Restructuring in Emerging Markets." www.iif.com/emp/principles.

International Capital Market Association. August 2014a. "International Aggregated Collective Action Clauses (CACs) for the Terms and Conditions of Sovereign Notes." www.icmagroup.org.

——. August 2014b. "Standard Pari Passu Provision for the Terms and Conditions of Sovereign Notes." www.icmagroup.org.

International Monetary Fund. 2002, July 30. "Fund Policy on Lending into Arrears to Private Creditors—Further Considerations of the Good-Faith Criterion," International Monetary Fund, International Capital Markets, Policy Development and Review and Legal Departments, Washington, D.C.

——. 2013, April 26. "Sovereign Debt Restructuring: Recent Developments and Implications for the Fund's Legal and Policy Framework." Staff Paper, Washington, D.C.

——. 2014, September 2. "Strengthening of the Contractual Framework to Address Collective Action Problems in Sovereign Debt Restructurings."

Kaiser, Jürgen. October 2013. *Resolving Sovereign Debt Crises: Towards a Fair and Transparent International Insolvency Framework*. 2nd rev. ed. Dialogue on Globalization Series. Berlin: Friedrich Ebert Stiftung.

——. 2016. "Making a Legal Framework for Sovereign Debt Restructuring Operational." In *Too Little, Too Late: The Quest to Resolve Sovereign Debt Crises*, ed. Martin Guzman, José Antonio Ocampo, and Joseph E. Stiglitz, chapter 12. New York: Columbia University Press.

Krueger, Anne O. 2001. "International Financial Architecture for 2002: A New Approach to Sovereign Debt Restructuring." Address at the American Enterprise Institute, Washington, D.C., November 26. www.imf.org/external/np/speeches/2001/112601.htm (accessed September 1, 2014).

———. April 2002. *A New Approach to Sovereign Debt Restructuring*. Washington, D.C.: International Monetary Fund.

Ocampo, José Antonio. 2014. "The Latin American Debt Crisis in Historical Perspective." In *Life After Debt: The Origins and Resolutions of Debt Crises*, ed. Joseph E. Stiglitz and Daniel Heymann, chap. 2.1. London: Palgrave-Macmillan.

Panizza, Ugo, Federico Sturzenegger, and Jeromin Zettlemeyer. 2009. "The Economics and Law of Sovereign Debt and Default." *Journal of Economic Literature* 47 (no. 3): 653–700.

Paulus, Chistoph G., ed. 2014. *A Debt Restructuring Mechanism for Sovereigns: Do We Need a Legal Procedure?* Munich: Beck.

Rakffer, Kunibert. 2016. "Debts, Human Rights, and the Rule of Law: Advocating a Fair and Efficient Sovereign Insolvency Model." In *Too Little, Too Late: The Quest to Resolve Sovereign Debt Crises*, ed. Martin Guzman, José Antonio Ocampo, and Joseph E. Stiglitz, chapter 15. New York: Columbia University Press.

Republic of Argentina. 2015. "Towards a Multilateral Legal Framework for Sovereign Debt Restructuring Processes." Proposal by Argentina presented to the UN negotiations.

Rhodes, William R. 2011. *Banker to the World: Leadership Lessons from the Front Lines of Global Finance*. New York: McGraw-Hill.

Schneider, Benu. 2014. "Sovereign Debt Restructuring: The Road Ahead." In *Life After Debt: The Origins and Resolutions of Debt Crises*, ed. Joseph E. Stiglitz and Daniel Heymann, chap. 3.3. London: Palgrave-Macmillan.

Spiegel, Shari. 2010. "Excess Returns on Emerging Market Bonds and the Framework for Sovereign Debt Restructuring." In *Overcoming Developing Country Debt Crises*, ed. Barry Herman, José Antonio Ocampo, and Shari Spiegel, chap. 6. New York: Oxford University Press.

Stiglitz, Joseph E. 2010. "Sovereign Debt: Notes on Theoretical Frameworks and Policy Analyses." In *Overcoming Developing Country Debt Crises*, ed. Barry Herman, José Antonio Ocampo, and Shari Spiegel, chap. 2. New York: Oxford University Press.

Suter, Christian, and Hanspeter Stamm. 1992. "Coping with Global Debt Crises: Debt Settlements, 1820 to 1986." *Comparative Studies in Society and History* 34, no. 4 (October): 645–678.

United Nations. 2002. "The Monterrey Consensus." International Conference on Financing for Development, held in Monterrey, Mexico, March 18–22. www.un.org/esa/ffd.

———. September 2009. *Report of the Commission of Experts of the UN General Assembly on Reforms of the International Monetary and Financial System* [UN Stiglitz Commission]. New York.

CHAPTER 11

Toward a Multilateral Framework for Recovery from Sovereign Insolvency

Barry Herman

From time to time, sovereign governments find themselves in a situation in which the repayment terms on at least some of their external debt must be eased or cancelled. Creditors cannot force repayment, whether from an impoverished sovereign or an irresponsible one. However strong the presumed contractual and moral obligation to repay, it cannot or will not be fully done in some cases. Instead, distressed or even recalcitrant sovereigns almost always restructure their debt, albeit in ad hoc negotiations that mainly reflect power differences at the time of negotiation. The world should do better. There ought to be some principled way to restructure sovereign debt repayment obligations. The process should function independently of judgments by creditors about what the leaders of the defaulting government "deserve." It should be especially mindful of the heavy harm debt crises impose on the people of the indebted country. As agreed by all the world's governments in the "Monterrey Consensus," it should "provide for fair burden-sharing between public and private sectors and between debtors, creditors and investors" (UN, 2002: para. 51).

In other words, sovereign debt restructuring is a fully political process. Some internationally agreed principles should govern how it works. In fact, some principles have regularly been invoked as accepted international law, such as "creditor rights" to enforce contracts that borrowing governments have signed, or more generally, *pacta sunt servanda* (agreements must be honored). But who should enforce this principle? Once upon a time, governments threatened to send warships on behalf of their bankers and investors to collect debt servicing owed by bankrupt governments. This practice is no longer deemed acceptable; nor is it deemed necessary. Creditors instead mainly rely for repayment on the appreciation that the indebted government will want to borrow again, which is generally sufficient incentive. Similarly, regaining access to financial markets is assumed to be the operative incentive for a bankrupt sovereign to reach agreement with its creditors to restructure repayment of the debt.

In this regard, enforcement of "creditors' rights" is driven by creditors withholding new loans, something the market usually does quickly when it realizes the debtor is in difficulty and something that official creditors may threaten. As the debtor government is usually desperate for some form of external finance, *pacta sunt servanda* operates today by creating the strong debtor incentive to try to delay acknowledging that it cannot pay as long as possible and then, when insolvency leaves creditors no option but to reduce their claims somewhat, accepting the generally insufficient debt relief offered so as to regain market approval and resume access to market finance. The debtor government's only countervailing power is to survive without new external credits for some period of time or to mortgage future export revenues for cash or essential imports (a kind of barter trade) or to mobilize support from an official lender that is not cooperating with the private and mainstream official lenders.

It is possible that the sovereign debtor and its creditors reach no restructuring agreement and arrears accumulate, possibly leading to formal repudiation of the debt. In fact, little sovereign debt, if any, has been repudiated in recent decades, and so it may be inferred that the debtors and creditors find the current processes for sovereign debt restructuring to have been a tolerable or unavoidable way out of a debt crisis. Losses are taken by one group or another according to their respective negotiating prowess and power, and the parties move on. That, however, is a very low normative standard and one generally not accepted as sufficient by national legislatures when they write laws to cover bankruptcies of companies, households, or subnational public entities. They want to ensure that the workout from insolvency is economically efficient (e.g., maintaining operation of some of the physical plant, equipment, and employees of bankrupt companies when economically possible, instead of fully closing them down and selling off the assets); timely (i.e., ensuring that decisions are not unnecessarily postponed by one party or another); and fair to the relevant stakeholders (i.e., that the burden is appropriately shared among creditors and the debtor). Could we not ask that the sovereign debt workout also aim to be effective, timely, and fair?[1]

Governments or private creditors have at various times sought to define principles to govern sovereign debt restructuring, and the UN General Assembly has recently adopted such a set, albeit without the participation or agreement of the developed countries (Muchhala, 2015). Those principles thus need to be considered a work in progress, an invitation to global dialogue. This paper suggests how that dialogue might proceed.

In addition, the usual proposal to reform how sovereign debt is restructured imagines establishment of an international authority that would apply the agreed principles in a proceeding that would emulate how national bankruptcy laws and courts bring all the parties together to resolve the debt distress of the covered entity. And yet governments are rarely willing to cede sovereignty to an international authority, except perhaps as a last resort. It should not surprise us that borrowing governments, let alone creditors, have not supported such proposals. This chapter instead proposes a better way to carry out the decentralized approach.

The rest of the chapter first reviews the complex organization of sovereign debt workouts to offer a perspective on the political and legal frameworks in which those processes are embedded.[2] This is intended to set the stage for a mental exercise on what an ideal political/legal framework might look like, leading to a reform proposal. The main innovation is not my own but one suggested more than a decade ago by Christoph Paulus of the law faculty of Humboldt University in Berlin.[3] I think it might be time to look again at that idea, which I try to fit into an international political framework.

THE DECENTRALIZED AND COMPLEX REALITY

As other chapters in this book have also noted, an insolvent sovereign usually owes money in a variety of currencies, including its own, and it owes it to a variety of lenders, usually including commercial banks, investors in bonds, other sovereign governments, and various international financial institutions (IFIs), almost always including the International Monetary Fund (IMF).

It is useful to focus for a moment on the IMF role. Most debtor governments will work with the IMF on the design of an economic recovery program for the country meant to bring about a sustainable fiscal situation. The IMF will also help formulate a financing plan for the duration of the adjustment program, including giving an indication of the overall amount of temporary relief needed from debt servicing and whether and how much permanent relief is needed for the country to reach a sustainable debt scenario over the medium term. The IMF operates under guidance of its boards of governors and executive directors, whose views most heavily reflect the views of the Fund's own main creditors, an approach that is widely and justly criticized (IMF, 2014). The debtor government is then formally on its own to negotiate the restructuring of its debt-servicing obligations or obtain outright debt reduction with each of its creditor classes. However, political pressure may be put on different official and private groups of creditors so the overall anticipated level of relief is attained, although not all creditors need be accommodating. At the same time, the recommended IMF target level of relief may reflect the Fund's judgment of what the different classes of creditors are willing to give, which may be insufficient to give the debtor a "fresh start."

The debtor thus opens negotiations with its external creditor banks (usually in an informal arrangement called a London Club), also with the holders of the various series of its foreign currency bonds (some of whom sometimes organize themselves into creditor committees), perhaps as well with its domestic banks and bondholders, and with its foreign government creditors (most of which will come together in the informal Paris Club). Although restructuring of obligations to IFIs is unusual, it has been essential over the past two decades for the debt restructuring of a group of thirty-nine heavily indebted poor countries (HIPCs). Such a process could again become necessary for poor and vulnerable countries that owe a large share of their debt to those institutions. Each of the restructuring bodies works under a largely ad hoc and uncoordinated set of procedures. Not surprisingly, outcomes of the different processes need not amount to appropriate burden sharing between the debtor and its creditors or among the creditor classes. This is not satisfactory.

In sum, each debt crisis country arranges a workout program containing some combination of government-spending austerity, tax reform to raise public revenues, additional loans from IFIs or governments, and restructuring of one or more classes of debt obligations. Citizens may also replace the government that was in charge during the descent into crisis, as also happens in corporate restructuring, where the defaulting management may be fired. But sometimes official creditors prefer for geostrategic reasons that governments remain in power despite being responsible for a debt crisis, and the key officials may survive—indeed, have survived—many a financial crisis.[4] The proportions between economic adjustment, new financing, and debt relief will differ among country cases, depending on the size of the debt "overhang," the political importance of the indebted sovereign to the global powers, and the skill of the sovereign's negotiators relative to that of its creditors.

THE POLITICAL FRAMEWORK

One may see that there is a political framework among states and IFIs within which the debt workout takes place. There is also a legal framework, which largely pertains to the contractual relations between the indebted state and its private creditors. We return to that below. Here it is sufficient to say that every effort is made to voluntarily resolve unpaid sovereign debt obligations to private creditors. The courts may get involved in aspects of difficult cases, and creditor governments will involve themselves when there is a pressing policy concern.

Consider, for example, the sovereign debt crises of the early 1980s, which mainly involved syndicated loans to middle-income countries from commercial banks, especially the "money center banks" that operated the international currency markets. The governments of the world's major economies feared the consequences that recognizing sovereign debtor insolvency would have had on the balance sheets of the money center banks and thus pushed them to make "concerted" loans to the otherwise-defaulting sovereigns. The debtor countries thus met their debt-servicing obligations with these forced loans, at least for a time, while the financial regulators applied "forbearance" in their supervision of the banks. The feared collapse of the international currency markets appears to have been a good enough reason for the governments to intervene at the time (Devlin, 1993). It took the rest of the decade and considerable policy intervention to arrange the final workout. That is, ending the sovereign debt crisis of the 1980s involved a political deal (the Brady Plan), not a market-led process (Garay Salamanca, 2010).

Government intervention in the workouts from excessive sovereign obligations to private creditors continues to the present day, with borrowing from the private sector mainly taking place through bond issuance. Initially, governments—but especially the IFIs—involved themselves in "important" cases by lending to the overindebted sovereigns, as during the Asian financial crisis of the 1990s. This bailout strategy generally prevented outright default, although it happened anyway in the case of Russia in 1998. Private creditors did not object to these bailouts, although voters in creditor countries frowned on the practice. The creditor governments, acting through the IMF, thus revised their approach by the end of the 1990s to give more emphasis to "private sector participation" or "bail-ins" in workouts from excessive obligations to private creditors (IMF, 2002). As has been clear in the recent series of Greek restructurings, this sets up a three-way struggle between the debtor government (wanting the least austerity), the private lenders (wanting their money back), and the official international community (wanting the least threat to its bondholding banks, the least voter criticism, and the least threat to its own bailout loans).[5]

If there have been greater and smaller political interventions in resolving distressed sovereign debt obligations owed to private creditors, the restructuring of sovereign debts owed to official creditors has been entirely political. Although interofficial loans are formalized in contracts, the decisions to alter the repayment obligations in those cases are in practice taken politically. The bilateral official creditors that meet in the Paris Club agree to bind themselves a priori to specific norms for the relief that they offer to countries in different income groups, revising the relief standards from time to time as deemed warranted. However, they actually accord relief on a case-by-case basis, as they have some flexibility in how much relief they give any specific country. For example, within an agreed framework for relief, the Paris Club can reduce current and future debt servicing by more or less by deciding where to position the "cutoff point" after which date obligations are not restructured. Also, after the Paris Club reaches its joint creditor decision on these terms of relief, called the Agreed Minute, the debtor needs to renegotiate each specific loan with each member country of the club, allowing further differences in treatment to creep into the final detailed arrangement. Moreover, from time to time the Paris Club substantially departs from its standards for politically strategic cases, as for Egypt, Indonesia, Poland, and Turkey at one time or another (Cosío-Pascal, 2010). Finally, the club has also offered to unilaterally delay debt repayments to countries harmed by disasters, including the tsunami of December 2004 and the internal conflict that wracked Liberia.[6]

The 1996 initiative to reduce the debt of the HIPCs was a uniquely comprehensive set of political arrangements for debt restructuring. To begin it, an eligible debtor government had to approach IMF and indicate a willingness to undertake macroeconomic and structural policy reforms, and since 1999 it has had to draft a standardized "Poverty Reduction Strategy Paper." Typically the government would adopt an austerity and policy liberalization program that would be supported by new loans on concessional terms from IMF, other IFIs, and bilateral donors, along with cancellation of 67 percent of Paris Club debt servicing falling due during the adjustment period and long-term rescheduling of the rest.

Typically, after three years of a country staying "on track" with its adjustment commitments, the IMF and World Bank executive boards would jointly graduate the country to its "decision point," when additional policy reform commitments would be made by the debtor, including to start implementing its poverty reduction strategy; in addition, a plan for permanent debt relief would be prepared, including reduction of obligations to the IFIs. An "interim phase" then ensued in which the Paris Club would cancel 90 percent of the debt servicing falling due to its member governments and reschedule the rest, while other official and commercial creditors would be asked to provide comparable relief. The IFIs would start giving annual relief of debt servicing, which would be made permanent at the next stage.

When the adjusting poor country earned sufficient creditor confidence (originally only after another three years), the IMF and the World Bank would graduate the country to the "completion point," when the Paris Club and multilateral creditors would agree to reduce the stock of debt and when other official and private creditors would again be asked to grant comparable treatment. The final amount of HIPC relief was intended to put the country on a path to fiscal sustainability, but that was often based on optimistic projections. A further step was thus added to the HIPC Initiative in 2005, when major IFIs adopted the Multilateral Debt Relief Initiative (MDRI), agreeing to essentially wipe out all remaining obligations to the IFIs of each completion-point HIPC on condition that the additional savings in debt servicing would be applied to antipoverty programs meant to help the country achieve the UN's Millennium Development Goals.

As HIPCs have borrowed anew after receiving their HIPC and MDRI writedowns, their debt-servicing obligations have begun to grow again and have become a significant burden for some of them. IMF reflected this concern when it announced in February 2015 that it was giving special relief from debt servicing owed to the Fund to the three West African countries hit by the Ebola outbreak. It will not actually reduce the repayments but will draw grant monies to cover the debt-servicing obligations from a new Catastrophe Containment and Relief Trust at IMF (IMF, 2015).

THE LEGAL FRAMEWORK FOR PRIVATE CREDIT

As noted already, private lending to a sovereign today usually takes the form of a bond issued by the government and sold on a particular financial market. The bond contract specifies the country whose laws will govern the bond, typically the country in which the market is situated. The contracts also specify the possibilities and limitations for changing the repayment terms. Purchasers of the bonds are thus relatively confident that if a repayment problem arises, the contractual clauses of the bonds will win them sympathetic treatment in the relevant courts if litigation becomes necessary.

Pension funds, insurance companies, banks, and other lenders prefer to buy bonds in markets having creditor-friendly legal and regulatory systems, for example, where standardized and reliable information on the borrower is filed with the market oversight authority and the depth of the market makes the purchased bond liquid. In addition, economies of scale and competition in large markets hold down the cost of raising funds in those centers. Borrowing countries will thus prefer to issue their bonds in such jurisdictions to minimize the interest rates they have to pay and to be able to issue bonds with longer maturities. On the other hand, countries will likely want to diversify their obligations and so might issue in multiple currencies on multiple markets, including the domestic market, where there would be no exchange-rate risk but a possible rollover risk if the market were not very deep.

Thus the world has and will continue to have multiple financial markets that trade the bonds of different sovereigns, each market governed by its own domestic laws. The desirability of issuing in a particular financial market can change with changes in its laws or in how they are interpreted by their courts. A case in point is the United States, where the attraction of being able to issue in its deep markets has even led governments to waive their sovereign immunity from being sued in U.S. courts by their bondholders. However, the attractiveness of the New York market may have fallen somewhat owing to the strange treatment of Argentina in the U.S. courts. As noted elsewhere in this volume, the courts privileged the claims of a small group of uncooperative bondholders—aptly named "vulture funds"—against those of the overwhelming majority of Argentina's other bondholders, including those holding bonds issued under the laws of the United Kingdom, Japan, and Argentina itself. Not surprisingly, this has been highly controversial.

The evolution of the legal treatment of sovereign bonds in the U.S. market also highlights how the courts in interpreting the law can make policy independent of the foreign policy priorities of the government. In the case of Argentina's bonds, the U.S. government submitted a number of amicus briefs in support of Argentina's position against the vulture funds as the case percolated up from the district court to the Supreme Court.[7] This was to no avail. In other words, there seems to be a measure of separation between the legal regime in the United States governing the sovereign debtor's relationship with its private creditors and the policy regime of the United States regarding its priorities in sovereign debt restructuring. Still, the U.S. government has the power to change the law that its courts apply in their decisions, and thus the political framework can trump the legal one in the end.

All in all, one may see that the system works in a fashion, in that it produces debt workouts. However, this is hardly a satisfying criterion. In fact, if the debt restructuring produced by this system worked well, then Greece would not have sought another restructuring in 2015 after having restructured its privately held bond debt in 2012. Jamaica would not have had to restructure its obligations to domestic banks again in 2013 after having restructured them in 2010. Gabon would not have defaulted in 2002 on the external bank debt that had been restructured in 1994. And so on.

AN IDEAL FRAMEWORK

Let us now try to imagine an ideal system. To begin, one might want to see a system in which some respected neutral global authority—a philosopher king, as Plato would have it—was responsible for oversight and coordination of the overall restructuring of the obligations to private and public creditors of all indebted states. It would ensure that the end point of the debt restructuring was a fresh start, a situation in which no further debt restructuring would be expected for many, many years (natural or economic catastrophes aside). It is also necessary that essential social services are maintained during the crisis period. In particular, the philosopher king would make sure that the "social protection floor" was maintained in each country and that economic recovery was possible. The king would also entertain complaints from insolvent states or the creditors that believed they were not being treated according to the king's principles of effective, timely, and fair restructuring.

However, the king would not need to intervene directly with each of the public and private classes of creditors in most instances. A principle of subsidiarity could apply. The philosopher king in considering the overall amount of needed relief could set the target for the degree of restructuring of the official and private claims of any state. Official creditors could then decide among themselves how to offer the specific terms of relief to meet the king's target. Moreover, a judge from a national bankruptcy court could oversee the workout with the private creditors, guided by the king's principles and rules. As the king appreciates that there will be multiple financial markets in which sovereign bonds would be issued, he could mandate that essentially the same law governs the relations with the private creditors in each state, including that of the borrowing government. Moreover, in this ideal world, the courts would perform competently, independently, and honestly in each jurisdiction. In this way, domestic investors and banks purchasing domestic currency issues of the government's securities would face the same legal protections as purchasers of its bonds issued in foreign markets. Similarly, foreign investors in the bonds issued under domestic law could also settle any claims in the domestic court.

Still at the level of the ideal, we can imagine that the foreign and domestic creditors would find the resulting sovereign insolvency regime attractive. Creditors would feel that their property rights were protected fairly, that is, that they would recover the maximum possible amount of their investments, including interest, and that there was a reasonable way to reach decisions that were enforceable on all creditors in their class (e.g., no more "vultures" to destabilize an otherwise agreed restructuring). Nevertheless, unhappy creditor groups could appeal to the king for review.

A PATH TO REFORM

We have no philosopher king to set guidelines, but we have an international political process in the United Nations, whose member states have agreed in the General Assembly to various guidelines for international political and economic behavior that are widely accepted (admittedly with sometimes distressingly common violations). Examples of already existing guidelines include those on business and human rights, gender equality, peaceful settlement of disputes, and sustainable development.

As noted at the outset, the General Assembly undertook another such exercise in 2015 when it drafted a set of "basic principles" on how sovereign debt crises should be addressed. The principles address relations between the sovereign debtor and its creditors, stating that the sovereign has a right to restructure its debt, although it should do so only as a last resort in view of creditors' rights. The principles also call for "good faith" negotiation by the debtor and its creditors, transparency of negotiating partners, impartiality of involved international and regional institutions,

equitable treatment of different classes of creditors, and limited exceptions to sovereign immunity before foreign courts. They also specify very
general requirements for considering the institutions that facilitate debt
workouts as internationally legitimate. They further stipulate that debt
workouts should be completed in a timely and efficient manner and lead
to a stable debt situation that promotes sustained growth and sustainable
development, and that agreements that are reached by qualified majorities
should be protected from disruption by minority creditors or other states
(UN, 2015).

Unfortunately, not only were these basic principles not discussed or
approved by the creditor countries, but they lack precision and in some
cases ambition. For example, while principle 8 says that the debt workout
should minimize economic and social costs and respect human rights,
it could more specifically have called for protecting the social protection floor of the indebted country. In other words, it is not enough to
minimize the cost, as the imposed cost could still be substantial. Calling
for respect for human rights is correct but too vague in this context.
No one should be made hungry by a debt workout, nor should a child
be deprived of quality schooling, nor should people be left vulnerable
to disease because health clinics had to close. Owing to this and many
other shortcomings in the drafting, further work is needed to devise an
adequate set of principles that might actually serve as guidelines for sovereign debt workouts.

To this end, the General Assembly could start a new intergovernmental deliberation and invite all classes of stakeholders to contribute
their views on a strengthened set of principles for sovereign debt workouts. It could invite legal scholars to help draft the text; indeed, it could
request drafting assistance from the highly respected and long-established
intergovernmental body on commercial law, the UN Commission on
International Trade Law (UNCITRAL). On the basis of such deliberations, the General Assembly could then reach global consensus on a set of
principles it would adopt, with those principles becoming a part of what
legal scholars call "soft law."

The key point is that the formal step of adoption would reflect an
actual political consensus that had grown during the deliberative discussion stages. Governments and international institutions should then
agree, ipso facto, to apply the principles when they undertake workouts
from sovereign insolvencies. In other words, adoption of the principles
should reflect actual political commitments to employ them.

The IMF, in particular, as the already designated international intermediary on sovereign debt crisis workouts, should agree to be guided by them. This would not represent an instruction from the United Nations to the IMF, which is not allowed by mutual agreement of the two institutions, but rather would reflect an actual consensus among all UN and thus IMF member governments. However, the IMF executive board should formally adopt the principles for the sake of clarity.[8]

Henceforth, there would thus be an international standard against which to assess sovereign debt workouts. It would also create opportunities through public or peer pressure (as there is no philosopher king) to draw back relevant actors that depart from the guidelines. The essence of the proposal is that because workouts from sovereign debt crises are political in nature, involving relations between states and with IFIs, the guidance for appropriate functioning needs to be governed politically.

As with the philosopher king, the world's governments should also want their agreed principles to govern the relations of the sovereign debtor with its private creditors. One of the principles could thus specify the priority for repayment of obligations. The principle might be stated as repayment of IFI obligations first (as is the current practice), then repayment to government creditors, and finally repayment to private creditors. This would subordinate the standing of private claims and might raise the risk premium embedded in the interest rates of these instruments. But that seems a fair deal, as taxpayers in lending countries must cover losses on official loans. On the other hand, private creditors might propose a different order of priority, with government creditors having lower priority on the argument that private creditors lend on the firm expectation of repayment whereas government lenders are undertaking a public policy action that more easily accommodates the risk of nonpayment. The point here is not that one is a priori right and the other wrong. The point is that this is something to discuss.

Furthermore, recognition of these principles could be placed into the standard "boilerplate" (fine print) of bond contracts. But they should also be reflected in how the relations of private creditors and the sovereign borrower are governed should creditors bring cases to court. This would require reform of court practice in at least some countries so as to be in harmony with the guidelines.

One way to bring that about would be for the General Assembly to ask UNCITRAL to draft a "model law" that if adopted by national legislatures would implement the principles as they relate to the claims of private creditors in domestic courts. UNCITRAL is the appropriate body to undertake this task owing to its deep expertise, including on insolvency issues and in drafting model laws. UNCITRAL is also politically well balanced, with 60 members selected by the General Assembly to reflect the various geographical regions and principal economic and legal systems of the world. The commission operates through working groups, including one on insolvency law, which currently focuses on cross-border issues in corporate insolvency (UNCITRAL, 2013). The draft model law to implement the sovereign debt principles in domestic courts should then be endorsed by the General Assembly, signaling its global political acceptance, on the basis of which each country would then be expected to adapt the model law to fit its constitution and institutions and then adopt it into its legal system.

Each country would then have a comparable process to treat creditor claims against a troubled sovereign, including claims against its own government. Private creditors could still seek a voluntary restructuring agreement, but it would now be explicitly in the "shadow of the court." The adoption of the model law would thus give greater confidence to sovereign bondholders and other private creditors as to the extent and limitations of their rights to repayment. Not only would this discourage the practice of "forum shopping" to find the most creditor-friendly courts in which to press an unhappy bondholder's claims, but it would simplify restructuring bonds issued in different markets that might otherwise be subject to widely different domestic laws.

This innovation could be valuable in itself. There is already a strong growth in issuance of government as well as private securities in domestic markets in domestic currencies and under domestic laws. There is also a strong international investor interest in holding such securities (Akyüz, 2015).

Finally, the proposal needs a real-world counterpart to the right of appeal to the philosopher king from the official and/or private participants in the workout. In fact, a relevant forum already exists in the Permanent Court of Arbitration (PCA). It was created in 1899 at The Hague Peace Conference to assist states in peacefully settling disputes. The conference reconvened in 1907 and adopted several additional treaties, including one on using arbitration to settle sovereign debt disputes, with a view to ending "gunboat diplomacy." The PCA, which is not a court but an international organization with 116 member states, helps parties to a dispute set up arbitral panels for cases encompassing territorial, treaty, and human rights disputes between states, and commercial and investment disputes, including disputes arising under bilateral and multilateral investment treaties. It administers arbitration, conciliation, and fact finding in disputes involving various combinations of states, private parties, state entities, and intergovernmental organizations.[9] In sum, the PCA has a very old mandate to address sovereign debt workouts, a mandate that might be revived.

AND NOW A FIRST STEP

Perhaps we are not so far from being able to take the first step in the reform proposal, that is, reaching global consensus on the principles. Various proposals could inform the consultations. To start, the UN Conference on Trade and Development (UNCTAD) convoked an expert group, which formulated a set of principles on responsible sovereign borrowing and lending to sovereigns (UNCTAD, 2012), and a successor group deliberated on the desirable characteristics of a sovereign debt workout mechanism.[10] The UNCTAD Secretariat then synthesized these efforts in a comprehensive report (UNCTAD, 2015) that informed the debate in the General Assembly's ad hoc group on sovereign debt workouts. Also relevant, the Human Rights Council adopted "Guiding Principles on Foreign Debt and Human Rights" in 2011.[11] Although the guiding principles were adopted by vote in the Human Rights Council, this seemed to reflect less on the content of the proposals (which seem quite good) and more on the decision to undertake such an exercise in that forum. The Institute of International Finance (IIF), an organization of major private financial institutions, could also contribute to the principles discussion, as it had formulated a set of "Principles for Stable Capital Flows and Fair Debt Restructuring and Addendum" (IIF, 2012).

The principles could be guided as well by the agreed conclusions on sovereign debt in the Addis Ababa Action Agenda, adopted at the Third International Conference on Financing for Development in July 2015 (endorsed by the General Assembly in Resolution 69/313 on July 27, 2015), and by the overall policy imperatives of the 2030 Agenda for Sustainable Development that was adopted on September 25, 2015 at the heads of state summit meeting in the General Assembly (Resolution A/70/1). In this regard, the new principles could accord high priority to poverty eradication, to the creation and maintenance of decent work and rising incomes, and to progress in protecting the planet.

To take the first step, the world's governments need to agree that the current global system for addressing sovereign insolvency is unacceptable. The preference for staying with the status quo seems weak. It is a preference for the system we know with all its faults rather than taking the risk of attempting reform. That view could change. Nothing in politics is immutable.

NOTES

1. Incentive and equity aspects of a desirable sovereign insolvency regime are reviewed by Guzman and Stiglitz (2016).

2. For a more detailed historical review, see Ocampo (2016).

3. I apologize if I have distorted Professor Paulus's views to make them fit my framework. Readers can find the original in a number of papers, including two written by Paulus (2002, 2003).

4. Reflect, for example, on the case of Zaire during the career of Mobutu Sese Seko (e.g., Callaghy, 1986).

5. For a good discussion in an already vast literature on Greek debt, see Xafa (2014).

6. The unilateral cases are listed by the Paris Club secretariat at http://www.clubdeparis .org/en/communications/page/exceptional-treatments-in-case-of-crisis, last accessed December 18, 2015.

7. For example, see Supreme Court of the United States, "Brief[s] for the United States as Amicus Curiae in Support of Petitioner," Republic of Argentina, Petitioner v. NML Capital, Ltd (Case No. 12-842), December 4, 2013, and March 3, 2014; United States Court of Appeals for the Second Circuit, Brief for the United States of America as *Amicus Curiae* in Support of Reversal," NML Capital, Ltd. [et al.]. v. The Republic of Argentina (10-1487), December 28, 2012; April 4, 2012; and November 3, 2010.

8. An additional principle for the board to adopt, as James Boughton might specify, is that powerful member states not pressure IMF staff or management to include specific policy obligations of interest to those states in adjustment programs or distort the judgments of the institution (Boughton 2015: 11).

9. For additional information, see the PCA website at www.pca-cpa.org.

10. For a record of its discussions, see www.unctad.info/en/Debt-Portal/Project -Promoting-Responsible-Sovereign-Lending-and-Borrowing/About-the-Project /Debt-Workout-Mechanism, last accessed on February 25, 2015.

11. The principles are contained in a report to the UN Human Rights Council (2011). They were adopted by the council in Resolution 20/10 on July 5, 2012.

REFERENCES

Akyüz, Yilmaz. 2015. "Internationalization of Finance and Changing Vulnerabilities in Emerging and Developing Economies." Research Paper No. 60 (January), South Centre, Geneva.

Boughton, James M.2015. "The IMF as Just One Creditor: Who's in Charge When a Country Cannot Pay?" CIGI Papers No. 66 (April), Waterloo, Ont.

Callaghy, Thomas M. 1986. "The International Community and Zaire's Debt Crisis." In *The Crisis in Zaire: Myths and Realities*, ed. Georges Nzongola-Ntalaja, 221–244. Trenton, N.J.: Africa World Press.

Cosío-Pascal, Enrique. 2010. "Paris Club: Intergovernmental Relations in Debt Restructuring." In *Overcoming Developing Country Debt Crisis*, ed. Barry Herman, José Antonio Ocampo, and Shari Spiegel, 231–276. Oxford: Oxford University Press.

Devlin, Robert. 1993. *Debt and Crisis in Latin America: The Supply Side of the Story.* Princeton, N.J.: Princeton University Press.

Garay Salamanca, Luis Jorge. 2010. "The 1980s Crisis in Syndicated Bank Lending to Sovereigns and the Sequence of Mechanisms to Fix it." In *Overcoming Developing Country Debt Crisis*, ed. Barry Herman, José Antonio Ocampo, and Shari Spiegel, 111–139. Oxford: Oxford University Press.

Guzman, Martin, and Joseph E. Stiglitz. 2016. "Creating a Framework for Sovereign Debt Restructuring That Works." In *Too Little, Too Late: The Quest to Resolve Sovereign Debt Crises*, ed. Martin Guzman, José Antonio Ocampo, and Joseph E. Stiglitz, chapter 1. New York: Columbia University Press.

Institute of International Finance. 2012. "Principles for Stable Capital Flows and Fair Debt Restructuring and Addendum." In *Report of the Joint Committee on Strengthening the Framework for Sovereign Debt Crisis Prevention and Resolution.*October), annex II. Washington, D.C.

International Monetary Fund. 2002. "Fund Policy on Lending into Arrears to Private Creditors—Further Consideration of the Good-Faith Criterion" (Document number SM/02/248). www.imf.org/external/pubs/ft/privcred/073002.pdf (accessed February 23, 2015).

——. 2014. *IMF Response to the Financial and Economic Crisis.* Washington, D.C.: IMF Independent Evaluation Office.

——. 2015. "IMF to Provide Grants for $100 Million in Debt Relief to Ebola-hit Countries." *IMF Survey*, February 5.

Muchhala, Bhumika. 2015. "UN Adopts Landmark Debt Resolution on Principles for Sovereign Debt Restructuring." *Third World Network Info Service on Finance and Development*, September 11. www.twn.my/title2/finance/2015/fi150901.htm (accessed October 2, 2015).

Ocampo, José Antonio. 2016. "A Brief History of Sovereign Debt Resolution and a Proposal for a Multilateral Instrument." In *Too Little, Too Late: The Quest to Resolve Sovereign Debt Crises*, ed. Martin Guzman, José Antonio Ocampo, and Joseph E. Stiglitz, chapter 10. New York: Columbia University Press.

Paulus, Christoph G. 2002. "Some Thoughts on an Insolvency Procedure for Countries." *The American Journal of Comparative Law* 50 (No. 3, Summer): 531–553.

——. 2003. "A Statutory Procedure for Restructuring Debts of Sovereign States." *Recht der Internationalen Wirtschaft* 6 (June): 401–406.

United Nations. 2002. *Report of the International Conference on Financing for Development, Monterrey, Mexico, 18–22 March 2002* (A/CONF.198/11), chap. 1,

resolution 1, annex. http://www.un.org/ga/search/view_doc.asp?symbol=A/CONF.198
/11&Lang=E.
———. 2015. General Assembly Resolution 69/319, "Basic Principles on Sovereign Debt
Restructuring Processes," adopted September 10. http://www.un.org/en/ga/search
/view_doc.asp?symbol=A/RES/69/319.
United Nations Commission on International Trade Law. 2013. *A Guide to UNCIT-
RAL: Basic Facts About the United Nations Commission on International Trade Law.*
Vienna: United Nations. http://www.uncitral.org/pdf/english/texts/general/12
-57491-Guide-to-UNCITRAL-e.pdf.
United Nations Conference on Trade and Development. January 2012. *Principles on
Promoting Responsible Sovereign Lending and Borrowing* (document UNCTAD/
GDS/DDF/2012/Misc.1), Geneva. http://unctad.org/en/PublicationsLibrary
/gdsddf2012misc1_en.pdf.
———. April 2015. *Sovereign Debt Workouts: Going Forward Roadmap and Guide*
(document UNCTAD/GDS/DDF/2015/Misc.1), Geneva. http://unctad.org/en/
PublicationsLibrary/gdsddf2015misc1_en.pdf.
United Nations Human Rights Council. 2011. "Guiding Principles on Foreign Debt
and Human Rights." In *Report of the Independent Expert on the Effects of Foreign Debt
and Other Related International Financial Obligations of States on the Full Enjoy-
ment of All Human Rights, Particularly Economic, Social and Cultural Rights, Cephas
Lumina* (A/HRC/20/23), annex. http://www.ohchr.org/Documents/HRBodies
/HRCouncil/RegularSession/Session20/A-HRC-20-23_en.pdf.
Xafa, Miranda. June 2014. *Sovereign Debt Restructuring: Lessons from the 2012 Greek
Debt Restructuring.* CIGI Papers No. 33, Waterloo, Ont.

CHAPTER 12

Making a Legal Framework for Sovereign Debt Restructuring Operational

THE CASE FOR A SOVEREIGN DEBT WORKOUT INSTITUTION

Jürgen Kaiser

Ever since the beginning of the "Third World debt crisis" in 1982 the need for (individual or collective) debt relief for sovereigns has been an issue. It has also rightly been asked whether the international community has the appropriate instruments at its disposal to resolve debt crises quickly and fairly. The United Nations General Assembly (UNGA) resolution of September 9, 2014, provided a unique opportunity to redesign the institutional setup of debt restructuring, which academics, nongovernmental organizations, UN institutions, and some governments have been working for since the 1980s. The "legal framework" that the resolution envisages implies two essential innovations:

- it avoids assigning the responsibility for procedural reform to the IMF or to the creditors in institutions like the Paris Club; and
- it pays tribute to the fact that the key player in any debt restructuring is indeed the debtor government.

Here, I would like to discuss not the substance of the proposal, nor the legal framework in the strict sense of the word, but rather its "institutionalization." In other words: How can a new framework for sovereign debt restructuring function in practice to help overcome sovereign debt crises in a speedy and efficient manner? I shall make one specific proposal beyond a mere "framework."

SUBSTANCE

Without going into any detail on the substance of the legal framework, the following proposal for an institutionalization assumes that it will comply with three basic principles, which need to distinguish a new framework from the ways and means currently available to deal with sovereign overindebtedness:

- it needs to restructure debt in a single comprehensive process, with no payment obligations being exempted from the process;
- it needs to allow for impartial decision making about the terms of any debt restructuring; and
- this decision must be based on an impartial assessment of the debtor's situation.

HISTORICAL PRECEDENT

There are not many historical precedents for a sovereign debt restructuring that comply with these conditions, but the case of Indonesia in 1969 may be inspiring.[1]

In that year Indonesia was a low-income country with a per capita income of US$109. Its external debt was in the range of US$2.1 billion. Even in the absence of strict sustainability thresholds like the ones being applied today, there was broad agreement that this debt was unsustainable. The single biggest creditor was the Soviet Union, due to its earlier extensive support to President Soekarno's policies as a leader of the non-aligned movement.

Four years earlier Indonesia had undergone a bloody regime change with some 500,000 (alleged) communists killed by the pro-Western military. Consequently the political setup for a debt restructuring with Eastern and Western creditors was difficult. The (Western) Paris Club and the Soviet Union were in a mutual standoff, with each of them calling for concessions from the other. As the situation deteriorated, the parties agreed to look for a neutral mediator. At first the Paris Club suggested the freshly inaugurated World Bank president Robert McNamara. However, no consensus could be reached. Finally, the task was assigned to the director of Deutsche Bank, Hermann Josef Abs. However, he assumed the task not in his capacity as a private banker but as a board member of the official German development bank Kreditanstalt für Wiederaufbau. KfW also assumed the costs of his mission.

After a period of shuttle diplomacy, Abs made a proposal, which foresaw the full repayment of the capital and the full cancellation of past-due and current interest uniformly on all claims. In broad terms this implied a 50 percent NPV reduction of Indonesia's foreign debt payment obligations. With a (creditors') face-saving deviation of an across-the-board interest rate of 0.5 percent rather than full cancellation, Abs's proposal was implemented from 1971 onward.

The agreement was a speedy solution to a complex problem, and it led to a sustainable debt situation in Indonesia until the Asian crisis struck in 1998.

LESSONS FOR TODAY'S EFFORTS

Was "Indonesia 1969" a historically unique success story that escapes any application to today's sovereign debt problems? Or would it be possible to translate the episode's key elements into a legal and institutional general framework for debt restructuring? As one German government official put it in 2014: "Can Abs be institutionalized?" Who can a critically indebted sovereign turn to in order to trigger a fair and transparent debt restructuring in the absence of a generalized and binding legal framework?

Without any recourse to this particular historical experience, some of the more recent proposals for a sovereign debt restructuring mechanisms have referred to informality and ad hoc arrangements not as weaknesses but rather as valuable assets in a complex restructuring. Outstanding among these is the proposal of a sovereign debt forum (SDF), launched by Richard Gitlin and Brett House.[2] The SDF goes a long way in designing an institution that would be informal and ad hoc and that would serve as a facilitator of a meaningful dialogue between the debtor and the entirety of its creditors.

In this short text I do not want to match the profound and detailed proposals by Gitlin and House, but I do want to add one element of institutionalization to their proposal. However, this requires one additional piece of justification.

PRESERVING THE POLITICAL DYNAMICS

As stated at the beginning, the new quality of the present debate over past debt management rules and regulations such as the various "terms" of the Paris Club, the Heavily Indebted Poor Countries (HIPC) and Multilateral Debt Relief (MDRI) Initiatives, and the (failed) SDRM proposal by the IMF stems from the fact that it takes place at the United

Nations. While the above-mentioned mechanisms and proposals were developed and driven by creditors—and consequently solved *their* problems before anything else—the United Nations is a place where debtor country interests have at least as much weight as creditors' interests. Therefore the G-77's decision to launch the present debate at the United Nations, despite the rich countries' insistence on the IMF as the sole and exclusive host for it, was key to any progress that might be achieved in 2015 against the background of the new buildup of sovereign debt crises in the global South as well as the persisting crisis in the eurozone.

On the other hand, the United Nations is less well organized, resource rich, and homogenous than creditor-dominated institutions such as the IMF. So UN resolutions on global finance very often have been excellent but lacked any material consequences. Given the opposition to the present initiative by powerful UN members, in September 2015 nothing more than some positive but nonbinding "Principles for Sovereign Debt Restructuring" were the only visible outcome. They would not effect much of a change for any country that runs into payment problems from October 2015 onward.

This is where the need for substantial progress regarding the design of future sovereign debt workouts and the need to have a visible and material outcome of the present UN process in order to prevent it from getting lost in endless consensus-seeking processes coincide. What follows is a proposal of what that could mean in practice.

THE "INSTITUTION"

Establishing an institution with a mandate comparable to Abs's mandate in Indonesia, that is, to function and further emerge as the contact for any sovereign seeking a fair and comprehensive restructuring, can at the same time secure visibility and a continued reform dynamic.

ITS MANDATE . . .

The institution's involvement in cases of repayment problems on sovereign debt would not be compulsory. Rather the institution would be a visible *option* for any sovereign who wants/needs to trigger a restructuring process and wishes to avoid the shortcomings of existing frameworks. It would not be an attorney or advocate on behalf of the debtor with regard to the *outcome* of a restructuring process; however, it would support the debtor in the *process*, because the debtor is key for an efficient process in the interest of all parties. Its mandate therefore encompasses the following elements:

- It receives the request for a restructuring from the sovereign, mandates a time-limited standstill, and if so agreed among the parties, receives token good faith payments from the debtor.
- It facilitates the organization of exploratory meetings between the debtor and all creditors.
- It suggests providers of expertise/independent assessment with regard to debt sustainability for the consideration of and agreement on by the parties.
- It mediates a conciliatory solution between a sovereign and all its creditors upon request by the parties
- It organizes a more formal and binding debt arbitration process based on UN Commission on International Trade Law (UNCITRAL) principles and rules,[3] if more informal instruments such as facilitation, mediation, and conciliation fail.

It does not have to be ready-made when the sixty-ninth session of the UNGA ends, but can start existing as an option from the end of the sixty-ninth session onward, with rules, bylaws, standard procedures, and infrastructure developing over time. However, from the very first day it would be able to fulfill its purpose upon request by an indebted sovereign.

. . . AND ITS EVENTUAL INSTITUTIONALIZATION

Proposals for such a catalytic institution have been raised in various forms in the recent past, for instance under the roof of the Permanent Court of Arbitration in The Hague by the Dutch government or for an international debt arbitration court under Scottish insolvency law by the regional government of Scotland. For various political reasons none of these proposals has been implemented. However, their proponents may still be asked to become part of a debate on the best possible design and location of the institution.

For the institution to start functioning, there does not have to be any international treaty or other statutory underpinning, though at a later stage it may be advisable to define and agree on one. However, this should then be the formalization of an already tested and functioning informal international practice and not the prerequisite for a new arrangement.

The institution needs to have at least an informal UN mandate, such as a resolution, that welcomes its creation and encourages sovereigns to seek its support. Even with this mandate, however, it does not have to be part of the UN system, although affiliation with a UN body is an option. It needs to be governed by public interest, so it cannot be a private for-profit organization, but it can be organized under private law. An option is a board of "eminent persons."

It would have a very small technical staff but would be able to mobilize experts, facilitators, mediators, and arbitrators quickly, reliably, and efficiently.

It could be called "sovereign debt restructuring liaison office" or something more fanciful.

ENFORCEMENT OF AD HOC AND INFORMAL AWARDS?

The institution would not be a superbureaucracy, able to enforce compliance with its awards through legal end executive powers. In fact, no international body presently is in that position, and often enough asking for full-scale legal binding power has rather been an attempt to outmaneuver reform proposals than to find solutions to a debt problem. It needs to be kept in mind that sovereign debt management has largely been free of any legally binding and executable instruments. This is a deficiency and an opportunity at the same time. An opportunity because it allows for pragmatism when designing individual solutions or general frameworks (such as this "institution") that may best serve common interests. This does not mean, however, that informal awards could not be enforced. Generally, wherever the institution engages in cases of debt restructuring there can be three levels of enforcement of the results of processes organized by the institution:

- Domestic law enforcement in all jurisdictions, particularly the ones under which debt is contracted; specific legal regulations can include the type of "anti–vulture fund laws" in force in Britain and Belgium; the institution would encourage and support the creation of such laws.
- Enforcement of arbitral awards under the New York Convention on the Recognition of Foreign Arbitral Awards of 1958, and eventually under other national laws, providing enforcement for consensually organized processes below the level of arbitration.
- De facto enforcement through the cessation of payments and the impossibility of attaching debtors' assets.

ADDITIONAL FUNCTIONS

Beyond the immediate services the institution can provide to indebted sovereigns, it can serve additional purposes in the context of global debt management:

- It can manage an inventory of best practices, rules, and regulations on debt sustainability and on procedures for creditor aggregation.
- It can produce a standard reference on global debt data.
- It can serve as a rallying point for information exchange regarding debt problems and debt management practice.

URGENCY

It should be kept in mind that sovereign debt is no problem of the past or of just a few remote and almost failing states, or one of any distant future. Out of seventy-four low-income countries and small island developing states, fifteen countries (i.e., more than 20 percent) are considered by the IMF[4] to be at high risk of debt distress. Out of these six are post–completion point HIPCs, that is, countries that have just been relieved of a big chunk of their external debt in a multilateral process. An additional thirty-three countries (i.e., 45 percent) are at "moderate risk," which means any negative deviation from the development path assumed by the IMF in its debt sustainability analysis can trigger a debt crisis.

As a matter of illustration: the severely indebted small island developing state Grenada was in default from April 2013 until December 2015, because powerful creditors in the Paris Club were only prepared to negotiate individually and after concessions from other bilaterals. In the end Grenada obtained a restructuring far below the level it required to restore debt sustainability. What if the tiny Spice Isle had the option at the start of its economic crisis to ask a "sovereign debt restructuring liaison office" for its support in realistically assessing its future payment capacities as an extremely vulnerable small economy and in suggesting a feasible restructuring? Eventually, someone like Mr. Abs would have had a proposal.

NOTES

1. For a short summary of the Indonesian case, see: Kaiser (2013). A more detailed presentation can be found in Hoffert (2001).

2. Gitlin and House (2014).

3. UNCITRAL principles and rules would not be the only option here. Other legal references could be used (see Howse 2016).

4. See the IMF's "List of LIC DSAs for PRGT-Eligible Countries as of October 01, 2015," www.imf.org/external/Pubs/ft/dsa/DSAlist.pdf.

REFERENCES

Gitlin, R., and B. House. January 2014. "A Blueprint for a Sovereign Debt Forum." CIGI, Waterloo, Ont.

Hoffert, A. 2001. "The 1970 Indonesian Debt Accord." Discussion Paper No.05-01, Fakultät für Wirtschaftswissenschaften der Ruhr Universität, Bochum, Germany.

Howse, Robert. "Toward a Framework for Sovereign Debt Restructuring: What Can Public International Law Contribute?" In *Too Little, Too Late: The Quest to Resolve Sovereign Debt Crises*, ed. Martin Guzman, José Antonio Ocampo, and Joseph E. Stiglitz, chapter 14. New York: Columbia University Press.

Kaiser, J. October 2013. *Resolving Sovereign Debt Crises: Towards a Fair and Transparent International Insolvency Framework*. 2nd rev. ed. Dialogue on Globalization Series. Berlin: Friedrich Ebert Stiftung, 26–27.

United Nations Commission on International Trade Law. 2010. *Arbitration Rules* [as revised in 2010]. Vienna.

CHAPTER 13

Perspectives on a Sovereign Debt Restructuring Framework

LESS IS MORE

Richard A. Conn Jr.

Initiatives to improve sovereign debt restructuring (SDR) began long before recent Argentine bond decisions but were redoubled in the aftermath of these rulings. At first glance, these cases identify problematic contract language that could be rectified by redrafting critical boilerplate provisions such as the pari passu and collective action (CAC) clauses. But given the effects of disorder and delays in restructuring foreign sovereign debt upon debtor countries, creditors, and the bond market itself, it is understandable that some are uncomfortable leaving such matters largely in the hands of private parties to contracts without a framework that assists in minimizing damage to contracting and noncontracting parties alike.

The creation of an agreed-upon framework that interacts with private party contracts or restricts contractual options ex ante is a logical alternative to the status quo if this approach can provide greater stability and efficiency in the restructuring process while allowing for sufficient flexibility and certainty (traditional benefits of the iterative development of contract language) for market participants. There are a broad variety of options to consider and cost/benefit analyses, particularly relating to political feasibility, to be performed before implementing a framework that would be akin to an international bankruptcy court with substantive powers to affect the rights of contracting parties. There are, however, procedural frameworks that could add value to the restructuring process with less risk of treading on the political terrain of sovereigns.

THE CATALYST FOR RECENT EFFORTS TO CREATE
A FRAMEWORK FOR SDR: ARGENTINA

The Argentine litigations feature several attention-grabbing aspects. These include the Second Circuit's one-two punch: its interpretation of pari passu and its granting of unusually broad injunctive relief.

The court's very limited discussion of competing interpretations of pari passu is curious given the centrality of that issue to the decision. In the context of foreign debt restructuring, there are principally two competing theories regarding interpretation, one limited to "ranking" (which is the traditional meaning in other contexts) and the other including the concept of "ratable." The court's lack of discussion of these competing meanings or of contractual interpretation rules in the case of ambiguity raises questions regarding whether there was a generally accepted meaning of the term in the market. The market's reaction to the court's decision suggests that there was and that the meaning did not include the "ratable" concept. It is not clear whether the court considered the argument that market participants (including the buyers of bonds at deep discounts in this specific case) knew that "ranking" was the common meaning of pari passu. Such would naturally then support arguments based on unjust enrichment and other equitable theories to counter the court's eventual conclusion that its decision merely held parties to their bargain under state contract law.

As a remedy for breaching the pari passu clause, the court prohibited Argentina from making payments on its restructured bonds unless it paid the holdouts on a "ratable" basis. The courts defined "ratable" to require that when Argentina pays 100 percent of the amount owed to the restructured bondholders (i.e., the periodic coupon payment), it must also pay 100 percent of any amount owed to the litigating holdout creditors (i.e., all past-due principal and interest in an amount aggregating approximately US$1.6 billion). This does not sound like pari passu as that term commonly is used in the bankruptcy context, but this was not a bankruptcy case. Indeed, the court appeared to be saying that subsequent bonds are not in fact pari passu with the bonds at issue. The court concluded that the deal was that the relevant bonds would be paid come hell or high water prior to any subsequent issuance being serviced. There is, of course, nothing that would prevent future bonds from containing different language clarifying the meaning of pari passu and even limiting the scope of injunctive relief, but the decision does for the time being make SDR of bonds with similar language problematic due to the enhanced leverage of holdouts.[1]

In the context of the Argentine rulings, the UN General Assembly overwhelmingly decided on September 9, 2014, to begin work on a multilateral legal framework—effectively a treaty or convention—for SDR to improve the global financial system. Discussions regarding how to address the Argentine decisions focus upon the following alternatives: (1) creating a new legal/statutory framework as envisioned by the United Nations, (2) letting the market simply revise problematic contractual terms, or (3) some hybrid of these two alternatives. I will focus upon issues surrounding a new framework recognizing that contractual revisions are already occurring and will continue to take place in the private market.[2]

CONTEXT FOR EVALUATING AN SDR FRAMEWORK

Any framework to address SDR will be a piece in the mosaic of international law and will be evaluated based on its perceived fairness. Fairness, like beauty, is of course in the eye of the beholder, but the desire for fairness is universal, and the perceived lack of it can lead to conflict. Russia's President Putin, for example, is in the midst of an international campaign to underscore his perception of deep-rooted unfairness in economic and political relations and institutions. In Valdai, he continued his efforts to form coalitions to alter the rules of the game and/or establish competing international organizations and economic levers. Simultaneously, he sends the same message by taking various types of military action.

Putting aside the irony of Putin lecturing on fairness, the sentiment strikes a chord of truth in many parts of the world. Several nations have established competitors to major international financial institutions. China, for example, after long complaining that the International Monetary Fund (IMF), World Bank, and Asian Development Bank were dominated by the interests of the United States, Europe, and Japan, established the Asian Infrastructure Investment Bank (AIIB) with the support of many nations. The IMF and United Kingdom announced their desire to cooperate with the AIIB, but the United States has voiced strong opposition and pressured others not to provide support. The New Development Bank very recently formed by the BRICS (Brazil, Russia, India, China, and South Africa) also was expressly designed to counter the unfairness perceived by these nations in the governance of the IMF and World Bank.

Whether or not it is merited, there is certainly some degree of skepticism regarding the fairness of Western institutions outside the Western world. If the framework to address SDR is to be perceived broadly as fair, proponents must take this into account by, for example, making extraordinary efforts to gather the perspectives of market participants, including those of debtor nations and potential debtor nations. On the other hand, for an SDR framework to move from conceptual to functional, proponents must understand and address the political and market-based objections of the United States and other established powers whose support is vital to the adoption and implementation of a framework. In short, crafting an SDR framework evokes the long history of weaker nations seeking to gain power over their fates and of more powerful nations resisting ceding power. The last major effort to adopt a framework was led by the IMF. The IMF's proposed Sovereign Debt Restructuring Mechanism (SDRM) was voted down, however, in 2003. Countries, including the United States, did not wish to cede the power necessary to the IMF or other multilateral bodies to allow the SDRM to function.

STRATEGY AND TACTICS FOR ADOPTING AN INITIAL FRAMEWORK FOR SDR

Given the inability to garner support for SDRM in the past, what is the best shot at adopting a framework now? Clearly we must address the objections of those who opposed SDRM in the past while at the same time carefully considering fairness issues if we want a framework to be viewed as a legitimate dispute resolution tool even by critics of Western institutions who have begun setting up competing institutions. We need to (1) identify clearly which problems we are trying to solve through a framework (and which we are not), (2) make the case for its need (meticulously explaining why the current contract-based system is insufficient), and (3) demonstrate how a framework can better address the problems identified in point 1 through narrowly drafted provisions. Each element is addressed briefly below.

PROBLEMS TO BE SOLVED BY A FRAMEWORK FOR SDR

It is difficult to find consensus on precisely which problems a framework should be designed to address and which problems should not be within its purview. This is due in part to the different approaches taken by public versus private institutions. The public sector measures the success of restructuring largely by the effect on the debtor economy (focusing on the timing of initiation of restructurings and various economic results), while the private sector focuses upon the negotiation elements and effects on bondholders. Moreover, there is little consensus on the breadth of the powers a framework should possess.

Nonetheless, here is my list of problem areas relating to the initiation as well as negotiation of restructurings that a framework should address in its initial incarnation:

the coordination of restructurings;
the speed of restructurings;
the efficiency of restructurings; and
the process and predictability of restructurings.

It is also important to identify problems outside the purview of even of a fully matured framework for SDR. These include in my view:

Moral hazard: an SDR framework will be unlikely to limit debtors who borrow irresponsibly counting on using the leverage of contagion/ systemic risk and political harm to obtain bailouts and possibly gain leverage over existing bondholders to accept haircuts. (As discussed later, this may be better addressed through upfront regulatory issues.)

Politics: an SDR framework will be unlikely to infringe upon political territory. The political process does and will have a tremendous impact on the course of significant defaults and restructurings, so politicians are highly unlikely to support any framework that limits their options or powers. Taking Greece as an example, the resolution of this crisis affects the viability of the eurozone and even the prospects for success of the EU itself as well as Europe's ability to remain united in responding to the Ukraine crisis. For these reasons, SDR and related bailouts are integral parts of a political response and hence unsuitable for resolution by a judicial decision maker.

DEFICIENCIES OF THE CURRENT PRIVATE CONTRACT SYSTEM

The arguments against maintaining only the current private contract system include:

- It fails to address voting among different bond issuances (absent aggregation provisions), thereby complicating restructuring. This suggests a short-term need to deal with language in existing bonds that allows for holdouts.

- It fails to allow for new funding resulting in default or bailouts by IMF or regional institutions.
- It fails to provide a common forum for all parties to address restructuring.
- Most importantly, it is concerned only with the interests of contracting parties, not systemic threats ("too big to fail" issues, contagion) that affect noncontracting parties.

HOW CAN A FRAMEWORK ADDRESS THE IDENTIFIED PROBLEMS?

A framework granting substantive powers to a decision maker would, like a bankruptcy court, adjudicate disputes that could not be negotiated successfully. While an international bankruptcy court for SDR may be the ultimate goal of the international community, it not likely achievable at the outset for the political reasons mentioned earlier and the additional reasons discussed later. If limited in power, consensual, and consistent with contract rights of bondholders, however, the first iteration of a framework might be feasible politically and practical. If all goes well, it could foster trust sufficient to enable it to take on additional responsibilities.

Accordingly, here are suggested features of an SDR framework that is designed to be broadly acceptable:

1. It is consensual.
2. It provides a mechanism to invite all relevant parties, including the IMF, to one forum.
3. It provides rules and procedures for restructuring.
4. It utilizes substantive law only to the extent contracting parties adopt it.
5. It provides impartial, expert SDR decision makers who make decisions only with consent of relevant parties. Otherwise, they play the role of expert SDR facilitators.
6. It permits discussion regarding contagion risk, sustainability of the debtor's economy, and debt service.
7. It provides for mechanisms to create creditors' committees.
8. It focuses upon procedure, not enforcement.
9. It would pursue the support of leading participants in the market by showing that the framework would speed up restructuring, create greater predictability, and ultimately increase liquidity.

PROSPECTS FOR A MORE SUBSTANTIVE FRAMEWORK

Several scholars have proposed draft frameworks that seek to do more than establish a procedural framework without enforcement mechanisms such as that outlined earlier.[3] These can best be described as setting up an international bankruptcy tribunal specializing in SDR. Though it may not be feasible to implement such frameworks initially, it is important to be working to develop them now for several reasons, including the need to think through a multitude of complex issues (some of which are referenced later) and the desirability of laying out next stages in the maturity of a framework.

The starting point is to identify which problems a substantive rather than procedural framework would seek to address. What principles would then guide a tribunal? Would these include promoting liquidity in the bond market generally, helping existing bondholders get paid, safeguarding the economies of debtor nations, promoting IMF goals of structural reforms by debtors, authorizing new debt of higher priority than existing debt, and/or authorizing loans for the sake of avoiding contagion or meltdown? A decision maker needs to rely upon laws defining the principles to be applied and the extent of jurisdiction and powers and clarifying how to balance the competing goals. To agree upon such fundamental matters will be very challenging.

The mechanics of bankruptcy also present myriad practical issues that will take time to address. To establish an international bankruptcy law, which we arguably have been inching toward in the United States with the replacement of Section 304 with Chapter 15 of the U.S. Bankruptcy Code (the Code), would be an extraordinarily complex undertaking. If based on U.S. concepts embodied in Chapters 9 and 11 of the Code, this would imply that the key features of those chapters, such as the ability of courts to alter contractual terms in order to promote the greater good of restructuring, would be applied to SDRs. On what basis would bond terms be altered without creditor consent, a typical feature of unsecured claims in bankruptcy? Balancing the interests of all parties in this process requires massive societal buy-in, even in the comparatively simple context of domestic U.S. bankruptcies. Such consensus and support will be all the more difficult to achieve on an international scale. Moreover, who will adjudicate and enforce international bankruptcy law? Just as all politics is local, so is bankruptcy law, in the sense that bankruptcy rulings have real effects upon employment and wealth in specific jurisdictions, all of which can result in forum shopping. As we consider the concept of international bankruptcy, we must keep in mind the practical reality of how home court advantages will play out.

It is worth keeping in mind Alex Rosenberg's work[4] in exploring how the human mind developed cooperative behavior. His theory is that cooperation reflects a tit-for-tat process; I will trust you next time if you acted honorably this time and will not trust you this time if you burned me last time. How does this potentially apply to creating a framework, such as international bankruptcy laws, to address SDR? As we broaden the community interacting in applying a set of laws (moving from national to international in the case of SDRs), we will be relying at some level upon enforcement of rulings in the domestic courts of various nations and must therefore consider how tit for tat will play out in order for an SDR framework to be perceived as fair. Similarly, the procedures, laws, and decision-making procedures under an SDR framework must also be perceived as fair if we expect parties to participate.

Then there are "the rubber meets the road" problems to take into account, such as the willingness of attorneys to advise their clients to include in their documents dispute resolution for SDR in an untested, complex new forum. At least initially, an international bankruptcy court would likely need to apply some existing substantive law, since creating a new body of substantive law will deprive market participants of the comfort of precedent (seeing how that law has been applied in the past).

For these reasons, it makes more sense to create a procedural framework as the first step, rather than a more ambitious substantive framework, and see whether trust and confidence emerging from that allow for certain matters to eventually be decided by some authority. Much of the Code in the United States is procedural, so effectuating this first step should not be taken lightly or viewed as a small accomplishment. Such a framework could be under UN auspices but remain consensual, like the International Court of Justice. It is, however, important to begin focusing on the substantive laws that could be added and to consider a pilot SDR framework to test out substantive provisions. This may be feasible for the eurozone, where the partial surrender of sovereignty that has already occurred may make substantive statutory rules less controversial.

This can all be viewed as leading toward a standing international bankruptcy court tasked with addressing SDR and recognized by domestic courts through treaties or otherwise. How far can this go before becoming politically impractical to adopt? Nations have shown some recognition that it serves narrow national interests to have international disputes addressed through widely respected consensual dispute resolution mechanisms, but there is a long way to go before this perspective becomes politically popular in domestic settings. The desire to be heard in an independent forum by a fair decision maker will always be present, so a well-conceived SDR framework has a role to play in the expansion of civilized international dispute resolution. But it will take the development of precedent, enforcement mechanisms, and trust that arises from positive tit-for-tat experiences for a new framework to grow and function effectively.

CONCLUDING COMMENTS

A final thought—our task was to explore a framework for the improvement of SDR. But the very term SDR may too narrow to actually address the problems of contagion and systemic risk that are the undercurrents of SDR. If we were instead to consider how to avoid, limit, or minimize the impact of sovereign defaults (rather than just how to restructure), then regulation before debt is incurred would have been a major focal point of my discussion. Just as countries regulate "too big to fail" financial institutions, so the international community should seek consensus on proper regulation of sovereign debt offerings to limit systemic risk. For example, consensus might be reached that bonds must contain CACs and aggregation clauses to avoid holdout problems such as those faced by Argentina. Another example is a standstill clause to provide contractually authorized breathing space under certain conditions. More creative concepts would doubtless also emerge. In short, it seems logical to focus not just upon SDR but also upon front-end regulation to address the public policy concerns of contagion and systemic risk that result from private contractual arrangements.

Such provisions would raise questions of national sovereignty, such as the freedom of nations to seek to borrow on whatever terms they wish. But if a global solution to sovereign debt crises is the goal, some elements of sovereignty must be on the table. Moreover, while financial networks are interrelated and hence difficult to tinker with, the advantage of setting contractual requirements is that they focus only upon the content of private agreements. Though private parties may not want any regulation, at least they would be able to take the requirements into account as they negotiate their deals. The substance of required contractual terms would be limited to those few provisions around which consensus could be built, such as CACs or standstill clauses. If such provisions were approved by the United Nations, this would constitute a positive precedent that may allow for the gradual adoption of additional regulatory provisions and add legitimacy to the proposition that competition among sovereigns for debt should not be based in part on whether or not systemic risk prevention clauses appear in debt instruments.

The stakes are high in establishing a new framework for SDR, not just because of the relationship of this undertaking to sensitive international themes but also because sovereign defaults are so commonplace and lending to developing countries so important. The opportunity is at hand to build stronger international relationships by exploring together and implementing a framework that can add value immediately to SDRs and offer the prospect of even greater effectiveness as the framework's role expands over time.

NOTES

1. See Chodos (2016).
2. See Gitlin and House (2016).
3. See Guzman and Stiglitz (2016) and Kaiser (2016).
4. See Rosenberg (2011).

REFERENCES

Chodos, Sergio. 2016. "From the Pari Passu Discussion to the 'Illegality' of Making Payments." In *Too Little, Too Late: The Quest to Resolve Sovereign Debt Crises*, ed. Martin Guzman, José Antonio Ocampo, and Joseph E. Stiglitz, chapter 4. New York: Columbia University Press.

Gitlin, Richard, and Brett House. 2016. "Contractual and Voluntary Approaches to Sovereign Debt Restructuring: There Is Still More to Do," in Guzman, *Too Little, Too Late*, chapter 7.

Guzman, Martin and Joseph E. Stiglitz. 2016. "Creating a Framework for Sovereign Debt Restructuring That Works," in Guzman, *Too Little, Too Late*, chapter 1.

Kaiser, Jurgen. 2016. "Making a Legal Framework for Sovereign Debt Restructuring Operational," in Guzman, *Too Little, Too Late*, chapter 12.

Rosenberg, A. 2011. *The Atheist's Guide to Reality: Enjoying Life Without Illusions*, 128–131. New York: Norton.

CHAPTER 14

Toward a Framework for Sovereign Debt Restructuring

WHAT CAN PUBLIC INTERNATIONAL LAW CONTRIBUTE?

Robert Howse

By resolution of the General Assembly, the United Nations adopted this fall the principles to underpin a multilateral framework for sovereign debt restructuring.[1] While they are still not accepted by the United States and are controversial in some European countries, the principles represent the clearest acknowledgement so far that the resolution of sovereign debt crises in a manner that balances fairly and efficiently the rights and responsibilities of debtors, creditors and other stakeholders is a matter of concern to the global community. The purpose of this brief paper is to analyze the possible international-law elements of a possible framework for sovereign debt restructuring, taking into account the UN Principles; this exercise requires first understanding how international law affects or shapes at present the resolution of sovereign debt crises. This paper draws extensively from the deliberations and publications of the UN Conference on Trade and Development (UNCTAD) Working Group on a Sovereign Debt Workout Mechanism,[2] of which I am a member, and especially the efforts of the three other public international-law specialists in the group, Juan-Pablo Bohoslavsky, Matthias Goldmann, and Marie Sudreau.

International law is drawn from several fundamental sources that are set out in Article 38 of the Statute of the International Court of Justice: treaties, custom,[3] general principles of law of "civilized nations," and as secondary sources, decisions of courts and tribunals and the views of scholarly authorities. Traditionally international law has been understood as made by states, binding only on states, and only conferring rights on states, at least directly. With areas like international criminal law and human rights law, this is changing;[4] international investment law is a dramatic example of such a change, with private investors being enabled to directly sue states for violations of treaty protections of investment and enforce a monetary judgment in domestic courts around the world. It is notorious that apart from some exceptional mechanisms such as the one just mentioned with respect to investment, enforcement of international law tends to be diffuse and often dependent upon the cooperation of domestic authorities. In some legal systems, international law may be given "direct effect" by domestic courts and other authorities; in others, such as that of the United States, it is a very complex matter to determine whether and in what way an international-law norm will have effect and whether intermediate action such as legislative implementation is necessary (the case of so-called non-self-executing treaties).

At the same time the conduct of international relations has been shaped in important ways by what many international lawyers call "soft law" norms that are not formally binding as a matter of international law on states but guide the behavior of state, and increasingly non-state, actors in various specialized domains. As Ruti Teitel and I have noted, it may often be the case that soft law–type norms attract greater compliance than formally binding rules of international law: one example is the Basle Committee norms on capital adequacy for financial institutions, which are not binding as international law but have gained considerable legal force through their implementation by domestic regulators.[5]

SOVEREIGN DEBT AND THE EXISTING INTERNATIONAL LEGAL LANDSCAPE

Although it is sometimes claimed that there is an underlying rule of customary international law that a sovereign is required to repay its debt in full, even despite fundamental transformations such as regime change, the notion of "maintenance of obligations," to the extent this norm exists, is grounded in the obligation of *pacta sunt servanda*. As Michael Waibel and I have pointed out, this concept concerns *treaty* obligations. It could apply to obligations under the International Monetary Fund (IMF) Articles of Agreement, for example, which is a treaty; but it is rare that the obligation to repay is treaty based. These obligations are largely, and entirely so in the case of private, non-state creditors, created by contract rather than by treaty. Where treaty law does come into the picture is where contractual debt obligations are protected as "investments" under bilateral investment treaties. In such instances, nonpayment or partial payment of such obligations could constitute an "expropriation" or a violation of the norm of fair and equitable treatment. In the *Abaclat v. Argentina* case,[6] in an award on jurisdiction, the majority of the tribunal held that restructured Argentine bonds constituted an "investment" in Argentina, thus allowing the bondholders to pursue their claim on the merits under the Italy-Argentina Bilateral Investment Treaty (BIT). However, a vigorous dissenting opinion by Professor George Abi-Saab contested this interpretation of the meaning of "investment," arguing that as purchasers of restructured bonds on the international secondary market the bondholders in question did not have the requisite connection to Argentina to be considered as investors there for purposes of the treaty. In a subsequent award in an investor-state dispute, *Postova Banka v. Greece*,[7] the majority supported a position akin to Abi-Saab's, finding that given the special nature of sovereign debt one could not assume as a general matter that it was to be included even in a relatively broad definition of an investment. At the same time, the defense of necessity under Article 25 of the International Law Commission (ILC) Articles of State Responsibility may be available to justify a suspension of performance of international obligations during a crisis that rises to a state of "necessity" within the meaning of Article 25. In the litigation arising out of Argentina's financial and economic crisis of the 1990s, some investor-state arbitral tribunals found that Argentina had met the conditions of a necessity defense under Article 25, whereas others did not. More generally, any obligation to repay under a treaty, even if reinforced by the customary norm of *pacta sunt servanda*, would still have to be reconciled with a debtor state's human rights obligations to its own citizens under, for example, the Covenant on Economic, Social and Cultural Rights. These obligations would have equal status under international law with those under any other treaty, and on some theories of international legal obligation, a higher status, in the sense that international human rights obligations are owed to the international community as a whole (as opposed to the bilateral obligations of an investment treaty, for instance).

Because the underlying obligation to repay sovereign debt is contractual in almost all relevant cases, the applicable law is the domestic law of the contract, which will usually also specify the courts of that jurisdiction as a dispute forum. However, there is nothing inevitable in that. There are precedents, in the area of investment law for example, for also putting into a contract that international-law principles will apply as well as domestic law; similarly, the parties could specify binding international arbitration as an alternative to recourse to domestic courts. Generally, such clauses have been honored by domestic courts, which have refused jurisdiction where the parties agreed in advance to an international arbitral forum.

In any case, even with arbitration, domestic courts are the ultimate enforcement mechanism, as is illustrated by international investment law. Enforcement of obligations of sovereigns in domestic courts engages at least two bodies of international law, that of sovereign immunity and that which pertains to the recognition and enforcement of foreign judgments. In the case of sovereign immunity, sovereign debt contracts would either contain waivers of sovereign immunity with respect to the jurisdiction of the domestic courts over the sovereign or, in any case, the so-called commercial exception to sovereign immunity would likely apply. The Court of Justice has recently ruled in the case of *Germany v. Italy* that there is a core of sovereign immunity that all states are bound to respect as a matter of customary international law.[8]

However, the court was decidedly unhelpful in indicating the content of that core as opposed to what is left to each state to determine under its sovereign immunity statutes, including any exceptions to immunity. Immunity with respect to execution of a judgment against state assets is not the same thing as immunity from jurisdiction, it should be noted. There are often significant limits on the ability of a creditor to obtain execution against state assets. Moreover, the ILC Draft Articles on Jurisdictional Immunities of States and Their Property (1991), Article 18, provide that for a state to be subject to "measures of constraints" by the court of another state, including attachment and execution against property, it must either have consented to be subject to those specific "measures of constraint" or "allocated or earmarked the property for the satisfaction of the claim that is the object of that proceeding" or it must be the case that "the property is specifically in use or intended for use by the State for other than government non-commercial purposes and is in the territory of the State of the forum and has a connection with the claim which is the object of the proceeding or with the agency or instrumentality against which the proceeding was directed." While it is unclear to what extent the draft articles reflect customary international law today, it is fairly clear that some of Judge Griesa's orders against Argentina in the New York court would constitute "measures of constraint" not contemplated by the narrow exceptions to immunity from "measures of constraint" in Article 18. In particular, Judge Griesa's attempt to prevent Argentina from making payments to restructured creditors does not, on its face, appear to fall within any of the exceptions in Article 18. Here UN principle 6 would reinforce such an reading, as it requires that sovereign immunity be interpreted "restrictively."

This leads to another respect in which international legal obligation may be relevant to the enforcement of sovereign debt contracts. Such enforcement by the courts of a state must be consistent with the international legal obligations of that state to others. Where BITs exist, foreign restructured creditors might be able, for example, to sue the United States on the expropriation or on the grounds of fair and equitable treatment provisions of the BITs, due to Judge Griesa's order, which has disrupted Argentina's payments to these creditors. This would depend upon whether the restructured creditors could be considered "investors" in the United States within the meaning of the particular treaty in question, thereby acquiring standing.

Finally, enforcement of sovereign debt contracts is affected by the Hague Convention on the Recognition and Enforcement of Foreign Judgments. This multilateral treaty would apply where a creditor obtains a judgment in one jurisdiction, typically that of the contract, but wishes to enforce it in another state, usually because the sovereign debtor has assets there of the kind not protected by sovereign immunity. Under the Hague Convention the courts of a state may refuse recognition or enforcement where it is "manifestly incompatible" with public policy. It is up to the courts and other authorities of the state in question to determine the content of public policy.

But if we look at the "big picture" of the management of sovereign debt crises up to now, it is quite clear that it is informal norms, which international lawyers might in some cases call "soft" international law, that have played a predominant role. These norms have emerged in an ad hoc, diffuse way through the establishment and evolution of institutions such as the London and Paris Clubs, the bargaining methods of creditors and debtors, the practices of the IMF, and the largely unwritten principles on the basis of which private law firms have shaped the clauses, including the jurisdictional provisions, in sovereign debt contracts. Neither the norms nor the epistemic community or elite group that emits them and actualizes them operate in so doing under the authority of public international law, generally speaking (except the Fund to the very limited extent that its mandate in this area can be derived from the Articles of Agreement). The norms in question included, until Argentina's unilateral restructuring, the notion that a sovereign has no entitlement to a restructuring that involves reduction in its levels of indebtedness and that any restructuring must involve the IMF. The eventual acceptance of the restructuring by the almost all of the relevant actors is an example of a very effective change in an informal norm through the initiative of one debtor state.[9] Judge Griesa's orders are a counterexample of a unilateral action by one state that threatens the norm change. However, many of the insiders, the epistemic community (including the IMF), have expressed serious concerns about his judgment. Along these lines, today "soft law" also includes the UNCTAD Principles on Responsible Sovereign Lending and Borrowing[10] which declare that "a state of economic necessity can prevent the borrower's full and/or timely repayment" (Principle 9) and "the restructuring should be proportional to the sovereign's need and all stakeholders (including citizens) should share an equitable burden of adjustment and/or losses." These norms are reinforced now by UN Principle 8 on sustainability.

As creditors and debtor states and other actors have responded to crises from the 1970s and 1980s onward, they have grasped on to the norms, "experts," and other intermediaries that presented themselves, more or less ad hoc or willy-nilly available; it is perhaps an implication of Coase that bargaining in a normative and institutional vacuum is perhaps impossible or prohibitively costly. There was no necessary alignment between the norms, elite agents, and institutions that presented themselves as available and appropriate to deal with sovereign debt crises, either with international law or/and a socially and economically optimal approach to addressing such crises. But there was often a sense of inevitability, especially on the part of debtor states, that they had no choice but to work within this constellation of informal norms, elite agents, and institutions or face unacceptable consequences, such as being cut off from the international financial system altogether. Argentina's bold move to restructure outside that framework was referred to earlier. This move has disturbed the sense of inevitability; but the Griesa orders show it is messy and can introduce new uncertainties, increasing the transaction costs of bargaining to sustainable debt restructuring.

MOVING FORWARD UNDER THE UN RESOLUTION

One approach to moving forward on the UN resolution would be to attempt to replace the existing "framework" as just described with a framework of alternative norms and institutions that through the creation of a multilateral treaty would be binding as a matter of international law, and would impose the principles in the resolution as formal treaty rules. In addition to the general difficulties of multilateral treaty making, and the opposition of the United States to this exercise, the fundamental nature of sovereign debt obligations as contractual obligations under domestic law creates a formidable enforcement challenge with respect to any such framework. The framework could easily be undermined, or regarded in any case as legally insecure, if it were not implemented in the domestic law of any country under whose legal system such debt has been issued and/or whose courts are authorized by contract to enforce sovereign debt obligations or settle disputes concerning them. Given the amount and range of current sovereign debt instruments where the contract specifies US law, the non-adhesion of the United States could create significant difficulties for operating a debt workout under the framework, as creditors with debt instruments under US law could effectively escape its disciplines.

With respect to *new* debt obligations, however, sovereigns could choose to insist that contracts contain a clause stating that the party accept the multilateral framework as a basis for their contractual relations. Such a clause would be honored by the courts of the jurisdiction that is selected in the debt contract and also by courts of other states if a creditor attempted to enforce in another jurisdiction pursuant to the Hague Convention, as discussed earlier. But as shall be discussed later, to become enforceable through the choice of the parties to a sovereign debt contract, there would be no need for the multilateral framework to be in and of itself binding in *international* law. Multilateral treaty negotiations are plagued by many collective action problems; the attempt to achieve agreement among a very large number of states to a binding instrument can be hijacked by holdouts. Also, those who have a vested interest in the existing "framework" of informal norms and so on described earlier would be given a single "target" to attack; a process that even a few states might well be able to hobble. And, as the example of credit default swaps suggests, there are fast-moving developments in international finance that may well affect sovereign debt restructuring: a multilateral treaty is hard to amend to address a moving target.

As an alternative I would recommend an informal "counterframework" using the UN Principles and other soft law instruments of a kind generated by various UN processes and institutions, including the ILC, the UN Commission on International Trade Law (UNCITRAL), and the UNCTAD. The counterframework would offer alternative norms, fora, legal mechanisms, expertise, and analysis to those that dominate the existing informal framework (IMF, Paris Club, U.S. Treasury, financial industry associations, private law firms, creditors' groups, etc.). The alternative framework would offer a different option to a sovereign debtor with the determination to insist that it be used for its restructuring and to states that could be sources of new finance and that do not want to conform to the existing informal framework (China, perhaps).

Based in part on UN Principle 6, The UNGA could charge the ILC with the clarification, on a priority basis, of the application of international-law concepts of sovereign immunity and extraterritoriality to the role of domestic courts and other legal actors in relation to sovereign debt restructurings. The ILC would need to directly address concerns under international law about some of the orders of the Griesa court, concerns expressed, for instance, by France. Imposing a short deadline at the ILC, which has sessions only at certain times of the year, would probably require forming a special working group there on sovereign debt and principles of international law.

Secondly, the UNGA could give the UNCITRAL the task of creating a model domestic law applicable to sovereign debt rescheduling. This law could include provisions for a standstill during the course of negotiations and for priority being given to creditors who provide new financing to maintain liquidity during the workout, as well as anti-vulture provisions; such provisions would reflect UN Principles 1 (on avoidance of abusive measures); 2 (on good faith) and 5 (on intercreditor equity). Of course, it would be up to individual states to adapt their existing domestic legislation to bring it into accord with the model law. (The UNCITRAL already has a model law on cross-border insolvency.) The UNCITRAL could also have the task of developing principles for sovereign debt contracts. These principles could include norms or best practices for new sovereign debt, including the form of collective action clauses, redefining the notion of "default," standstill provisions, and so forth. The principles could also address proper interpretation of certain provisions of existing sovereign debt contracts, for example, pari passu. As with the existing UNCITRAL model law on cross-border insolvency, the task could be fast-tracked through informal consultations between the UNCITRAL Secretariat and appropriate experts and stakeholders, rather than being put into a formal working group process, which is more cumbersome and more vulnerable to blocking.

Third, an independent institutional facility could be established to facilitate sovereign debt restructuring, based on inclusiveness and the rule of law (UN Principle 7). Such a facility might have the following roles:

- It could both issue early warnings concerning debtor nations and aid those nations in the area of sovereign debt management. Experts within the institution would follow the debt situations of countries with a certain de minimis ratio of debt to gross domestic product. The institution could give advice about ongoing restructuring or renegotiation of debt, that is, crisis avoidance rather than crisis response. The institution could give early warning of situations in which debt might not be sustainable unless rescheduled. It could also act as a clearinghouse for alternative sources of financing.

- The institution could also determine a kind of insolvency trigger, at which point there would be an obligation for all debtors to negotiate with creditors on restructuring, a standstill being put in place during these negotiations. It could also, taking into account social, economic, and human rights considerations, make determinations about what is a sustainable level of sovereign debt and how burdens might be shared among the sovereign debtor and the creditors to bring to ensure debt is at sustainable levels. I underline that none of these judgments would be legally binding on creditors or the sovereign debtor, and in the case of the standstill would have to be made effective through the domestic courts staying enforcement by holdouts. What I have in mind is a kind of "counter-IMF" role, which the UNCTAD has already been playing in some cases of debt management. The institutional facility's judgment would have legitimacy from: (1) the quality of its expertise (it would need to be led by highly respected, well-known individuals); (2) support from civil society, sympathetic governments, foundations, and celebrities; (3) the willingness of debtor states (that are in a position to do so) to insist that debt management/debt restructuring will take place under the institution; and (4) reliance on the UNCTAD "Principles on Responsible Sovereign Lending and Borrowing."

- The proposed institution could also arbitrate settlement of between debtors and creditors and possibly between different creditors by means of mediation or arbitration. The existing UNCITRAL rules could apply in the case of arbitration. Arbitral awards could be made binding through applying the New York Convention. Arbitration would, however, ultimately have to be by consent between the parties, and the institution's relationship to the choice of forum in existing debt contracts would need to be addressed.

CONCLUSION

A counterframework to the one dominated by the U.S. Treasury/IMF /private sector that emerged in the 1980s for dealing with sovereign debt crises is long overdue. The older framework has already been shaken by Argentina's out-of-framework restructuring, among other events. Its basis was that a sovereign must repay in full despite the economic and social reality of unsustainability; this was supposed to be enforced by cutting off a defaulting sovereign from international markets. The older framework was nested in a particular epistemic community and operated through mechanisms of semiformal coordination like the Paris and London Clubs, and perhaps above all the Fund and the private law firms and bankers designing sovereign debt instruments. A counterframework would be difficult to achieve through a binding multilateral treaty, but might mimic the older one in its decentralized, semiformal character. It will not impose itself through law from the top down but rather through responding more adequately to economic and social realities, through the courage and vision of debtor nations, and as a consequence of the dehegemonization of global finance, most dramatically illustrated in the last weeks through the European nations' decision to join China's alternative development bank.

NOTES

1. The Principles are as follows:

a. A Sovereign State has the right, in the exercise of its discretion, to design its macroeconomic policy, including restructuring its sovereign debt, which should not be frustrated or impeded by any abusive measures. Restructuring should be done as the last resort and preserving at the outset creditors' rights.

b. Good faith by both the sovereign debtor and all its creditors would entail their engagement in constructive sovereign debt restructuring workout negotiations and other stages of the process with the aim of a prompt and durable reestablishment of debt sustainability and debt servicing, as well as achieving the support of a critical mass of creditors through a constructive dialogue regarding the restructuring terms.

c. Transparency should be promoted in order to enhance the accountability of the actors concerned, which can be achieved through the timely sharing of both data and processes related to sovereign debt workouts.

d. Impartiality requires that all institutions and actors involved in sovereign debt restructuring workouts, including at the regional level, in accordance with their respective mandates, enjoy independence and refrain from exercising any undue influence over the process and other stakeholders or engaging in actions that would give rise to conflicts of interest or corruption or both.

e. Equitable treatment imposes on States the duty to refrain from arbitrarily discriminating among creditors, unless a different treatment is justified under the law, is reasonable, and is correlated to the characteristics of the credit, guaranteeing intercreditor equality, discussed among all creditors. Creditors have the right to receive the same proportionate treatment in accordance with their credit and its characteristics. No creditors or creditor groups should be excluded ex ante from the sovereign debt restructuring process.

f. Sovereign immunity from jurisdiction and execution regarding sovereign debt restructurings is a right of States before foreign domestic courts and exceptions should be restrictively interpreted.

g. Legitimacy entails that the establishment of institutions and the operations related to sovereign debt restructuring workouts respect requirements of inclusiveness and the rule of law, at all levels. The terms and conditions of the original contracts should remain valid until such time as they are modified by a restructuring agreement.

h. Sustainability implies that sovereign debt restructuring workouts are completed in a timely and efficient manner and lead to a stable debt situation in the debtor State, preserving at the outset creditors' rights while promoting sustained and inclusive economic growth and sustainable development, minimizing economic and social costs, warranting the stability of the international financial system and respecting human rights.

i. Majority restructuring implies that sovereign debt restructuring agreements that are approved by a qualified majority of the creditors of a State are not to be affected, jeopardized or otherwise impeded by other States or a nonrepresentative minority of creditors, who must respect the decisions adopted by the majority of the creditors. States should be encouraged to include collective action clauses in their sovereign debt to be issued.

2. UN Conference on Trade and Development, *Sovereign Debt Workouts: Going Forward Roadmap and Guide (April 2015),* available from http://unctad.org/en /PublicationsLibrary/gdsddf2015misc1_en.pdf. The record of the Working Group can be found here: http://unctad.org/en/pages/MeetingDetails.aspx?meetingid=889.

3. Article 38 of ICJ: "The Court, whose function is to decide in accordance with international law such disputes as are submitted to it, shall apply:

a. international conventions, whether general or particular, establishing rules expressly recognized by the contesting states;

b. international custom, as evidence of a general practice accepted as law;

c. the general principles of law recognized by civilized nations;

d. subject to the provisions of Article 59, judicial decisions and the teachings of the most highly qualified publicists of the various nations, as subsidiary means for the determination of rules of law."

4. See Ruti Teitel, *Humanity's Law* (Oxford: Oxford University Press, 2010).

5. Howse, Robert L., and Ruti Teitel, *Beyond Compliance: Rethinking Why International Law Really Matters. Global Policy (Online),* Vol. 1, No. 2, 2010; NYU School of Law, Public Law Research Paper No. 10-08. Available at SSRN: http://ssrn.com /abstract=1551923.

6. Abaclat (formerly Beccara) v. Argentine Republic, ICSID Case No. ARB/0715, Decision on Jurisdiction and Admissibility (Aug. 4, 2011).

7. Poštová Banka, a.s. and Istrokapital SE v. The Hellenic Republic, ICSID Case No. ARB/13/8. (April 9, 2015).

8. Jurisdictional Immunities of the State (Ger. v. Italy), Judgment (Feb. 3, 2012), http://www.icj-cij.org/docket/files/143/16883.pdf.

9. Robert Howse, "Concluding Remarks in the Light of International Law" in *Sovereign Financing and International Law: The UNCTAD Principles on Responsible Lending and Borrowing*, ed. Carlos Esposito, Yuefen Li, and Juan Pablo Bohoslavsky, 385–390. Oxford: Oxford University Press, 2013.

10. Available at http://unctad.org/en/docs/gdsddf2011misc1_en.pdf.

CHAPTER 15

Debts, Human Rights, and the Rule of Law

ADVOCATING A FAIR AND EFFICIENT SOVEREIGN INSOLVENCY MODEL

Kunibert Raffer

Court decisions against Argentina and the recent resolution of the UN General Assembly (UNGA) forcefully recalled a well-known glaring gap in the international financial architecture and the limits of the contractual approach. Demanding debt reductions, the newly elected Greek government again raised the issue of insolvency. So far, official claims already have been quietly reduced—for instance by lowering interest rates, deferring debt service, or canceling the European Financial Stability Facility (EFSF) guarantee fee—while stating that official haircuts would be impossible.

The UN resolution demanded the elaboration of "a multilateral legal framework for sovereign debt restructuring processes" (UNGA, 2014). Regretting the absence of appropriate mechanisms, the UN Human Rights Council spoke of the "unjust nature of the current system, which directly affects the enjoyment of human rights in debtor States" (UNHRC, 2014: 3). If debtor states can no longer finance their obligations under human rights laws, people are denied basic human rights. Unlike under any civilized municipal law, debtor protection continues to be refused to the poorest by those creditor governments safeguarding debtor protection at home. All domestic legal systems have established insolvency as the only economically efficient (on this issue, see also Guzman and Stiglitz 2016) and fair solution. Historical record and the fact that no one wants to abolish it prove this solution right.

As early as the eighteenth century, Adam Smith ([1776] 1979: 930) saw the need for "a fair, open, and avowed bankruptcy" of states, being "both least dishonourable to the debtor, and least hurtful to the creditor." Many proposals to follow Smith's advice were made around 1982 (Rogoff and Zettelmeyer, 2002); all were shunned by official creditors. While legal systems have evolved since the days of debtor prisons and debt slavery, the generally acknowledged first, best solution to debt problems continues to be refused to people in debtor countries. Clumsy attempts to emulate parts of insolvency (e.g., the Paris Club's "comparable treatment"), skirting full proceedings, exist. Predictably, success is limited.

Official lending has usually prolonged and worsened crises, postponing and eventually increasing unavoidable haircuts. Greece is one extreme example: "rescue operations" increased debts from about 120 percent to roughly 175 percent of gross domestic product. The illegal and economically absurd bailout of speculators rather than Greece has already afflicted would-be "rescuers" themselves. A quick haircut, as proposed early on, also by people from the financial sector, would have contained losses (not least the budgets of those illegally bailing-out speculators) and spared the Greeks unnecessary hardship. In most jurisdictions, penal law sanctions delaying insolvency, precisely because it makes things worse for all.

Argentina is another example of problems created because official creditors prevented the first, best solution. Its unilateral debt reduction was an emergency solution, necessary because proper proceedings were unavailable, a second-best solution or optimization under restrictions (see also Chodos 2016). Fair and rule of law–based insolvency proceedings would definitely have been better. More and more countries have resorted to unilateral actions. Ecuador put pressure on creditors via its debt audit commission, receiving a large reduction after quite an unpleasant debate. Enumerating several examples, Richards (2010) identified a clear trend toward unilateral exchange offers as a technique for restructuring sovereign debt. When Congo (Brazzaville)—after a series of restructurings in which creditors were either completely bypassed or slighted after initial overtures for dialogue—responded favorably to promoting a negotiated solution over unilateral exchange offers, Richards called this "a ray of sunshine cutting through the shadow cast by the cases of Ecuador and Argentina" (298). Without a fair solution, debtor countries had to become more assertive. Iceland refused to socialize the debt of her private banks, resisted considerable pressures, exited from the crisis quickly, and is meanwhile called a success by the International Monetary Fund (IMF, 2011). Fair insolvency proceedings are no longer uniquely of interest to debtors, but increasingly also to the private sector.

The UNGA did not specify details. It is therefore necessary to draw attention to the essential and indispensable features of any procedure one can rightly call insolvency, all the more so as proposals definitely not meeting these minimum requirements have been propagated as such.

The necessary features of any insolvency procedure are:

- *No creditor diktat*: equality of both parties, debtor and creditors; a neutral and independent entity without any self-interest must chair the proceedings. Unlike present practice or the proposed Sovereign Debt Restructuring Mechanism (SDRM), creditors must not be allowed to be judge and party. Other arguments apart, economic efficiency prohibits deciding in one's own cause.
- *Debtor protection*: some resources must remain exempt to allow a humane existence and a fresh start
- *Best interest of all (not just some) creditors*: as recent cases have shown, private creditors are increasingly discriminated against. Greece is arguably the worst case, where only the private sector—lured into lending by absurdly low capital weights—had to suffer big haircuts.

Sovereignty is an additional issue with sovereign debtors. It was used as a valid counterargument against proposals to adapt Chapter 11, Title 11 U.S. Code to sovereigns after 1982. But there is an easy solution. The main and essential points of the special insolvency procedure for municipalities in the U.S. (Chapter 9, Title 11, U.S.C.) can be easily applied to sovereigns, as was shown in 1987 (Raffer, 1989, 1990).

A solution to an overhang of sovereign debts is needed, one that differs markedly from debt relief that creditors previously granted, which usually prolonged and deepened crises. A proper mechanism to solve a sovereign debt overhang must comply with minimal economic, legal, and humane requirements, and must be fair to all involved. Impartial decision making and debtor protection are the two essential features of insolvency, both denied to debtor states nowadays, even though debtor protection is no longer totally absent. Impartial decisions are also denied to private creditors. This paper presents a model of sovereign insolvency fulfilling these conditions, the Raffer proposal, also called FTAP (Fair Transparent Arbitration Process) by many nongovernmental organizations (NGOs) advocating it. As it has been described in detail already (Raffer, 1989, 1990, 2005, 2010), only its essential points are sketched against the background of recent evolutions.

SOVEREIGNTY, EQUALITY OF PARTIES, AND IMPARTIAL DECISIONS

The difference between Chapter 11 and Chapter 9 is fundamentally important. Chapter 9 is the only procedure protecting governmental powers and thus applicable to sovereigns. Section 904 ("Limitation on Jurisdiction and Powers of Court," Title 11 U.S.C.) states with utmost clarity that the court must not interfere with

1. any of the political and governmental powers of the debtor,
2. any of the property or revenues of the debtor, or
3. the debtor's use or enjoyment of any income-producing property.

The concept of sovereignty does not contain anything more than what Section 904 protects. The court's jurisdiction cannot be extended beyond the debtor's volition, similar to the jurisdiction of international arbitrators. Unlike in other bankruptcy procedures, liquidation of the debtor or receivership are impossible. No trustee can be appointed (Section 926, avoiding powers, if seen as an exception, is very special and justified). Section 902(5) explicitly confirms: " 'trustee,' when used in a section that is made applicable in a case under this chapter . . . means debtor." Change of "management" (removing elected officials) by courts or creditors is not possible, nor should it be in the case of sovereigns. Obviously, similar guarantees are absent from Chapter 11, where debtor-in-possession financing is not unusual too. Public interest in the functioning of the debtor safeguards a minimum of municipal activities under Chapter 9. Limits to tax increases exist. When creditors insisted on higher payments by the City of Asbury Park, the U.S. Supreme Court clearly stated that a city cannot be taken over and operated for the benefit of its creditors.

Chapter 9 was passed during the Great Depression, precisely to avoid prolonged and inefficient negotiations and reschedulings and to allow quick, fair, and economically efficient solutions. Lawmakers rejected a first draft not barring intervention into the governmental sphere as unconstitutional. A new version containing Section 904 passed. Creditor interventions similar to those usual in developing or eurozone countries nowadays were considered unacceptable. "Debt management" as practiced internationally for decades was to be avoided. Technically, the essential features of Chapter 9 allow implementing an economically sensible, fair, efficient, and legally correct solution.

The formally powerful position of the debtor might make non-economists wonder whether Chapter 9 actually works. More than 500 cases within the United States show it does. Needing a solution, the debtor must make a proposal acceptable to creditors. As history has shown, sovereign debtors also cannot be forced to comply by courts. The situation is similar. Composition plans should be fair, equitable, and feasible. To be confirmed the plan has to be reasonable and also in the best interest of creditors. They must be provided the "going concern value" of their claims. A plan can only be confirmed if it "embodies a fair and equitable bargain openly arrived at and devoid of overreaching, however subtle" (Raffer, 1990: 302).

An ad hoc panel of arbitrators nominated by both parties plus one further person elected by nominees should play the role of domestic courts, a traditional method in international law. This arbitration model was granted to Germany by creditors, including Greece and Ireland, in 1953 (Raffer, 1989: 60): Rule of law and arbitration instead of troika and arbitrary creditor diktat. As several problematic court cases have illustrated, courts in creditor countries may not always be a good solution. Arbitrators would mediate between debtors and creditors, chair and support negotiations with advice, provide adequate possibilities to exercise the right to be heard, and if necessary, decide. As all facts would be presented by both parties and the representatives of the population (see section "Protecting Debtors and Democracy") during a transparent procedure, decisions would be unlikely to affect substantial sums of money but would rather resolve deadlocks. Agreements between the debtor and creditors would need the panel's confirmation. Ideally, arbitrators would just rubber-stamp plans agreed upon by creditors and the debtor.

Institutionalized arbitration is, of course, technically also feasible. But ad hoc panels give more say to the parties and do not need the long process of negotiating and ratifying a treaty. The parties can nominate arbiters for each case. Acceptance by the main, important countries, admittedly a big problem in practice, suffices.

Arbitration has become quite popular. The World Trade Organization and many bilateral investment treaties now including debts use it. The International Centre for Settlement of Investment Disputes (ICSID) has widened the concept of investment to include debts, arguably in a problematic way. There is no longer any logical reason why arbitration should not be used in a sovereign insolvency procedure, as foreseen in Germany's de facto case.

Unfortunately, one specific subtype of arbitration—investor-state dispute settlement (ISDS)—has created considerable and justified scepticism against the mechanism as such. The fact that ICSID increasingly shows a "corporate bias" (Broad, 2014) does not help either. The *Economist* (October 11, 2014) called ISDS "a way to let multinational companies get rich at the expense of ordinary people," arguing correctly that remedies—for example, precise and restrictive definitions of "investment," greater reliance on precedent, and more transparency— are easy.

Arbitration pursuant to my proposal is fully transparent.

Arbitration is always based on legal norms, for example, Bilateral Investment Treaties (BITs) or the North American Free Trade Agreement. If treaties are stipulated in a way that gives undue leeway to problematic interpretations and apparently abusive arbitral awards, allowing legally harassing governments, this is the fault of the treaties. If one includes blurry concepts such as "expected future profits," failing (deliberately?) to include norms that protect (exempt) general political decisions (such as environmental or regulatory norms or health issues like antismoking legislation), present outcomes are to be expected. ISDS was—deliberately one might assume—shaped so as to turn "entrepreneurs" into rent seekers, allowing them to cash in on off taxpayers' money on the cheap. The arbitration mechanism is not to be blamed; its concrete base, a treaty or agreement allowing undue practice, is.

As sovereigns have usually been unwilling or at least reluctant to accept courts of other sovereigns (the famous exception, waivers of immunity in debt contracts, is relatively new, a few decades old only), arbitration has been *the* way of solving problems peacefully and efficiently over centuries. It has been much more widely used than ISDS, which gave arbitration a bad name, even within the private sector. Until 1945 arbitration was stipulated in the case of sovereign lending, without complaints such as those raised against ISDS. The problems now rightly seen with one subtype of arbitration have not occurred in all other cases. Miscarriages of justice that do occur or problematically formulated laws have not led to general scepticism against courts and laws as such but to appropriate reform and redress. The same applies in the case of arbitration, a generic expression defining a mechanism wherein arbiters decide. The basis of any arbitral proceedings must be soundly formulated, as in my proposal. Advantages of the proposed ad hoc tribunals are that debtors codetermine this basis as one party, and both parties can nominate arbiters they trust to be fair and unbiased. If organized properly—as it was before ISDS—arbitration is a useful method to solve problems.

PROTECTING DEBTORS AND DEMOCRACY

Human rights and human dignity enjoy unconditional priority, even though insolvency only deals with claims based on solid and proper legal foundations. All insolvency laws guarantee insolvent debtors humane standards of living, and usually a "fresh start," exempting resources that could be seized by bona fide creditors. Debtors, unless they are countries in distress, cannot be forced to starve their children in order to be able to pay more. Debtor protection, one main principle of all civilized insolvency laws, had remained largely absent internationally. Due to massive pressure by NGOs, the second Heavily Indebted Poor Countries Initiative (I IIPC II) finally acknowledged the principle of debtor protection, not necessarily always fully honored by practice, but with visible improvements. An official antipoverty focus was established, and antipoverty programs were introduced for the first time. The Multilateral Debt Relief Initiative (MDRI) confirmed this.

Multilateral debt reductions were seen as a necessary condition for reaching the UN's Millennium Development Goals (MDGs), goals accepted by virtually all countries. Fully financing the MDGs can thus be interpreted as a form of debtor protection, although it differs from the protection enjoyed by domestic debtors. Even fully reaching those MDGs directly affecting poor people's lives does not yet satisfy the standard set by human rights and within countries. Not all goals and targets even aim at eliminating unacceptable living conditions. MDG 1 is a particularly good example. In spite of its wording ("Eradicate extreme poverty and hunger") MDG 1 only intends to halve the proportion of the extremely poor (target 1) and the proportion of people suffering from hunger. There remain people who go hungry or live under unspeakable conditions.

In virtually all poor debtor countries poverty existed before the debt crisis. With some justification, creditors can argue that a sovereign insolvency mechanism cannot resolve all development problems of a country that already existed before and independently of debt problems; in other words, insolvency procedures cannot substitute development policy.

In the search for an international standard, the MDGs thus offer a solution. Determining debtor protection, the MDGs prove useful and predestined to serve as the measuring rod. They are an internationally accepted standard capable of preventing excessive debt service from constituting an obstacle to the realization of human rights. Resources necessary to finance the MDGs should be exempt, although the MDGs ensure, strictly speaking, less than standard debtor protection as with other debtors because not each and every person in a debtor country is as fully protected.

The MDGs have been accepted by virtually all countries. Creditor governments, too, promised to "spare no effort" to free people from "the abject and dehumanizing conditions of extreme poverty," and "committed" themselves to realizing the right to development for everyone as well as to "freeing the entire human race from want." If that is a true statement rather than a political truth, important creditor governments cannot but enthusiastically embrace the MDGs as an acceptable debtor-protection standard. The proof of the pudding is always in the eating. The MDGs may continue to be useful as a yardstick after 2015, if no other goals protecting the poor in a similar way would be accepted.

Chapter 9 knows two instruments to protect debtors:

(1) exempting a minimum of resources needed to allow a debtor to go on functioning and to provide essential services to its inhabitants and

(2) the right to be heard of the affected population. If electoral approval is necessary under nonbankruptcy law to carry out provisions of the plan, it must be obtained before confirmation of the plan pursuant to Section 943(b)(6).

U.S. municipalities must be allowed to go on functioning and to provide essential services to their inhabitants (presently, Bill H.R. 870 wants to extend Chapter 9 protection to Puerto Rico). Resources necessary to assure this are exempt. This principle must be applied to sovereign countries. Resources necessary to finance minimum standards of basic health, primary education, and so on, must be exempt. Eventually, antipoverty measures under HIPC II have formally recognized this principle. Private creditors have always been aware that some money simply cannot be collected due to public resistance against social expenditure cuts. The SDRM, by contrast, fell back behind this minimum standard, not mentioning any kind of debtor protection at all. In Greece people have to die in hospitals because necessary medication can no longer be bought due to the troika's decisions. The absence of sovereign insolvency protection allowed forcing Greece, against the law, to shoulder the costs of rescue programs Germany or France would have had to finance for their banks if Article 125, the "no bailout clause," would not have been violated. ATTAC (n.d.) showed that "at least 77.12 percent" of "rescue" funds went to the financial sector. According to the *Washington Post* (January 28, 2015), only 11 percent went to Greece's government. Greece suffers from this illegal activity on the part of other member states, paying for banks and speculators, something a sovereign insolvency procedure would prohibit. Finally, the private sector (not necessarily each private creditor) suffered larger losses.

Of course, no insolvent debtor can just go on as before, saving and economizing are unavoidable. The question is uniquely which services are exempt, or have to be assured, though on reduced levels.

As Iceland proved, protecting the population is possible, and adjustment pains can be cushioned (Bohoslavsky, 2014). The IMF (2011) put it in a nutshell: "Iceland set an example by managing to preserve, and even strengthen, its welfare state during the crisis." In stark contrast to the standard IMF recipe, Iceland introduced capital controls, did not tighten its fiscal policy during first year of the program, and had referenda to determine whether the debts incurred by its three liberalized and deregulated banks should be paid in full by taxpayers. The people decided against. Iceland returned to capital markets in 2011. Differences from orthodox "debt management" are obvious.

According to Kentikelenis and colleagues (2014) the weakness of regional health systems was one "major reason" why Ebola spread so rapidly. IMF conditionalities requiring spending cuts had eroded healthcare systems over the years. The IMF denies this, pointing at increases in health spending "from 2010 to 2013" (Gupta, 2014), apparently effects of HIPC II. Without any doubt stronger health systems would have reduced Ebola's international impact. This illustrates that no debtor protection in debtor countries can create international externalities. Apart from diseases, too strict austerity is also likely to affect migration flows.

Stiglitz and colleagues (2015) pointed out: "Any framework for sovereign debt restructuring has to take account of the primacy of the functions of the state, its obligations to its citizens, and the 'social contract' the state has with its citizens."

Participation of the municipality's inhabitants is guaranteed: in domestic Chapter 9 cases the affected population has a right to be heard. Internationally, this would have to be exercised by representation. Trade unions, entrepreneurial associations, religious (Christian, Muslim, etc.) or nonreligious NGOs, or international organizations such as UNICEF could represent the debtor country's population, presenting arguments and data before the panel. Affected people would thus have the right to defend their interests, to present estimates and arguments, to show why or whether certain basic services are necessary. The openness and transparency usual within the United States should become the norm of sovereign insolvency.

Besides preserving essential services to the population, my proposal gives the affected population and vulnerable groups a right to be heard. It gives voice to those who have been denied participation and have therefore often "participated" by rioting in the streets. HIPC II already practices NGO participation; transparency and NGO participation in debt issues are thus facts. I propose to apply the same legal and economic standards to all debtors, to guarantee equal treatment of indebted people everywhere, irrespective of nationality or skin color. There is no logical reason why someone living in an insolvent U.S. municipality is treated in a more humane way than people living in another public debtor, such as Greece.

Further participation by parliaments or the electorate could easily be integrated. The debtor government can choose to leave the task of nominating panel members either to the parliament or the people. Voters could, for example, elect arbitrators from a roster on which experts reaching a minimum of supporting signatures by voters would be listed. One arbitrator might be chosen by parliament, the other by voters. The parliament might establish a special committee to handle insolvency, including members of the cabinet, as proposed in a bill drafted on the initiative of Argentine congressman Mario Cafiero. This bill would have established a commission consisting of members from both Houses and the executive power; it was to nominate panel members and represent Argentina during the proceedings. Solutions to sovereign debt problems need not destroy democracy as the EU does at present. Sovereign insolvency proceedings would have been much better for anyone than Argentina's unilateral action, necessary because insolvency was unavailable.

Compared with HIPC II, debtor participation has declined again. Those really affected by adjustment have no voice at all, referenda (if considered) are prevented both in debtor countries (as in Greece) and in countries whose taxpayers are to finance bailouts covering losses of their own banks. The democratic sovereign is gagged. This problem goes beyond debt, destroying the very essence of democracy. "Democratic processes must entail open dialogue and broadly active civic engagement, and it requires that individuals have a voice in the decisions that affect them, including economic decisions," as Stiglitz (2000: 20) put it. These "people, who would inevitably face much of the costs of the mistaken policy" are "not even invited to sit in on the discussions; and I often felt myself to be the lone voice in these discussions suggesting that basic democratic principles recommended that not only should their voice be heard, but they should actually have a seat at the table" (1). U.S. Chapter 9 shows how this problem can be solved.

Creditors, of course, have the right to demand selling some of the debtor's assets to reduce their losses. This is part and parcel of any insolvency case, fair and justified. Quick-fire sales under enormous pressure and within a stipulated short time frame as presently requested from Greece are not. They are likely to yield unfairly low prices (as illustrated by euro countries), damaging both bona fide creditors and the debtor, though allowing some lucky (or well-connected) few to get these assets on the cheap.

FAIR AND EQUAL TREATMENT OF ALL CREDITORS

The last point of my proposal is fair and equal treatment of *all* creditors. Multilateral debts must no longer enjoy illegal preference. All creditors must be treated equally, in line with the statutes of multilaterals. So far, the private sector has been forced to bear most or all losses. Official creditors, even when and if delaying haircuts by their actions, thus increasing damages, have enjoyed economically undue and illegal preference. This is patently unfair and economically wrong and must stop. Especially the poorest countries must get meaningful multilateral haircuts. Particularly problematic and a grave violation of the rule of law is any form of ex post seniority. The IMF (2012: 54) put this new discrimination of private creditors in a nutshell: "The ECB's [European Central Bank's] exemption from the Greek so-called Private Sector Involvement (PSI) reflected a net expected transfer of value from private sovereign bond holders to the ECB." Economically, this is vulture behavior.

All debts of the sovereign, domestic and foreign, must be included in one, single procedure. Erce (2014: 23) showed that discriminating against domestic creditors or "IMF-sanctioned heterogeneous treatment of sovereign creditors can have negative effects on growth." Including domestic claims may thus be in the purely economic interest of foreign creditors.

Insolvency laws usually allow preferential treatment of certain types of claims. Ladders of priority are plain vanilla. Treating all creditors equally is not a procedural necessity, but in my model all creditors are to be treated equally. Except creditors lending during the procedure to keep the country afloat—whether public or private—all private and public creditors must get the same haircut. This avoids unfair burden sharing. Demanding that those official creditors aggravating damages by illegal lending must not enjoy preference is extremely justified and indispensable. One may even demand subordination of insolvency-delaying public lending. Greece illustrates this most clearly: a quick haircut early on would have cost the private sector less.

Equal haircuts, arguably subordination of abusive public credit, is therefore an important feature of my sovereign insolvency model, which is based on specific economic, legal, and ethical reasons: the necessity to establish the equivalent of national liability and tort laws, and fairness to bona fide creditors who, like debtors, would otherwise have to pick up part of the bill for failures by official lenders.

The present situation encourages "overoptimism" of those determining haircuts (see Raffer, 2010: 204ff; Guzman, 2014: 35ff). More realistic forecasts would demand larger reductions and more losses to the public sector. Delaying is thus the "optimal" strategy of governments hoping that another, new government might have to tackle this problem later and acknowledge losses occurred long before it came to power. The preparedness to stretch Greece's amortization period seems explained by the fact that present political decision makers will be retired when the impossibility of repayment finally has to be recognized. Other cabinets will officially have to take losses of the past veiled over years and the blame for what was basically not their fault. Equal treatment would provide a strong disincentive.

SNAIL-SPEED PROGRESS

Although opposition is still quite strong, changes for the better exist, although deplorably slow progress has occurred at snail speed since the first proposals of sovereign insolvency around 1982.

No one would still defend illusory approaches such as the Baker Plan or the Venice Terms (all must and can be repaid plus interest), except the EU. The need for debt reduction is no longer debated. Even in the case of Greece, where this illusion has been kept alive longest, the tide seems to be turning. Changes in terms and conditions constitute an official sector haircut on the sly.

Recognizing the existence of unpayable debts, bond issuers are trying to substitute collective action clauses and the Paris Club tries to substitute comparable treatments for proper insolvency proceedings. Some countries have passed laws against professional holdouts, aka "vulture funds." The problems created by the absence of Adam Smith's first, best solution, a glaring gap in the international financial architecture, have become quite obvious. The UNGA's call for a sovereign insolvency mechanism is an evolution obviously propelled by Argentina's litigation and debatable decisions by a federal judge, who continued to be unfamiliar with essential facts after presiding for over a decade (see *New York Times*, July 24, 2014).

Recalling the objections against my proposal during the 1980s, most forcefully made by international financial institution (IFI) staff, one notes movements, especially so after Krueger's proposal. Krueger (2001) recognized the necessity of an orderly framework, pointing out that this reduces restructuring costs, echoing Raffer (1989). As if touched by Harry Potter's wand, the IMF immediately turned from a fierce enemy to an ardent advocate of sovereign insolvency. Nevertheless, its SDRM is no insolvency mechanism: the IMF's executive board would have continued to determine haircuts and debtors' policies (see Raffer, 2005: 365; on the SDRM, see also Brooks and Lombardi 2016), and only the private sector would have had to take losses, both in stark contrast to the first proposal to arbitrate (Raffer, 1989) shaped after and inspired by Germany's London Agreement.

Verification (Raffer, 1990: 309), often called impossible in earlier discussions with IMF staff, was eventually demanded by the IMF (2002: 68). "Agreements between debtor and creditors would need the confirmation of the arbitrator, in analogy to Section 943" (Raffer, 1990: 305; similarly Krueger, 2002: 7). Krueger (2001, cf. Raffer, 1990) proposed stays or standstills, even though the IMF (2002: 33ff) backtracked under criticism, modifying Krueger's bolder proposal. Arbitration was proposed, though only for private creditors, possibly for bilateral but not for multilateral creditors (e.g., IMF, 2002: 56ff). But this body would not have been allowed to decide the two really important issues.

Debt arbitration has become quite popular meanwhile. Creditors use ICSID and BITs to sue debtor nations. Only when it comes to fair and efficient solutions of sovereign debt distress is arbitration shunned by the same governments eagerly pushing it anywhere else. In 2005, however, the Norwegian government explicitly expressed the intention to support arbitration on illegitimate debts.

HIPC I already recognized the need for multilateral debt reduction, a great merit of James Wolfensohn's, breaking this taboo. Nevertheless, undue preference is still granted to IFIs instead of treating them in accordance with their own statutes. Finally, the MDRI demanded substantial cuts of some multilateral debts to provide additional support in reaching the MDGs. This can be interpreted as a form of debtor protection: money that could be paid to creditors is used to finance social expenditures. The principle of debtor protection has already been accepted by HIPC II, with visible results.

Summing up, one may say: change is painfully slow, but it exists. More speed is urgently needed.

REFERENCES

ATTAC. n.d. "Background Material: Three Years of 'Greek Bail-Out': 77% Went Into the Financial Sector." www.attac.at/fileadmin/_migrated/content_uploads/backgroundmaterial_bailout_english.pdf.

Bohoslavsky, Juan Pablo 2014. "End-of-Mission Statement by Mr. Juan Pablo Bohoslavsky, United Nations Independent Expert on the Effects of Foreign Debt and Other Related International Financial Obligations of States on the Full Enjoyment of all Human Rights, Particularly Economic, Social and Cultural Rights. Mission to Iceland, 8–15 December 2014." www.ohchr.org/EN/NewsEvents/Pages/DisplayNews.aspx?NewsID=15420&LangID=E.

Broad, Robin. 2014. "Corporate Bias at the World Bank Group—The World Bank Group's International Centre for Settlement of Investment Disputes." www.brettonwoodsproject.org/2015/09/corporate-bias-at-the-world-bank-group.

Brooks, Skylar, and Domenico Lombardi. 2016. "Private Creditor Power and the Politics of Sovereign Debt Governance." In *Too Little, Too Late: The Quest to Resolve Sovereign Debt Crises*, ed. Martin Guzman, José Antonio Ocampo, and Joseph E. Stiglitz, chapter 3. New York: Columbia University Press.

Chodos, Sergio. 2016. "From the Pari Passu Discussion to the 'Illegality' of Making Payments." In *Too Little, Too Late: The Quest to Resolve Sovereign Debt Crises*, ed. Martin Guzman, José Antonio Ocampo, and Joseph E. Stiglitz, chapter 4. New York: Columbia University Press.

Erce, Aitor. 2014. "Banking on Seniority: The IMF and the Sovereign's Creditors." Working Paper 175, Federal Reserve Bank of Dallas, Globalization and Monetary Policy Institute. www.dallasfed.org/assets/documents/institute/wpapers/2014/0175.pdf.

Gupta, Sanjeev. 2014. "IMF Response to *The Lancet* article on 'The International Monetary Fund and the Ebola Outbreak.'" www.imf.org/external/np/vc/2014/122214.htm.

Guzman, Martin. 2014. "Understanding the Relationship Between Output Growth Expectations and Financial Crises." Initiative for Policy Dialogue Working Papers Series. Columbia University, New York

Guzman, Martin and Joseph E. Stiglitz. 2016. "Creating a Framework for Sovereign Debt Restructuring That Works," in *Too Little, Too Late: The Quest for Resolving Sovereign Debt Crises*, chapter 1. New York: Columbia University Press.

International Monetary Fund. 2002, November 27. "The Design of the Sovereign Debt Restructuring Mechanism—Further Considerations." www.imf.org/external /np/pdr/sdrm/2002/112702.pdf.

———. 2011. "Iceland's Unorthodox Policies Suggest Alternative Way Out of Crisis." *IMF Survey Online*, November 3. www.imf.org/external/pubs/ft/survey/so/2011 /car110311a.htm.

———. 2012. "Euro Area Policies: 2012 Article IV Consultation—Selected Issues Paper." Country Report No. 12/182. https://www.imf.org/external/pubs/ft/scr/2012 /cr12182.pdf

Kentikelenis, A., L. King, M. McKee, and D. Stuckler. 2014. "The International Monetary Fund and the Ebola Outbreak." *Lancet* 3 (no. 2). www.thelancet.com /journals/langlo/article/PIIS2214–109X%2814%2970377–8/fulltext.

Krueger, Anne. 2001. "International Financial Architecture for 2002: A New Approach to Sovereign Debt Restructuring." www.imf.org/external/np/speeches/2001 /112601.htm.

———. 2002. "Sovereign Debt Restructuring and Dispute Resolution." www.imf.org /external/np/speeches/2002/060602.htm.

Raffer Kunibert. 1989. "International Debts: A Crisis for Whom?" In *Economic Development and World Debt*, ed. H. W. Singer and S. Sharma, 51–63. London: Macmillan. (Papers of a conference at the University of Zagreb 1987.)

———. 1990. "Applying Chapter 9 Insolvency to International Debts: An Economically Efficient Solution with a Human Face." *World Development* 18 (no. 2): 301–313.

———. 2005. "Internationalizing US Municipal Insolvency: A Fair, Equitable, and Efficient Way to Overcome a Debt Overhang." *Chicago Journal of International Law* 6 (no. 1): 361–380.

———. 2010. *Debt Management for Development—Protection of the Poor and the Millennium Development Goals*. Cheltenham, U.K.: Elgar.

Richards, Mark B. 2010. "The Republic of Congo's Debt Restructuring: Are Sovereign Creditors Getting Their Voice Back?" *Law and Contemporary Problems* 73 (no. 4): 273–299.

Rogoff, K., and J. Zettelmeyer. 2002. "Bankruptcy Procedures for Sovereigns: A History of Ideas, 1976–2001." *IMF Staff Papers* 49 (no. 3): 470–508.

Smith, Adam. [1776] 1979. *An Inquiry into the Nature and Causes of the Wealth of Nations*, vol. 2, Glasgow ed., Oxford: Oxford University Press.

Stiglitz, Joseph. 2000. "Democratic Development as the Fruits of Labor." Keynote address at the Industrial Relations Research Association, Boston, Mass. Mimeo.

Stiglitz, J., M. Guzman, D. Lombardi, J. A. Ocampo, and J. Svejnar. 2015. "Frameworks for Sovereign Debt Restructuring." IPD-CIGI-CGEG Policy Brief. http://policydialogue .org/files/publications/IPD-CIGI-CGEG_Report_-_FSDR_Conference_R.pdf

United Nations General Assembly. 2014. "Towards the Establishment of a Multilateral Legal Framework for Sovereign Debt Restructuring Processes" (A/68/L.57/Rev.2).

United Nations Human Rights Council. 2014. "Effects of Foreign Debt and Other Related International Financial Obligations of States on the Full Enjoyment of All Human Rights, Particularly Economic, Social and Cultural Rights: The Activities of Vulture Funds" (A/HRC/27/L.26).

CONTRIBUTORS

Skylar Brooks is a PhD candidate at the Balsillie School of International Affairs, University of Waterloo. His research focuses on the global politics of money and finance, with particular emphasis on the international monetary system and sovereign debt governance.

Sergio Chodos, currently executive director for the Southern Cone countries at the International Monetary Fund. Previously, he held positions in Argentina, including secretary of finance, board member of the Central Bank of Argentina, and vice superintendent of Financial Entities. He holds a law degree from the University of Buenos Aires and an LLM from Columbia University. He was admitted to practice in Buenos Aires and in New York.

Richard A. Conn Jr. serves as managing partner of Eurasia Advisors LLC (www.eurasiadvisors.com), an advisory firm specializing in problem solving and deal making in Russia and other CIS nations, and as managing partner of Innovate Partners LLC (www.innovatepartners.com), a private investment fund. He delivered the keynote address before the UN General Assembly Ad Hoc Committee on Sovereign Debt Restructuring in April 2015.

Timothy B. DeSieno is a New York–based partner in the global financial restructuring practice of Morgan, Lewis & Bockius LLP. DeSieno advises institutional investors in protecting and restructuring their investments globally in cases of economic, political, financial, or other stress. He frequently represents creditors of sovereign states in connection with debt restructurings.

Anna Gelpern is a law professor at Georgetown and a fellow at the Peterson Institute for International Economics. She has published many articles on financial integration and debt and has coauthored a law textbook on international finance. Earlier he practiced law in New York and served in legal and policy positions at the U.S. Treasury.

Richard Gitlin is chair of Gitlin & Company, LLC and a senior fellow at the Centre for International Governance Innovation (CIGI). For many years he has been actively involved in efforts to improve systems for both sovereign and corporate cross-border debt restructurings.

Martin Guzman is a postdoctoral research fellow at Columbia University GSB (Department of Economics and Finance), an associate professor at the University of Buenos Aires, and a senior fellow at the Centre for International Governance Innovation. He is a cochair of Columbia University IPD Taskforce on Debt Restructuring and Sovereign Bankruptcy, and a member of the Institute for New Economic Thinking Group on Macroeconomic Externalities. He is also the editor of the *Journal of Globalization and Development.*

James A. Haley is an adjunct professor at McCourt School of Public Policy, Georgetown University, Washington, D.C. He previously served as executive director for Canada at the Inter-American Development Bank and led the Global Economy program at the Centre for International Governance Innovation (CIGI). He has held a number of senior positions in the Canadian Treasury and was research director at the International Department of the Bank of Canada. He also served on the staff of the Research Department of the International Monetary Fund and has lectured on international finance at the Norman Paterson School of International Affairs, Carleton University.

Ben Heller is a fund manager at Hutchin Hill.

Barry Herman. After almost thirty years of service, Dr. Herman retired from the United Nations Secretariat in December 2005 and now teaches part-time in the Julien J. Studley Graduate Program in International Affairs in the Milano School of International Affairs, Management and Urban Policy of The New School, New York.

Brett House is chief economist at Alignvest Investment Management in Toronto, senior fellow at the Jeanne Sauvé Foundation, and visiting scholar at Massey College in the University of Toronto. Previously, he worked on sovereign debt–related issues as senior fellow at the Centre for International Governance Innovation (CIGI), global strategist at New York–based hedge fund Woodbine Capital Advisors, principal advisor in the executive office of the United Nations' Secretary-General, and economist at the International Monetary Fund.

Robert Howse is Lloyd C. Nelson Professor of International Law at NYU Law School. He was a member of the UNCTAD Working Group on Sovereign Debt Workouts and is the author of the UNCTAD study "The Concept of Odious Debt in Public International Law," among many other works.

Jürgen Kaiser is the coordinator of erlassjahr.de (Jubilee Germany). Born in 1954, he studied geography and regional planning in Berlin and Karlsruhe; worked for ten years in development education for the Protestant Churches in Germany, working for the German debt crisis network from 1995 to 1997, then cofounder of Jubilee Germany; in 2005/6 debt relief and financial flows adviser for UNDP (New York).

Domenico Lombardi is director of the Global Economy Program at the Centre for International Governance Innovation (CIGI), Canada. He serves on the advisory boards of the Peterson Institute for International Economics and the Bretton Woods Committee in Washington. Earlier in his career, Lombardi was a senior fellow at the Brookings Institution and had positions on the executive boards of the International Monetary Fund and the World Bank. He has an undergraduate degree summa cum laude from Bocconi University, Milan, and a PhD in economics from Oxford University (Nuffield College). More information is available at www.domenicolombardi.org.

José Antonio Ocampo is professor at the School of International and Public Affairs and co-president of the Initiative for Policy Dialogue at Columbia University, and chair of the UN Committee for Development Policy. He has been UN under-secretary-general for economic and social affairs, executive secretary of the UN Economic Commission for Latin America and the Caribbean (ECLAC), and minister of finance, minister of agriculture, and director of the National Planning Office of Colombia.

Kunibert Raffer is associate professor in the Department of Economics, University of Vienna, and honorary professor at the Universidad Nacional de Rio Negro (Argentina). He serves as a member of the Study Group on Sovereign Insolvency of the International Law Association.

Brad Setser is the deputy assistant secretary for international economic analysis at the U.S. Treasury.

Joseph E. Stiglitz is an American economist and a professor at Columbia University. He is also the cochair of the High-Level Expert Group on the Measurement of Economic Performance and Social Progress at the OECD, the chief economist of the Roosevelt Institute and cofounder and co-president of the Initiative for Policy Dialogue. A recipient of the Nobel Memorial Prize in Economic Sciences (2001) and the John Bates Clark Medal (1979), he is a former senior vice president and chief economist of the World Bank and a former member and chairman of the (U.S. president's) Council of Economic Advisers.

Marilou Uy is director of the Secretariat of the Intergovernmental Group of Twenty-Four on International Monetary Affairs and Development (G-24). Previously, Uy worked at the World Bank, where she was director of Financial and Private Sector Development in various regional departments.

Yanis Varoufakis is professor of economic theory at the University of Athens and a former finance minister who led his government's negotiations on debt relief with the International Monetary Fund, the European Commission, and the European Central Bank. His latest book is entitled. *And the Weak Suffer What They Must? Europe's Crisis, America's Economic Future* (New York: Nation Books).

Shichao Zhou is research associate at the G-24 Secretariat. Previously, he worked on country economic analysis as an intern at the Institute of International Finance. Mr. Zhou graduated from the Paul H. Nitze School of Advanced International Studies at Johns Hopkins University.

INDEX

Abaclat v. Argentina, 243
Abi-Saab, George, 243
Abs, Hermann Josef, 224–26
abuse, 120
Addis Ababa Action Agenda, 219
ad hoc awards, 228
Africa, 214; China and, 41, *42*; Ebola in, 212, 261; GDP of, *35*; international bond issues in, *43*; Zaire, 220*n*4
agency, 62; Fiscal Agency Agreement, 78–79, 82*n*4, 164
aggregation, 131–32, 135; foreign-law bonds and, 134; SDRM and, 198–99, 203*nn*4–5; single-limb aggregation, 109, 124–27, 165–66; two-limb aggregations, 111, 123–24, 165–66
aggregation clauses, 109, 198–200, 203*nn*4–5
Agreed Minute, 211
agreements must be honored (*pacta sunt servanda*), 206–7, 242–43
AIIB. *See* Asian Infrastructure Investment Bank
American courts, 25*n*6; Griesa of, 15, 26*n*16, 27*n*17, 265. *See also* Argentine restructuring
April 2015 proposal. *See* Greek debt April 2015 proposal
Arab Coordination Group, *42*
arbitration, 249; in PCA, xx, 218–19, 227; from UNCITRAL, 227. *See also* Fair Transparent Arbitration Process
Argentine restructuring, 56, 81*n*1; *Abaclat v. Argentina* in, 243; Comisión

Representativa del Estado Nacional for, 262; consequences in, 28*n*32, 80–81, 111, 179; equilibrium and, 79, 81; GDP-linked bonds in, 26*n*9; holdout creditors in, 164, 171*n*5, 239; in ICMA CACs evolution, 117–18; ICMA CACs new model in, 121; *NML Capital, Ltd. v. Republic of Argentina*, 11, 44, 157; pari passu clause and, 11, 15, 26*n*16, 27*n*17, 77–80, 82*n*4, 83*nn*6–7, 117, 148–49, 164, 198, 203*nn*3–4; remedy in, 79–81, 254; SDR framework and, 232–33; sovereign immunity and, 244–45; U.S. on, 25*n*6, 51*n*24, 77, 213–14; vulture funds and, xvi–xvii, 11, 26*n*16, 77
Arrow, Kenneth J., 28*n*31, 168
Article 38, 241, 251*n*3
Articles of Agreement, 242
Articles of State Responsibility, 243
Asbury Park, 256
Asia: China, 41, *42*, 233; GDP in, *35*, 38; international bond issues in, *43*; Japan, 51*n*25, 145, 233
Asian financial crisis: governments in, 210; local currency bonds after, 38; proposals after, 195; voluntary reschedulings after, 191
Asian Infrastructure Investment Bank (AIIB), 233
attachment, *150*, 157, 244
austerity, 8; in Greek debt analysis, *88*, 88–89, *89*; in Greek debt history, 86, 104*n*8
Australia, 51*n*25
authority, 208, 214–15, 255
autonomy of decision, 131